The Politics of Extremism in South Asia

South Asia is home to a range of extremist groups from the jihadists of Pakistan to the Tamil Tigers of Sri Lanka. In the popular mind, extremism and terrorism are invariably linked to ethnic and religious factors. Yet the dominant history of South Asia is notable for tolerance and co-existence, despite highly plural societies. Deepa Ollapally examines extremist groups in Kashmir, Afghanistan, Northeast India, Pakistan, Bangladesh and Sri Lanka to offer a fresh perspective on the causes of extremism. What accounts for its rise in societies not historically predisposed to extremism? What determines the winners and losers in the identity struggles in South Asia? What tips the balance between more moderate versus extremist outcomes? The book argues that politics, inter-state and international relations often play a more important role in the rise of extremism in South Asia than religious identity, poverty and state repression.

Deepa M. Ollapally is Professorial Lecturer, and the Associate Director of the Sigur Center for Asian Studies at the Elliott School of International Affairs at the George Washington University, Washington DC. She is an expert on South Asian politics and international security and her publications include *Confronting Conflict: Domestic Factors and US Policymaking in the Third World*. She holds a Ph.D. in Political Science from Columbia University.

The Politics of Extremism in South Asia

Deepa M. Ollapally

George Washington University

CAMBRIDGE
UNIVERSITY PRESS

CAMBRIDGE UNIVERSITY PRESS
Cambridge, New York, Melbourne, Madrid, Cape Town, Singapore,
São Paulo, Delhi

Cambridge University Press
The Edinburgh Building, Cambridge CB2 8RU, UK

Published in the United States of America by Cambridge University Press,
New York

www.cambridge.org
Information on this title: www.cambridge.org/9780521699129

First published 2008

Printed in the United Kingdom at the University Press, Cambridge

A catalogue record for this publication is available from the British Library

Library of Congress Cataloguing in Publication data
Ollapally, Deepa Mary.
  The politics of extremism in South Asia / Deepa M. Ollapally.
    p.   cm.
  Includes bibliographical references and index.
  ISBN 978-0-521-87584-4 (hardback)
  ISBN 978-0-521-69912-9 (pbk.)
  1. Radicalism–South Asia.   2. South Asia–Politics and government.
  I. Title.
  DS341.O66 2008
  320.530954–dc22   2008020513

ISBN 978-0-521-87584-4 hardback
ISBN 978-0-521-69912-9 paperback

To Anand

Contents

Acknowledgements

At the end of the day, one of the best things about writing a book is being able to thank all those who have been a part of this enterprise, in print. This has been a three-year project, written over two continents, and many have made it possible.

On the personal side, I thank my daughter Kavi and son Siddharth, for not only putting up with an absentee and absent-minded mother, but for being so understanding about it. My husband Anand has gone way beyond the call of spousal duty in making this book a reality. I dedicate this book to him, with love and gratitude for graciously adjusting and re-adjusting his life to fit mine, despite the huge demands of his own work.

My sister Beena, my brother Phil, and my mother Thresiamma Ollapally, offered constant support. As always, my biggest cheerleader was my father Abraham Ollapally; I only wish he could have seen the final product. I want to thank my father-in-law, S. Gnanalingam, for his lively discussions with me on South Asian politics and his deep insights. My extended family in Bangalore, especially my aunt Thankamma Ollapally, was a source of strength, and early believer in my endeavor. I want to thank my friends in Bethesda, especially Supriya and Sanjay Dhar, Ruth and Mark Morrel, for stepping in and helping in so many ways given our inter-continental family circumstances while I was writing.

Informal discussions with colleagues and acquaintances have helped me much more than they know: special mention should be made of Samina Ahmed, Kanti Bajpai, Dipankar Banerjee, Jonah Blank, Rekha Chaudhary, Wajahat Habibullah, Rick Inderfurth, Tariq Karim, Amitabh Mattoo, C. Raja Mohan, Surender Singh Oberoi, Narendar Pani, Varun Sahni and Siddharth Varadarajan. Mizanur Rahman Shelley needs to be singled out for the tremendous professional courtesy and hospitality he showed me when I visited Dhaka. Over the years, I have gained much from interacting with students in my graduate courses on South Asia at George Washington University and Georgetown.

Institutionally, I would like to thank the US Institute of Peace, in particular, Paul Stares for supporting this project at the initial stage. The

Sigur Center for Asian Studies at George Washington University has continuously provided excellent facilities and company. I also want to thank my editor at Cambridge, Marigold Acland, for her keen eye and patience.

Finally, I need to answer a question – why another book on extremism? Post September 11, I found many colleagues rushing to write because they felt they had to "say something." I resisted that temptation until I felt that I had "something to say." I hope the readers agree.

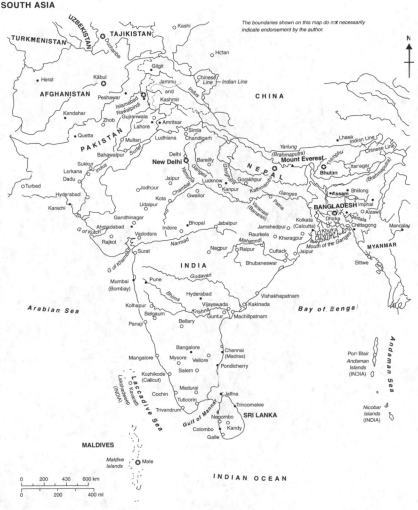

SOUTH ASIA

The boundaries shown on this map do not necessarily indicate endorsement by the author.

N

Note: Dotted line represents approximately the Line of Control in Jammu & Kashmir agreed upon by India and Pakistan.

1   Introduction: beyond and before the 9/11 framework

Re-examining extremism

In the popular mind, extremism and terrorism are invariably linked to ethnic and religious factors. Yet the dominant history of South Asia is notable for tolerance and co-existence, despite highly plural societies. What then accounts for the rise of extremist ethno-religious groups in societies that were historically not predisposed thus? What determines the winners and losers in the identity struggles that we see in South Asia, and what tips the balance between more moderate and extremist outcomes? Despite the unprecedented international attention South Asia has received in the wake of the terrorist attacks on September 11, 2001, we would be hard-pressed to conclude that our understanding of extremism and our capacity to combat it, have improved significantly. If anything, the situation has become more dire – from Afghanistan to Pakistan to Sri Lanka to Bangladesh, extremist violence is breaking out anew or remains unabated. Much of the post-9/11 analysis is from a US policy perspective with little theoretical or historical content, and for a region that has an overabundance of history and political complexity, such an approach is far too limited.

We need a new way to grasp the complex of political and geopolitical factors that have determined outcomes in South Asia over the contemporary period, pre- and post-9/11. It would seem vitally important to re-examine a phenomenon that shows little signs of receding, let alone being defeated. This book offers a fresh perspective to illuminate and explain the contours of extremism in South Asia, bringing together insights from international relations and domestic politics. While the book does not purport to offer a full-scale treatment of all forms of extremism in South Asia, it does attempt a fairly ambitious explanation that captures important tendencies in extremism across the region from Afghanistan, Pakistan, India, Sri Lanka and Bangladesh. Indeed, my analytical framework sees a cross-country and inter-linked process of extremism at work. This introductory chapter lays out the book's main line of argument, and shows why we need to go beyond a number of popular alternative explanations for extremism found in the literature.

Explanatory limitations

Broadly speaking, the conventional view posits religious ideology as the main driver of extremist violence in South Asia, especially "Muslim South Asia." In the larger South Asian context, we may add another factor, ethnic identity, as a chief motivator. Although both these so-called primordial explanations had been receding in the scholarly community, 9/11 has brought the religious explanation in particular back to the forefront. Referring to the ethno-religious hatred explanation, one analyst put it this way: "like the monster in slasher movies, just when you think that view is dead and buried, it springs up once more."[1] Samuel Huntington's *The Clash of Civilizations and the Remaking of World Order* remains the touchstone for many proponents of these models.[2] Yet, a closer look points to a puzzle: why do groups and individual leaders with shared religious roots or ethnic backgrounds and even similar initial objectives choose different strategies to achieve their aims? Why do some turn to extremism and even terrorist violence to promote their cause while others choose a more moderate path? Why are some groups more amenable to co-optation or participation in the larger political process than others? Why do we observe huge divergences across time in terms of the level of extremism expressed in any given region? These anomalies or puzzles clearly beg further explanation beyond ethnicity or religion.

An alternative explanation

This book argues that we can understand the trajectory of extremism in South Asia by considering a three-way identity struggle that repeats itself across the region between ethno-religious, secular, and what I term

---

[1] R. G. Suny, "Why We Hate You: The Passions of National Identity and Ethnic Violence," *Working Paper Series* (Berkeley Program in Soviet and Post-Soviet Studies) February 1, 2004, p. 22. He points out how Samuel Huntington takes the notion of a civilization and reifies it into a large cultural constellation. Examples of the post-9/11 primordial works include *The Age of Sacred Terror* (New York: Random House, 2002) by Daniel Benjamin and Steven Simon in which they argue forcefully for an apocalyptic religious conception of terrorism and violent extremism and Barry Cooper's *New Political Religions, or an Analysis of Modern Terrorism* (Columbia: University of Missouri Press, 2004). Jessica Stern takes a somewhat more equivocal stance in *Terror in the Name of God: Why Religious Militants Kill* (New York: Ecco/HarperCollins Publishers, 2003).

[2] Samuel P. Huntington, *The Clash of Civilizations and the Remaking of World Order* (New York: Touchstone, 1997).

"geopolitical identities."[3] This pattern of competition and convergence goes a long way in determining the evolution of either moderate or more extreme political outcomes, and a key objective of the book is to discover what tips the balance one way or the other. The book's underlying contention is that geopolitics has had far greater impact on the rise and persistence of extremism than generally believed, and the impacts of religion and ethnicity have been less so. There is a fairly good understanding of the *politics* of ethnic and religious movements. Less explored is the *geopolitics* of religion and ethnicity.

Competition between states and their power plays as set forth by a Waltzian realist framework have been enormously important.[4] However, in South Asia, geopolitics has to be seen as not simply occurring in a disconnected fashion at the international level, but rather as influencing and creating deeper social and political structures and orientations within states. This view is compatible with Peter Gourevitch's well-known approach, which points to the strong impact of the international system on domestic structures and preferences.[5] But he also cautions that the international arena does not determine outcomes outright, short of actual military occupation. Thus there is some leeway at the domestic level in responding to the international environment. What is important is the *interactive* nature of the international and domestic realms, a notion upon which my argument is based.[6]

South Asia is fertile ground for geopolitical influence in the domestic sphere with contested sovereignties; ethnic, religious and linguistic

---

[3] Secular and geopolitical identities need greater elaboration and are described later in the chapter. To anticipate, secularism is viewed in a more encompassing sense than a simple religious versus nonreligious dichotomy.

[4] For the definitive contemporary work on realism, see Kenneth Waltz, *Theory of International Politics* (Reading, MA: Addison-Wesley, 1979). One problem with Waltz's approach is that it operates at a fairly gross level in determining outcomes, and it remains firmly at the international level in terms of the independent and dependent variables.

[5] A more refined and useful approach that extends Waltz's theory for analyzing the influence of international factors on domestic structures is Peter Gourevitch's "second image reversed" ("The Second Image Reversed: The International Sources of Domestic Politics," *International Organization* 32.4 (Autumn 1978), p. 882, 900). The "outside-in" effects of external forces and actors on domestic politics and preferences is critical in South Asia, particularly his insight into how "domestic structure itself derives from the exigencies of the international system." James Alt, Peter Evans and Peter Katzenstein are a few of the well-known exponents of Gourevitch's model. See also Ira Katznelson and Martin Shefte (eds.), *Shaped by War and Trade: International Influences on American Political Development* (Princeton, NJ: Princeton University Press, 2002).

[6] As he put it, "The international system, be it in an economic or politico-military form, is underdetermining. The environment may exert strong pulls but, short of actual occupation, some leeway in the response to that environment remains." (Gourevitch, "The Second Image Reversed," p. 900)

minorities spilling across borders; and insecure political classes. The geopolitical interests and needs of regional and extra-regional states have increasingly had a deep impact on the shape of internal identities – and that impact has not been confined to the politico-military realm as traditional international analysis would have it. All too often, the results have been a polarizing of ethnic and religious identities with disastrous consequences. Yet, those identities had previously coexisted within a fairly open and secular historical tradition (described in Chapter Two). Across South Asia, perceived geopolitical and strategic needs have shaped and modified identities, as captured in the term "geopolitical identity." I suggest that conditions of weak secularism and a highly charged geopolitical environment tend to produce the most extremist outcomes. This is not to suggest that robust secularism will prevent war, but it is extremism, not inter-state warfare, that is under investigation.

Gaps in alternative explanations

Political violence or extremist violence takes place in different forms: insurgencies, civil war, communalism, terrorism and government repression. It is important to keep in mind that it is difficult to collapse all these forms of violence in any analytically meaningful manner. Conversely, it is nearly impossible to understand terrorism if it can encompass everything from government repression to inter-communal violence.[7] The literature on political violence is mostly characterized by domestic level explanations, with only a limited number also considering external variables.[8] The most important alternative explanations for radicalism are: ethno-religious identity; relative economic deprivation; elite manipulation; and state repression and lack of political institutional access. Their drawbacks and limitations are highlighted below to underscore the need for the alternative framework that this book offers. Further, the book shows how the proposed framework can subsume or supplement these explanations.

Donald Horowitz's studies on *ethno-religious conflict* remain classic works in the field.[9] For Horowitz, ethnicity is a key marker for groups in conflict,

---

[7] For a discussion of this dilemma, see, for example, Nicholas Sambanis, "Poverty and the Organization of Political Violence," *Brookings Trade Forum* (2004), pp. 168–170.

[8] One early work considering the role of external relations on ethno-political conflict is by Stephen Ryan, *Ethnic Conflict and International Relations* (Aldershot, England: Dartmouth Publishing Co., 1995), especially pp. 52–76.

[9] See for example, Donald Horowitz, *Ethnic Groups in Conflict* (Berkeley, CA: Univeristy of California Press, 2000); and *Deadly Ethnic Riots* (Berkeley, CA: University of California Press, 2001).

but challenges to this have come from a variety of sources.[10] If ethnic identity is given primary importance, then we would have to also explain how the hugely diverse populations of South Asia have co-existed without resorting to violence for long periods of time. Co-existence, not conflict, has been the reality of clearly differentiated groups in the subcontinent.[11] Similarly, if religious ideology is privileged in explaining political violence, how do we account for the large divergences *within* religious groups on political preferences? This factor is nearly always omitted in works making a strong religion-based argument.

For example, the book aptly titled *New Political Religions, or an Analysis of Modern Terrorism* argues that "new political religions" are launching spiritual warfare that does not recognize conventional cost-benefit analysis in its operation. The author uses a highly selective and narrow perception of Islamic tradition to argue that it never developed a pragmatic and realistic way to distinguish between religious and nonreligious aspects.[12] It is a reductionist argument that cannot account for the variations found in Islamic thinking or practice, and is, at bottom, an argument based on extremely shaky essentialist logic. In Kashmir, for example, Muslims are not united on either the means or the ends in their struggle. The ruling People's Democratic Party and its main opposition party, National Conference, are not insignificant and largely Muslim parties, yet they operate in entirely different ways than the militants. Even more pointedly, Muslims in the rest of India have shown little or no support for Kashmiri separatism. Clearly, more is at work than a simple attachment to ethnicity or religion.

Some proponents of the *relative deprivation* school, such as Ted Gurr, see the ethno-religious factor as an intervening variable, rather than a causal one. Others who make the relative deprivation argument have tried to establish a more direct causal link between inequality and violence, but, despite the huge literature on the subject, there is no consensus.[13] Gurr's more sophisticated notion is an expansion of his original view regarding individual psychological grievances about unfulfilled expectations, to one

---

[10] For an argument that takes issue with the very notion of ethno-religious conflict, see Bruce Gilley, "Against the Concept of Ethnic Conflict," *Third World Quarterly*, 25.6 (2004), pp. 1155–1166.

[11] Raju Thomas provides a good overview of the ethno-religious diversity of South Asia in "The 'Nationalities' Question in South Asia," in Amita Shastri and A. J. Wilson (eds.), *The Post-Colonial States of South Asia* (London: Curzon and Palgrave Press, 2001) pp. 196–211.

[12] Cooper, *New Political Religions*.

[13] For excellent summary discussions, see, for example, Sambanis, "Poverty," pp. 165–211 and Gudrun Ostby, "Horizontal Inequalities and Civil Conflict," paper prepared for the 46th Annual Convention of the International Studies Association, Honolulu, HI, March 1–5, 2005.

that sees how inequalities that coincide with ethnic cleavages may increase both dissatisfaction and group solidarity, resulting in greater chances to mobilize for conflict.[14] Still, in South Asia, even a cursory glance at some of the groups in conflict points to a gap: Tamils in Sri Lanka and Kashmiris do not fit the profile of groups that were relatively deprived economically. Terrorists of the 9/11 variety and others actually demonstrate a positive relationship between political violence and economic standing, calling this model into serious question.[15]

Explanations based on *elite manipulations* have taken us much further in explaining why conflict and extremism occurs in particular contexts and not in others, and how ethnic and religious factors come to the forefront in some cases and not in others.[16] However, ethnic and religious "elites" are far from uniform, so how is it that the interpretations of one set of elites on identity issues gains ascendancy over others? Inter-elite competition is frequent, and it is not always possible to predict the outcomes at the outset. For example, in the Indian case, there has been disagreement between the more Hindu nationalist Bharatiya Janata Party and Congress Party's Hindu and non-Hindu leaders alike on mobilizing political support by appealing to religious identity. In Pakistan, the leaderships of the Jamaat-i-Islami (JI) and Jamiat Ulema-e-Islami (JUI) have not been equally active on the Kashmir and Afghanistan conflicts, and have shown differences in the importance they attach to them and the manner in which they characterize the religious content of these conflicts.

An additional explanation for extremism is found at the state level: groups turn to violence in response to *state repression*, having no other effective recourse. In some instances, this seems to be a plausible explanation, as may be argued in the case of Sri Lanka. However, the causation is as likely to work the other way around, and it often depends on which point in the timeline the analysis begins. Of course, given the paramount position of the state and its potential coercive capacity, it does not necessarily take political repression as such to activate violent reactions; much less could do the same. Another state-level explanation

---

[14] Ted R. Gurr, *Why Men Rebel* (Princeton: Princeton University Press, 1970), Ted R. Gurr and Barbara Harff, *Ethnic Conflict in World Politics* (Boulder: Westview Press, 1994) and Ted R. Gurr, *Minorities at Risk* (Washington, DC: US Institute of Peace Press, 1993).

[15] Sambanis ("Poverty," pp. 168–170) is one of the few analysts who tries to explain this anomaly systematically, but it remains rather ad hoc.

[16] A foremost exponent of instrumentalism is Paul Brass, *Ethnicity and Nationalism* (New Delhi: Sage Publications, 1991), p. 15. See also Peter van der Veer, "Riots and Rituals: The Construction of Violence and Public Space in Hindu Nationalism," in Paul Brass (ed.) *Riots and Pogroms* (New York: New York University Press, 1996).

suggests that it does not require repression per se – denial or perception of denial of political access is often sufficient.

One study that partially supports this proposition is by Mohammed Hafez, whose work on Islamist groups suggests that institutional exclusion blocks avenues for political participation, and when it is combined with state repression, rebellions and insurgencies ensue.[17] His focus is on Egypt and Algeria, with only brief vignettes of many other cases including Afghanistan, Kashmir and Pakistan. But again we are left with the question as to why comparable groups react in different ways when faced with similar state actions, from high-handedness to outright repression. Moreover, we find extremist violence occurring even in open, democratic political systems, as the cases of India and Sri Lanka show. Indeed, despite being one of the strongest democracies, India is also the venue for a large number of sustained insurgencies and extremist violence.

Filling the gaps: external–internal encounters and mediating identities

As the above discussion shows, the most widely held explanations for extremism cannot account for the variations in outcomes that we observe in practice. We suggest that regional and global geopolitics have come to play an enormous role in shaping and influencing domestic structures and identities, and solely domestic level explanations are insufficient. The key to this external–internal interaction in South Asia is the role of the state, traditionally the only actor in such a mediating position, located at the intersection of internal politics and external geopolitics.[18] This pivotal position gives executive officials a special legitimacy in the formulation of national security policy that they lack in other more "domestic" areas of public policy. With this legitimacy, they can redefine previously domestic issues or define ambiguous international questions in a way that impinges on national sovereignty, security or threat perception, all generally conceded to be in the domain of the state.[19] Unlike liberal interpreters of the state who see it

[17] Mohammed Hafez, *Why Muslims Rebel: Repression and Resistance in the Islamic World* (Boulder, CO: Lynne Rienner Publishers, 2003).

[18] This privileged position of the state has been challenged in recent times by anti-statist groups, especially with the widespread use of the internet and other communication technologies that operate beyond the strict control of the state.

[19] This point, emphasized by G. John Ikenberry, David A. Lake and Michael Mastanduno, regarding foreign economic policy, is even more applicable in the national security arena. See "Introduction: Approaches to Explaining American Foreign Economic Policy," *International Organization* 42.1 (Winter 1988), p. 13.

only as a referee among competing societal interest groups, or captured entirely by class interests as Marxists would have it, this book adheres to the presumption of state autonomy as articulated by Theda Skocpol and others.[20]

Giving the state such significance and autonomy may seem contradictory in light of the near consensus regarding the weakness of states in South Asia.[21] Although the South Asian state's capacities may be weak in comparison to its counterparts in advanced industrial states, it still enjoys relative power among national actors (with the notable exception of the period of the internal wars in Afghanistan in the 1990s). As the dominant institution in what are universally diverse societies, the state is particularly well placed to influence, shape and perpetuate various identity formations. The state's capacity to define national identity in South Asia is also enhanced thanks to two other enduring realities: the region has been persistently vulnerable to wider geopolitical pressures; and the region has been plagued by unstable secularism as a result of historical factors. Both these conditions have given the state a significant mediating role as an autonomous and Janus-faced actor. This raises the question of why certain forms of identity are promoted (explicitly or implicitly) over others by the state. It is at this point that the external–internal relationship becomes critical; and it goes some way towards filling the gaps in current understandings of political violence and extremism.

If we assume that the autonomy of the state is fairly significant, it becomes possible to identify state preferences for "national identities." Identities that offer the greatest scope for statist conceptions would seem to be a natural preference. In South Asia, for example, we would expect that states with majority Muslim populations would opt

[20] Theda Skocpol's work has been decisive in understanding the critical notions of state autonomy and state capacity. State autonomy refers to the ability of the state to pursue goals independent of societal pressures or interests. State capacity relates to the ability of the state to carry out its objectives, which includes factors such as level of military control over territorial sovereignty, internal coherence and administrative and economic resources. It is especially useful in developing a historical–institutional and comparative perspective on the role of the state. Her early work remains highly relevant. See Theda Skocpol, "Bringing the State Back In: Strategies of Analysis in Current Research," in Peter B. Evans, Dietrich Rueschemeyer and Theda Skocpol (eds.) *Bringing the State Back In* (Cambridge University Press, 1985). See also Michael Mann, "The Autonomous Power of the State," in *States in History* (ed.) John A. Hall (Cambridge: Basil Blackwell, 1986).

[21] Vernon Hewitt offers one of the best constructed explanations of state weakness in South Asia. See *The New International Relations of South Asia* (Manchester: Manchester University Press and Palgrave Press, 1999), especially pp. 1–20. But despite talk of state failure or imminent collapse in parts of South Asia, the state as actor is still critical.

for more "officially" sanctioned Islamic identities rather than the traditional popular and folk Sufi versions. Some analysts have referred to these distinctive Islamic identities as "parcellization of Islam," a development that began with colonial authorities, but was extended under post-colonial elites.[22] Rather than a religious preference, it would appear to be a political one: Sufi concepts are diffuse, syncretic, inner-directed and as such are difficult, if not impossible, for the state to arrogate. They cannot be easily adapted for state purposes, nor easily destroyed for that matter. For example, while orthodox Islam was systematically purged during the anti-religious drives in Soviet Central Asia during the 1930s, Sufi mystical folk Islam managed to survive; likewise, Sufism continues to flourish in Afghanistan despite the onslaught of more radical Islamic strains in Afghanistan during the 1980s.[23] Conversely, it could be argued that the very fragmented nature of Hinduism makes it difficult for "official" versions to be developed or to take hold politically, despite attempts to do so. This discussion begins to give us a sense of how the state may operate in the context of identity politics, in particular, the creation or suppression of exclusionary political space. This has implications for nearly all the alternative explanations already discussed.

For instance, essentialist arguments that cannot explain why different ethno-religious groups engage in conflict when they have co-existed for long periods, may be overtaken by an understanding of the role of the state in constructing, or at minimum justifying, exclusionary social visions. In almost every South Asian country the state has done this at some point in the post-independence era. The effects have been felt most in Sri Lanka, Afghanistan, Bangladesh and Pakistan. Likewise, in the context of elite manipulations, which version of identity wins may be traced in large part to state sanction or opposition. In Pakistan, the trumping of mainstream elite conceptions of the Pakistan People's Party and the Muslim League, which have tended towards loose secular identities, by religiously motivated political ideology, cannot be understood without seeing the statist needs of the military. Even the relative economic deprivation argument may be supplemented by a

---

[22] Describing the historical developments in Bangladesh, Imtiaz Ahmed argues that the British authorities took the lead in trying to isolate Sufism from Islam, making the latter "thoroughly apathetic if not opposed to 'reason'." See "The Role of Education in Conflict: Bangladesh," in Pamela Aall and Deepa Ollapally (eds.) *Perspectives on the Role of Education and Media in Conflict Management in South Asia* (Washington, DC: US Institute of Peace Press, forthcoming 2008), p. 4.

[23] Brian Glyn Williams, "Jihad and Ethnicity in Post-Communist Eurasia: On the Trail of Transnational Islamic Holy Warriors in Kashmir, Afghanistan, Central Asia, Chechnya and Kosovo," *The Global Review of Ethnopolitics*, 2.3–4 (March/June 2003), p. 4.

state-oriented analysis: preferential or prejudicial economic policies can stimulate perceptions of future deprivation, as in the case of Sri Lankan Tamils, leading to a sharpening of grievances. In already polarized or potentially polarizing conditions, even benign economic neglect by the state can have a strong catalytic impact, as in Assam in northeastern India. Finally, the simple state repression argument needs to be refined. States have a variety of tools at their disposal that have been used, well short of repression, whether in proactive or reactive terms. The more complex institutional blockage argument made by Hafez is also not entirely convincing because he ignores the "political culture" surrounding institutions. The presence or absence of secular political culture often determines or conditions the level of institutional openness to various forms of grievances in the first place.

Nevertheless, this pivotal position of the state does not mean that it can dictate even security policy (an area in which it has no other serious competitor) on a whim. The external environment clearly sets some limits. For example, it is not an accident that the most violent conflicts have occurred on the borders or geographical peripheries in India. The Indian government cannot set policy in Kashmir, Assam or, earlier, Punjab without taking into account Pakistan, Bangladesh or China. Factoring in the geopolitical context allows us to make better sense of the state's chosen strategy in dealing with political violence in these cases. Going one step further beyond the domestic political sphere thus brings us to the central argument of this book.

The state and geopolitical identities

In South Asia, identities have underlying geopolitical components – the 1947 partition of India has left a legacy of clashing identities as well as territorial competition, best captured by the Kashmir conflict. Bangladesh is struggling to resolve its national identity between a Bengali and Bangladeshi definition, ultimately connected to regional relationships with India. Likewise, extremism in Sri Lanka reflects a chauvinistic Sinhalese nationalism wrapped up in a "majority–minority" complex understood only with reference to India.

The ongoing competition to redefine "national identity" in Afghanistan illustrates clashing preferences and interests vis-à-vis Pakistan and the US. Whether ethnic, religious or a more secular pan-Afghan identity dominates in the end will have implications for domestic and international relations. For the government, headed by Hamid Karzai, the latter is the most attractive for a host of reasons, not least because of exterior pressures.

Ethnic fragments, ethnic solidarity, religious affiliation, language rights, are all both internal and external challenges in South Asia. In other words, geopolitics is not just relevant in the military–strategic sphere. It has important implications for identity.

Preferences on national identity for state officials will vary – secular, religious or ethnic identification makes sense at different points for particular statist objectives or compulsions. (Among the countries of South Asia, only India has consistently had a secular constitution.) When national security, territoriality and national identity perceptions become merged, some of the most pernicious and counterproductive formulations of geopolitical identity can be created.[24] For example, purely economic factors can become translated into questions of dependency and control, perceived as affecting sovereignty and, by swift extension, national identity, as often happens in Bangladesh's policies towards India. In the Kashmir conflict, the preferences of the Pakistani state for an exclusivist Islamist identity – and its promotion of groups that project such – creates major regional dilemmas, even for Kashmiri Muslims, let alone, India. In the end, state actors may be expected to be power seekers – responding to, and, when possible, creating conditions that extend state power. Charles Tilly's well-known writings on the state and war may be paraphrased: war makes the state and the state makes war.[25] Even without going as far as war-making, we can see how competition and hostility in the region, supplemented by warlike mentalities and exclusionary identities, might serve the same purpose. We would expect this to be especially true for state actors who are weak or lack widespread legitimacy – all too often the situation across South Asia.

This discussion points to the key role of the state as "gatekeeper" in setting the terms of identity discourse and interpretation. What is important to recognize for our purpose is that the state plays a large role in defining national identity and threats, and in allowing or constricting political space for multiple interpretations. States have a variety of tools at their disposal, including the power not only to repress, but also to patronize and promote. For example, the formation of a more extremist religious identity in Pakistan over time cannot be understood without examining the way that Islamist groups

---

[24] This is consistent with Ali Riaz's portrayal of Bangladesh's identity transformation as a combination of religion, territoriality and national security. See his *Unfolding State: The Transformation of Bangladesh* (Ontario: de Sitter Publications, 2005), p. 218.

[25] See Charles Tilly, "Reflections on the History of European State Making," in Tilly, Charles (ed.) *The Formation of National States in Western Europe* (Princeton, NJ: Princeton Universty Press, 1972), especially pp. 73–76. See also Franz Schurmann, *The Logic of World Power: An Inquiry into the Origins, Currents and Contradictions of World Politics* (New York: Pantheon, 1974), especially pp. 3–30. For an application of Tilly's approach to contemporary foreign policy, see the author's *Confronting Conflict: Domestic Factors and US Policymaking the Third World* (Westport, CT: Greenwood Press, 1993).

have received state support. But it was the Pakistani military's specific geopolitical identity needs that led the state towards the Islamists in the first place. State actors as interlocutors between the international and domestic spheres will be investigated in detail later in the book, but at this stage, we need to add that the state in general has not escaped theoretical criticism. Indeed, criticism of the state is widespread in the literature on South Asia.

Ironically, some of the most trenchant criticism comes from two different ends of the spectrum: the post-modernists or critical theorists and the "traditionalists" (for lack of a better term). Both would like to see the state diminish if not disappear, although for quite different reasons.[26] Either way, states are seen as ineffective in dealing with extremism and violence of all sorts; in fact, the tendency would be to see the state itself as a root cause. These challenges are hardly surprising since the "state" in South Asian countries suffers huge shortcomings, from lack of legitimacy to weakness in the delivery of public goods. At the same time, of course, there is little to suggest that the abolition of the state would make separatists, extremists and other violent discontents any more amenable.

This book does not take an all-or-nothing view of the state; it recognizes that the state has been both protector and aggressor. Rather than abolition, what is needed is to subject it to strict accountability and examination. We do not necessarily need less of the state. We need a more responsive and transparent one. Practically speaking, there is no likelihood of the state disappearing any time soon, nor is there evidence that notions of sovereignty can be easily dislodged or replaced with some other international consensus.

Whatever position one takes, the state's influence is undeniable, and its role becomes even more pronounced when we add geopolitics into the mix in South Asia, whether via the war on terrorism, inter-state rivalries or other factors. In *Deadly Connections*, Dan Byman demonstrates

---

[26] While adherents to these schools might object to such simplification, I would argue that it captures an essential distinction. Having said this, it should be noted that the attack on modernity by those I have called traditionalists, cannot be critiqued as being nostalgic or backward-looking; it includes a strong attack against western hegemony and western particularism in its search for more authentic culture, thus partly sharing the postmodern outlook. See for example Ashis Nandy, *Bonfire of Creeds: The Essential Nandy* (New Delhi: Oxford University Press, 2004) and *Romance of the State and the Fate of Dissent in the Tropics* (New Delhi: Oxford University Press, 2003) and Bhikhu Parekh, "The Cultural Particularity of Liberal Democracy," *Political Studies* 40 (1992). Representative works on post-modernism include Jean-Francois Lyotard, *The Postmodern Condition* (Minneapolis: University of Minnesota Press, 1984), David Harvey, *The Condition of Postmodernity: An Enquiry into the Origins of Cultural Change* (Oxford: Basil Blackwell, 1989); and Pauline Marie Rosenau, *Postmodernism and the Social Sciences* (Princeton, NJ: Princeton University Press, 1992). See also Alex Callinicos, *Against Postmodernism* (New York: St. Martin's Press, 1990) and Robert J. Antonio, "After Postmodernism: Reactionary Tribalism," *American Journal of Sociology*, 106.2 (2000).

the importance of states that sponsor terrorist groups for foreign policy purposes and domestic politics.[27] While Byman's argument is not explicitly extended to domestic identity structures, the evidence he presents is supportive (and indeed goes against prevailing views of the fragmented and decentralized terrorist cells and networks dominating in the post-9/11 world).[28] The US war on terrorism since 2001 is only the latest manifestation of longstanding external forces acting on South Asia's domestic political structures. The extent of intrusiveness has varied from state to state in South Asia, with Afghanistan lying at one end of the spectrum and India at the other. Geopolitics casts its shadow deep into domestic political structures, either through direct military intervention and quasi-occupation as in Afghanistan after 2001, or in less tangible ways as in Bangladesh's ruling parties rejection of potentially profitable large-scale energy and economic proposals from India.

Geopolitics and internal politics have been inextricably linked in South Asia since the very emergence of states in the region. (The impact of colonialism on domestic structures and preferences cannot be understated, and is taken up in some detail in Chapter Two.) Yet, there is a dearth of research looking at these intersections in a systematic manner. Since 9/11 increasing work has been done on locating the sources of terrorism and political violence internationally by two schools of thought, briefly outlined below, one of which focuses on globalization and one on transnational networks.

Relevance of other external explanations

Analysts from the globalization school tend to emphasize economic inequality and new international divisions of labor as causal factors. Those from the transnational network school point to the diffusion of new technologies, breakdown of communication barriers, and/or the intensification of transnational religious movements, in particular, messianic interpretations of Islam that do not recognize national boundaries. To use a popular term, there has been a "flattening of the world," which is serving as a powerful stimulant according to the transnational approach.[29] There is also

---

[27] Dan Byman, *Deadly Connections: States That Sponsor Terrorism* (New York: Cambridge University Press, 2005).

[28] A strong proponent of the view that terrorist cells are fragmented is Marc Sageman, *Leaderless Jihad: Terror Networks in the Twenty-first Century* (Philadelphia: University of Pennsylvania Press, 2008). For a searing attack of this view, see Bruce Hoffman, "The Myth of Grass-Roots Terrorism," *Foreign Affairs* 87.3 (May/June 2008).

[29] This term has been popularized particularly by best-selling author and journalist Thomas Friedman, *The World is Flat: A Brief History of the Twenty-First Century* (New York: Farrar, Straus and Giroux, 2005).

emerging work on the involvement of diasporas but, for all practical purposes, this work may be subsumed under the transnational network approach.

The literature on globalization is extensive and theoretically well developed, but its attention to the impact on domestic economic structures and attendant social disruptions essentially brings us back to the relative deprivation model to explain extremist challenges.[30] In contrast, the transnational network framework addresses the issue of extremism more directly, but it remains ad hoc and often ethnocentric. Since 9/11, there has been an outpouring of work of this ilk. The transnational approach also fails adequately to examine domestic structural linkages to the international arena, as well as the critical role of state actors (an omission that is fatal as Byman demonstrates).[31]

Constructing the argument

In investigating recurring three-way identity contests across South Asia, this book looks at Afghanistan, Pakistan, India, Sri Lanka and Bangladesh. In each, the emergence and evolution of extremist groups is set against the broader congruence or competition between secular, ethno-religious and geopolitical identity formations. It is the outcome of this struggle (or convergence for that matter) that all too often tips the balance towards moderation or extremism. In line with my central proposition regarding the importance of the state, I examine how state actors have influenced the development of exclusive and polarizing identity conceptions. In doing so, the book relies on the notion of "political secularism" as a yardstick to measure state orientations. At this point, it becomes necessary to define how this book uses some key terms – secularism, extremism and moderation.

---

[30] See for example, Kevin Hewison and Garry Rodan, "Closing the Circle: Globalization, Conflict and Political Regimes," presented at the Conference on Asia Pacific Economies: Multilateral vs. Bilateral Relationships, City University of Hong Kong, May 19–21, 2004. See also Mohammad J. Kuna, "Nations Without States: States, Globalization and Identity Conflicts," a paper presented at the Conference on Globalization, Identity Politics and Social Conflict: Ethnic, Literary and Sociolinguistic Perspectives, at the Center for Black and African Arts and Civilization, Lagos, Nigeria, April 14–16, 2003.

[31] The tendency for those bringing in external linkages is to be additive to, rather than integrative with, the domestic sphere. See, for example, Kshitij Prabha, "Defining Terrorism," *Strategic Analysis* 24.1 (April 2000). An exception to this lack of integrative theory building is Gregory M. Maney, "International Sources of Domestic Protest," *Mobilization* 6 (2001), pp. 83–98. An excellent general study on transnational networks is by Margaret Keck and Katherine Sikkink, *Activists Beyond Borders: Advocacy Networks in International Politics* (Ithaca, NY: Cornell University Press, 1998).

Some terminology

The term "secular" has various connotations and numerous detractors, especially in South Asia. However, we need not be detained here by a philosophical, ethical or normative treatment of secularism. This has been done extensively and ably by others. For our purposes, what is most useful is the notion of "political secularism" as a viable, if imperfect, standard of a state's political behavior.[32] The idea is that complete secularism is elusive, if not impossible, for any state in the South Asian context; thus what needs to be evaluated is the extent of so called "principled distance" aspired to, and achieved by, the state from religious, ethnic and other chauvinistic tendencies in a multi-dimensional society. In the end, this would seem to be a most pragmatic way of assessing the relationship of the state to secularism, and the impact of secular space.

Given the predominance of fragmented and insecure identities across South Asia, the ideological sphere is available for political debate, rather than set in stone, which gives the state the opportunity, and sometimes even a requirement, to enter the arena. To measure the level of a state's political secularism, we consider its policy discourse and practice in key arenas: educational and legal domestic structures; political ideology; and informal or formal maneuvers towards and within coalitions. The premise is that the ideology that the state propagates ultimately affects the evolution of either inclusive or exclusive identity notions more broadly in society.

The terms "extremism" and "moderation" may not at first glance need elaboration, since they are so widely used. But as increasing scholarly work on moderation shows, this does not reflect a common understanding of the term.[33] When I use the term moderate, I mean

---

[32] Rajeev Bhargava has marshaled an impressive set of viewpoints to develop the notion of "political secularism." For an extended discussion of "ethical secularism" versus "political secularism," see Rajeev Bhargava (ed.) *Secularism and Its Critics* (New Delhi: Oxford University Press, 1999), pp. 492–511. See also Akeel Bilgrami's "The Clash Within Civilizations," *Daedalus*, 123.3 (Summer 2003), p. 89 on the practical notion of secularism as a "political doctrine."

[33] See for example, Jillian Schwedler, *Faith in Moderation: Islamist Parties in Jordan and Yemen* (New York: Cambridge University Press, 2006). *The Dictionary of Political Thought* (New York: Hill & Wang, 1982) defines extremism as "1. Taking a political idea to its limits, regardless of 'unfortunate' repercussions, impracticalities, arguments and feelings to the contrary, and with the intention not only to confront, but also eliminate opposition. 2. Intolerance towards all views other than one's own. 3. Adoption of means to political ends which show disregard for the life, liberty and human rights of others." Given the inherently ambiguous nature of the term extremism, it is difficult to offer a universally accepted definition. We can situate extremism along a spectrum and see it manifested in a number of different ways: from holding strongly exclusionary viewpoints to utilizing outright violence to promote them. Terrorism may be seen as one form of extremism.

that groups or leaders more or less adhere to the rules of the game as set out by the state in which they operate, especially democratic processes; that they do not directly utilize violence for political ends; and that the main thrust of their political discourse is not chauvinistically exclusivist. Context also matters. It is possible that a group or individual in one particular place may be characterized by some observers as moderate, whereas others might see them as more extremist.

In Afghanistan, for example, Gulbuddin Hekmatyar is regarded by nearly all as representing violent extremism, but opinion may be divided on Ismail Khan. According to our definition, he may be seen as towards the moderate end of the spectrum in the current political context while others might depict him closer to the extremist end. Despite the lack of a fine-grained, universally shared understanding of what it means to be extremist or moderate, we believe that these terms serve useful heuristic and practical purposes. The following discussion attempts to give some perspective to this debate, given this lack of consensus.

Beyond and before the 9/11 framework

Defining terrorism

The use of "extremism" as opposed to the blanket term "terrorism" is preferable for a number of reasons.[34] The term terrorism has suffered from the lack of a universally accepted definition, at both the academic and policy levels. Despite extended and repeated attempts by the United Nations in the aftermath of 9/11, it has proved nearly impossible to generate a definition of terrorism that satisfies all parties. Of course, in the face of the very real impact of violent extremism on victims, a purely semantic argument has its limitations. Nevertheless, I consider the term terrorism below in a manner that I hope will shed more light than heat in understanding our central concern of extremism in South Asia.

Terrorism as a term was first employed to describe a phase of the French Revolution – "The Reign of Terror" – in which the radical Jacobins, recently ascended to power in 1793, violently suppressed counter-revolutionaries. Despite the term's genesis in "state terrorism," it has over the years come to be used to identify non-state actors. This

---

[34] In any case, research shows that counterterrorism efforts not going beyond simple definitions of terrorism have not proven to be effective. See Audrey Kurth Cronin, *The Diplomacy of Counterterrorism: Lessons Learned, Ignored and Disputed*, Special Report 80, US Institute of Peace, Washington, DC, January 14, 2002.

makes some sense since states themselves are held to important standards such as accountability and representativeness, in contrast to non-state groups and individuals who may be unidentifiable, unrepresentative, and unaccountable except to themselves, their chosen circle, or, in the last instance, to a higher divine authority. State behavior is also circumscribed by rules of war under the Geneva Convention: protection of non-combatants, prohibition against taking hostages, treatment of prisoners of war, and diplomatic immunity. The state/non-state distinction holds particularly well for functioning democracies in which rampant human rights violations are hard to sustain with impunity.

Analysts have attempted to craft definitions of terrorism, none of which are fully satisfactory.[35] One widespread definition is the use of violence against random non-military targets in order to intimidate and create a generalized fear for the purpose of achieving political ends. For most of us, this is an acceptable characterization if we use the so-called "reasonableness standard," resorted to by juries in the legal context. For those who would like to recognize that some terrorists' grievances may sometimes be legitimate, this definition provides a way to reject their methods without rejecting their aims, although there will still be a tiny minority who argue that terrorist methods themselves are the weapons of last resort by the weak against the strong.

Two of the world's leading analysts of terrorism, Alex Schmid and Walter Laqueur, who have focused almost exclusively on arriving at a definition of terrorism, ultimately acknowledge their failure after several years' work. Schmid concedes that the "search for an adequate definition is still on," and Laqueur concludes that it is neither possible nor worthwhile to attempt a definition.[36] According to one exhaustive investigation, there

[35] A frequently cited expert is Martha Crenshaw who gives an extended definition of terrorism and other forms of political violence. See "The Psychology of Terrorism: An Agenda for the 21st Century," *Political Psychology*, 21.2 (2002), p. 406. One unconventional definition of terrorism as a mutating virus is put forward by Paul Stares and Mona Yacoubian, "Terrorism as Virus," *The Washington Post*, August 23, 2005. Their approach however is not developed, and remains at best suggestive. Mustapha Kamal Pasha suggests that one way to approach the definitional problem would be to distinguish between context-specific Islamic extremism and terrorism as a phenomenon in its own right in "Islamic Extremists: How Do They Mobilize Support?" Current Issues Briefing, US Institute of Peace, Washington, DC, April 17, 2002. For important general works on terrorism, see, for example, Walter Laqueur, *The Age of Terrorism* (New York: Little, Brown and Co., 1987), Yonah Alexander (ed.) *International Terrorism: National, Regional and Global Perspectives* (New York: Praeger, 1976) and Bruce Hoffmann, *Inside Terrorism* (New York: Columbia University, 1998). See also Mahmood Mamdani, *Good Muslim, Bad Muslim: America, the Cold War and the Roots of Terror* (New York: Doubleday, 2005).

[36] Quoted in Hoffman, *Inside Terrorism*, p. 39. Hoffman agrees, but suggests that it is possible to distinguish terrorism from other types of violence and terrorists from other types of criminals, and offers some distinguishing features.

are 109 different definitions of terrorism in the literature.[37] Does this mean that there is no way to define terrorism accurately and objectively? It would seem so if we want that definition to be universally accepted and normatively-shared.

A workable alternative is to see terrorism as one form of extremist political violence. Some might respond that substituting extremism is simply argument by displacement; but as we have seen, there is no optimal solution. This book uses the terms "violent extremism," "militancy," "jihadism" and "terrorism" depending on the context, with an eye for the local, widely accepted usage. This facilitates our analysis of a variety of groups without instantly getting mired in value-laden, first-order questions. Finally and most importantly, this book deals with broad trends in South Asia, making extremism a more sensible phenomenon to explore.

Contextualizing terrorism and America's role

For the large majority of analysts in the US and many external experts, 9/11 has become the decisive marker for studying global terrorism. Yet accepting a 9/11-centric framework to consider violent extremism worldwide, puts us in danger of losing sight of the nature and impact of America's own role. The Iraq case is the most obvious current example: almost no evidence of terrorist links or cells threatening the US could be found prior to the American invasion of Iraq. Post-invasion, groups in Iraq reactively attacking the US are regularly termed "terrorists," providing a justification for US military action, and in the process, blurring the lines between cause and effect. Most of all, this situation shows America's near hegemonic definitional power.

It is interesting that even for states that gain some utility from the post-9/11 "global war on terrorism" for their own legitimate national security reasons, there is a palpable distance from the US view. For example, in India, the Bharatiya Janata Party-led National Democratic Alliance that was in power until May 2004, consciously maintained a studied distance on the war in Iraq. The Indian decision not to send troops in July 2003, despite intense US pressure, was justified by citing the lack of a United Nations mandate, but there were two other underlying reasons as well: domestic opposition and strong doubts regarding America's approach to fighting

---

[37] Ray Takeyh, "Two Cheers from the Islamic World," *Foreign Policy* 128 (January–February 2002), pp. 70–71. See also Michael Kinsley, "Defining Terrorism: It's Essential. It's Also Impossible," *The Washington Post*, October 5, 2001.

global terrorism.[38] Soon after India's decision, a high-level official from the Ministry of External Affairs, in a candid statement, indicated that, while India fully agrees with the need to fight terrorism, the dominant belief among Indian policymakers is that America's current strategy in Iraq is likely to produce more, rather than fewer, terrorists.[39] Being too closely associated with an American agenda held potential dangers, something that was driven home during the taking of Indian hostages in Iraq and their subsequent successful release in 2004.

India's ambivalence is also derived from widespread domestic opposition, and the unstated but important need to be responsive to the sentiments of India's large Muslim minority. Despite having the second largest Muslim population in the world, India has not been a base for any al-Qaeda recruitment, a situation that has caught the attention of some well-known American commentators.[40] The major reason that al-Qaeda has not been active in India is the lack of local support. According to one high-level former counter-terrorism official in the Indian government, "It is a very privileged position which India has ... So when we want to cooperate with the United States, we have to do it in such a way that we preserve this."[41] A large number of influential Indian opinion makers and officials believe that it could be domestically counterproductive for India to follow, or be seen to follow, US anti-terrorism efforts too closely in Iraq.[42]

For a diverse country like India (as well as other South Asian neighbors), it makes little social or political sense to reproduce the American discourse given domestic realities. India's most sustained engagement with the discourse on terrorism since 9/11 has been to argue about perceived double standards in the US approach and the need for "comprehensive" versus "selective" definitions, alluding to the distinct impression that the US views militancy in Kashmir differently from violent extremists in the Middle East, or Afghanistan, and, in particular, Pakistan's role – reflecting America's narrow foreign-policy interests.

[38] For an expanded discussion of India's decision, see the author's *US–India Relations: Ties That Bind?* The Sigur Center Asia Papers 22 (Washington, DC: George Washington University, 2005), pp. 3–6.

[39] Background comments at an interaction organized by the Embassy of India in July 2003 in Washington, DC.

[40] Thomas Friedman of *The New York Times* was among the first to note this anomaly.

[41] B. Raman, "Managing the War on Terrorism in South Asia," paper presented at a conference on US–India Bilateral Cooperation: Taking Stock and Moving Forward, The Sigur Center for Asian Studies, George Washington University, Washington, DC, April 1–2, 2004.

[42] This conclusion is based on extensive interviews of leading policy analysts and government officials in New Delhi, conducted by the author during October and November 2004.

These distinctions matter because the American discourse has taken on a totalizing and purely military perspective, one that leaves little or no room for negotiations with "terrorists."[43] While the US might be able to sustain such a warlike policy given that its enemies are still largely externally based, the countries of South Asia are faced with militancy and extremism that have immediate internal repercussions. In other words, the "war" is being brought home, not just fought abroad. The government of Afghanistan and radical Pashtuns, the Indian government and militant Kashmiris, and the Sri Lankan government and alienated Tamils all face a central reality: unlike the US, these governments are dealing with their own populations.

Outline of the chapters

This introductory chapter has laid out the theoretical and methodological issues of the book and its main arguments. It has examined the major explanations for extremism found in the literature, pointing out why we need to go beyond them. It has also put forward an alternative explanation suggesting that outcomes are shaped in large part by the way in which ethno-religious, secular and what I term "geopolitical identities," compete or converge. In this interaction, the role of the state as a mediating actor is essential.

Chapter Two summarizes something invariably overlooked in current analyses of ethno-religious conflict in South Asia – the historical context that helps to illuminate the present. It offers an overview that suggests the unique nature of South Asian identity formation (religious and otherwise), especially the intermingling of traditions across the region. It sets the stage for discussions in subsequent chapters by noting the evolution of the secular models, their unstable character, ways they have been constricted or promoted, and how they may be viewed in relation to alternate religious and geopolitical identities to understand present-day extremism.

Chapters Three through Seven consider evidence from the region to illuminate the particular types of internal–external developments and interactions that have been characteristic over time. The extent of competition or confluence between religious, secular and geopolitical identities, mediated by the state, is posited in each case as significant in determining the level of extremism. Chapter Three takes up Afghanistan,

---

[43] According to well-regarded conflict resolution expert David Smock, "It is critical to talk to your enemies. Boycotting the opposing side just because you do not approve of what they do or say rarely advances the cause of peace." "Institute Vice President David Smock Advises President Bush," *PeaceWatch*, (July/August 2007), p. 4.

followed by chapters on Pakistan, Kashmir, Sri Lanka and Bangladesh (in which Assam is included due to its geo-strategic and identity role in Indo-Bangladesh relations).

The last chapter considers what the evidence tells us about the relationship between geopolitics, secular political space, and the role of the state in producing or perpetuating violent or moderate outcomes. How useful is it, in understanding extremism, to consider the competition or convergence between ethno-religious, secular and geopolitical identity conceptions that we find around the region? How interlinked are processes in South Asia? What type of lessons may be learned from this comparative study? What conditions may facilitate the construction of identities that undercut exclusive geopolitical conceptions? How generalizable are the findings for areas outside South Asia? What are the policy implications of our findings?

Limitations

A word on the limitations of this book is in order. Given its broad scope, this book cannot be exhaustive in presenting its evidence. Secondly, since this book deals with a spectrum of extremism, it may not appeal to those who want a clear-cut definition and focus on terrorism, as currently understood in official US discourse. I would contend that this approach has not detracted from the substantive arguments of the book.

From margin to epicenter: Locations and dislocations

In his testimony before the Senate Foreign Relations Committee's Sub-committee on Near Eastern and South Asian Affairs on November 2, 1999, Ambassador Michael Sheehan, Coordinator for Counterterrorism in the US, concluded that "The center of anti-American terrorism has moved from the Middle East to South Asia ... As direct involvement in terrorism by most Middle Eastern state sponsors and groups has declined, our attention has increasingly focused on Osama bin Laden and the alliance of groups operating out of Afghanistan with the acquiescence of the country's *de facto* rulers, the Taliban."[1] When viewed from a historical standpoint, however, South Asia's new status presents a serious anomaly.

Chapter One noted the major gaps and analytical shortcomings in ethno-religious explanatory frameworks for violent extremism in the region. This chapter will take a substantive look at a broad sweep of South Asian history to suggest that it is difficult to find any historically deterministic trend in ethno-religious extremism. It would be a mistake to take the current period as the touchstone and project backwards as many seem to do. The need for historical analysis becomes clear when we consider how many observers of South Asian politics and geopolitics either ignore, or do not understand, critical historical aspects. This chapter will provide context to the con-tention that, although violence in South Asia is certainly not a modern phenomenon, the fault lines along which violence occurred in the past cannot be reduced to religion or ethnicity. The nature of Islam and its encounters in South Asia over time will be emphasized to illustrate the point, although the analysis applies more widely than Islam.

The chapter begins by outlining a "syncretic" past for South Asia, from early India (that is, current South Asia) and the inter-connections between Hinduism and its offshoots. It then considers the key medieval period of Indian history and the intermingling of Islam with other

---

[1] Quoted in Ninan Koshy, "Qualifying as a Terrorist State," *Asia Times*, February 5, 2000.

religious traditions. Next, the discontinuities introduced by colonialism and post-colonial state construction in South Asia are elaborated. Finally, I suggest how a three-way interaction between ethno-religious, secular and geopolitical identities, mediated by the state, emerged in the contemporary period to produce conditions that either inhibited or promoted extremism.

Errors of conflation

A keen observer of South Asia has noted that "the geographic heart of Islam is in the Middle East, but the demographic heart of Islam is in South Asia."[2] Variations of Islamic practice and preaching are little understood beyond local arenas, yet there seems to be no hesitation in conflating Islam in the Middle East to Islam elsewhere. A closer look at the dominant 9/11 discourse shows why. There are some analysts from the liberal school who point to poverty and economic hopelessness as the root causes of extremism and terrorism. But a counter-argument is then made that the perpetrators of the attacks on the World Trade Center and the Pentagon were not drawn from the dispossessed classes, rather, their background was middle and upper middle class. Thus the religious commitment of the hijackers, not their economic status, is portrayed as the driving force behind their action. For some, this could make a fairly compelling argument for religiously motivated terrorism; on the other hand, approaches based on extrapolating from the 9/11 example, or conflating the regions of South Asia and the Middle East based on such evidence, do not hold up.

From the information that has been publicly released, we may note that the 19 suspected hijackers on 9/11 were entirely of Middle Eastern origin: 15 from Saudi Arabia, 1 from Egypt (identified as one of the key figures), 1 from Lebanon and 2 from the United Arab Emirates.[3] Significantly, none of the men were from any of the South Asian countries, despite Sheehan's characterization of the region in 1999. Several of the hijackers apparently had spent time in Pakistan and Afghanistan, thereby leading to scrutiny of these states and the particular ways they are implicated

---

[2] M. J. Akbar, well-known Indian journalist and author, has made this comment on numerous occasions.

[3] For a detailed description of the alleged hijackers, see Dafna Linzer, "A Year Later, the 19 Hijackers are Still a Tangle of Mystery," *Chicago Sun-Times*, September 8, 2002. While there is much that is not known about the suspected hijackers, what is clear is that they came from two of America's closest and longstanding allies in the Middle East: Saudi Arabia and Egypt. Instead of this irony stimulating a major foreign policy debate in the US, it appears to have been lost in the US popular imagination.

(to be taken up in later chapters). It is not enough to term these perpetrators "new terrorists," and characterize them as stateless, belonging to religious, international and nomadic networks.[4] To do so would be to leave them disembodied, without context or history and abandon the possibility of fully understanding and combatting their brand of extremism.

We now turn to the long-term historical specificities of South Asia that this book argues made it less likely for ethno-religious extremism to emerge from the region. This discussion thus sets the stage for the internal–external interactions that are posited to have produced the terrain for contemporary extremist violence, including jihadism and insurgency in South Asia.

South Asia's distinctiveness

Not only are Afghanistan, Pakistan, India and Bangladesh significantly different from the Middle East, but there are distinctions within the region itself. As the leader of the Jamaat-e-Islami of Bangladesh (and then Minister of Industry) has said "Remember one thing: Pakistan is Pakistan and Bangladesh is Bangladesh."[5] Nizami was speaking about the path of political development in the two countries, on which there can be no doubt, but it holds true in some ways at the religious level as well. At the same time, the nature of Islam in South Asia is drawn from shared roots, distinct from the Middle East in important ways. The Islamic identity of the region from Afghanistan across to Bangladesh has been enormously influenced by local tradition, from the pre-Islamic era, along with the manner in which Islam was introduced, and the intermingling of peoples, cultures and religions that occurred. While, throughout the ages, the region did look west to Saudi Arabia for religious direction, given its prominence as protector of the holy lands, it also managed to retain its own cultural confluences.

Part of the distinctiveness of South Asia has nothing to do with religion, but its hugely varying ethnic composition and regional and linguistic differences. Every state in South Asia is made up of a multiplicity of identities, and even a partial listing of these different groups is mind-boggling. In Afghanistan, while the Pashtuns are the majority, there are significant minorities of Tajik, Hazaras and Uzbek. Though largely Sunni, there is a sizeable Shia minority among the Hazaras. Pakistan's four major ethnic groups are the Punjabis (58%), the Pashtuns or Pathans (12%), Sindhis (13%) and Baluchis (4%), differentiated also by

---

[4] Steven Simon and Daniel Benjamin, "America and the New Terrorism," *Survival*, 42.1 (2000).
[5] Interview by the author with Maulana Matiur Rehman Nizami, Dhaka, July 2004.

language. Most Baluchis, for example, speak Baluch, a language that is similar to Persian, but about a fifth also speak Brahui, a Dravidian-derived language. The Urdu-speaking Mohajirs who migrated from India to Pakistan after partition tend to maintain a separate identity, thus forming a fifth ethno-linguistic group.

India's variations are too numerous to mention, but even within Kashmir, there are at least three regions comprising different identities: Kashmir, Jammu and Ladakh, respectively Muslim, Hindu and Buddhist, although even that is an oversimplification. Indian Muslims are approximately 13% of the country, outnumbering the Muslim populations of its avowedly Islamic neighbors, Pakistan, Bangladesh and Afghanistan. India's Christian communities are also heterogeneous, being drawn from various groups, including the majority of tribal people in the northeast. Bangladesh is the most homogenous in terms of ethnicity, but, even so, there is an important minority of tribal peoples in the Chittagong Hill Tracts. In addition, Hindus comprise approximately 12 percent of Bangladesh's population. Hindu and Christian Tamils, Sinhalese and Tamil Muslims form divergent communities in Sri Lanka. Among the Muslims in South Asia are Sunnis, Shias, Bohras, Khojas, Bahais and Ahmadiyas, hardly a monolithic religious grouping. Ismailis, though small in number, also comprise a powerful Muslim minority in a number of different South Asian states.

The point is that there is no South Asian equivalent to Germany, France or Japan, states formed on the basis of the same race, language, culture, religion and historical experience.[6] It is thus extremely difficult for a single definition of national identity (whether religious, ethnic, regional or otherwise) to be propagated or take hold. Conversely, the potential for ethno-religous movements to flourish in this context is arguably strong. This dilemma is summed up well by the sentiment of some Kashmiri Muslims: "India threatens our religious identity, Pakistan threatens our ethnic identity."

The accommodative historical impulses

South Asia's long historical trajectory prior to 1947 is notable for the lack of communal or religious conflict of any significant scale or duration. It would be inaccurate and misleading to denigrate this legacy of co-existence through a cynical, revisionist, or self-serving interpretation. There is ample compelling historical evidence to demonstrate that those

[6] For an extremely well articulated description of South Asia's plurality, see Raju G. C. Thomas, "The 'Nationalities' Question in South Asia." See also his "Competing Nationalisms," *Harvard International Review* 28.3 (Summer 1996), pp. 12–16.

analysts subscribing to the accommodative view are not just idealizing the past.

The syncretic tradition of early India is the legacy of all present-day South Asian states, whether it is officially acknowledged or not. The highly acclaimed historian of pre-modern India, Romila Thapar, concludes that "Early history suggests the existence of multiple communities based on various identities ... Even the sense of religious identity seems to have related more closely to sect than to a dominant Hindu community."[7] For example, there was little difference in culture and lifestyle between the Buddhists, Jains and Hindus, and the theological controversies that occupied pundits, priests or the political elite, rarely percolated down to the masses. In this context, it would have been hard to launch a mass crusade, inquisition, jihad or holy war; besides, dissidents could always opt to establish a new sect and this was not an uncommon practice.[8]

Conversely, by around the sixth century, Hinduism had gone as far as accepting the Buddha as the ninth avatar of Vishnu, the successor to Rama and Krishna.[9] Moreover, it was often the case that rulers allowed the various religious groups to function without trying to exercise control. For instance, in the Deccan area, Hinduism, Buddhism and Jainism co-existed easily from the third century onwards. The Hindu Satavahana kings promoted Buddhism during their 450-year reign, leading to a profusion of Buddhist art and architecture such as the renowned Ajanata and Ellora caves and the stupa of Amaravati. Emperor Ashoka converted from Hinduism to Buddhism in the third century BC, but without the religious wars which became such a regular feature of European history.

One of the most authoritative accounts of relations between different communities in pre-independence India is by a group of noted Indian historians whose extensive work based on primary data culminated in a well-received publication in 1999.[10] By and large, their research is significantly supportive of the syncretic thesis. Even at the height of the Islamic empire in India, it is the accommodative aspects that are most prominent. According to one leading historian, "The dominant picture of

---

[7] Romila Thapar, *Interpreting Early India* (Delhi: Oxford University Press, 1993), pp. 84–85.

[8] Even in the rare instances of religious persecution, it involved only particular segments of sects, rather than all Hindu sects. Romila Thapar provides an example of Saiva sects attacking Jaina establishments in the seventh century, but she emphasises that it did not include all Saiva sects in the area (Thapar, *Interpreting Early India*).

[9] Rajmohan Gandhi discusses the evolution of Buddhism in *Revenge and Reconciliation* (New Delhi: Penguin Books, 1999), pp. 65–67.

[10] S. Settar and P. K. V. Kaimal (eds.) *We Lived Together* (Delhi: Pragati Publications, Indian Council of Historical Research, 1999). Similar thinking is found in Asim Roy, "Introduction," in Mushirul Hasan and Asim Roy (eds.) *Living Together Separately: Cultural India in History and Politics* (New Delhi: Oxford University Press, 2005).

the seventeenth and eighteenth centuries is not of the Hindus and Muslims forming exclusive and antagonistic categories, but of their cooperating in cultural and social affairs."[11] The strength of historical co-existence in India lies in the multiplicity of sources from which it is drawn – political, social and religious.

The political fragmentation of pre-independence India remained remarkably resistant to change, with a semblance of unification occurring only three times: 260 BC under the Mauryan Emperor Ashoka, during Mughal Emperor Akbar's rule in the fifteenth century, and under the British from 1858. This geographical decentralization matched India's dominant feature of political flexibility from the very beginning. The Indian subcontinent was more often a fluid political entity than a distinct political unit. The social and religious realms only reinforced this situation, with caste, community, language, religious orientations and cultural practices strongly differentiating groups that may or not have been congruent with a particular political authority at any given point in time. The point is that it is difficult, if not impossible, for historians to create any generalized social categories that cannot be at once challenged in terms of authenticity or historicity.[12] From today's vantage point, it is the religious divisions in South Asia that need to be re-examined, and what emerges can only be described as counter-intuitive, or at least alien to current popular worldviews based around concepts like "the clash of civilizations." What follows below is an extensive discussion of historical Hindu–Muslim encounters, particularly in what must be the most incompatible sphere: religion.

Contact and co-existence at the official level

Islam's entry and integration into South Asia has to be viewed against the complex social setting that India presented at the time. In the context of "Muslim South Asia," the dominant face of Islam has been, and continues to be, liberal. Looking into the everyday practices of ordinary people, reveals a convincing portrait of the accommodating and adaptive aspects of Hinduism and Islam. Juxtaposed to this, is the reaction in recent years of some Islamists who are denouncing longstanding

---

[11] Mushirul Hasan, "Competing Symbols and Shared Codes: Inter-Community Relations in Modern India," in Sarvepalli Gopal (ed.) *Anatomy of a Confrontation: The Babri Masjid-Ramjanmabhumi Issue* (New Delhi: Penguin Books, 1991), p. 103.

[12] How accurate would it be to characterize the diverse Christian population of India in a single religious category, for example, the Christians of Goa and the Christians of Kerala? Similarly, the Muslims of Tamil Nadu and Kashmiri Muslims, the Hindu Lingayats of Karnataka and the Rajputs of Rajasthan. The list is endless.

practices as un-Islamic, especially in Pakistan and Afghanistan.[13] In order to understand the nature of Islam in South Asia, it is important to recognize that the frontiers of Islam established by the early eighth century defined the area in which its fundamental features were developed and instituted. This area did not include South Asia; it was a relative latecomer to Islam and as such, the manner in which Islam developed in South Asia cannot be understood without considering the local context.

The earliest arrival of Islam into India was through Arab traders on the western coast, but they came to trade, not to settle, conquer or convert. In any case, Arab traders had already been journeying to this region for centuries as key middlemen in the spice trade, before being displaced by the Portuguese once Vasco da Gama landed in India in 1498. The more important entry point for Islam was through the north and northwest, beginning with the conquest of Sind by Arab armies in 712 AD. For several hundred years after that, various raids were conducted, mostly originating from Central Asia. Although life for the ordinary masses was relatively undisturbed, the eleventh century witnessed some particularly destructive raids led by Mohammed Ghaznavi and Mohammed Ghori from Afghanistan. A series of new invasions began in the twelfth century, from a complex of Turkish people who, unlike earlier invaders, came to stay, not just to loot.

These conquerors pushed all the way down to the southern Deccan region of India, and led to a period of sultanates under which local Hindu kingdoms continued as tributaries. For instance, the Bahamani sultanate in the Deccan region followed a non-discriminatory policy by not imposing the *jiziya* (tax imposed on non-Muslims according to Islamic law) on its Hindu subjects. By doing so, it anticipated the much celebrated Mughal Emperor Akabar's religious tolerance 200 years later.[14] Various kingdoms did, however, manage to strike out on their own, once again leading to a period of political fragmentation of India, although this time under Muslim rule. But by then, Islam had become clearly entrenched. The most formidable Muslim rule was established in 1526 by Babur, who defeated the Muslim sultanate in Delhi and began the Mughal empire finally supplanted by the British in the mid-nineteenth century.

---

[13] There is a dearth of writing on Islam in South Asia as opposed to the Middle East. While books on South Asia after 9/11 have proliferated, they tend to be purely policy oriented. A recent book explaining the distinctions of South Asian Islam is Imtiaz Ahmad and Helmut Reifeld (eds.), *Lived Islam in South Asia: Adaptation, Accommodation and Conflict* (New Delhi: Social Science Press, 2004).

[14] Sarojini Regani, "We Lived Together – Deccani Culture and the Qutb Shahs of Golkonda," in Settar and Kaimal (eds.), *We Lived Together*, p. 219.

By the eighteenth century the Islamic empire covered an impressive area from North Africa to Sind, but local tradition and culture continued to persist. The latter was most apparent in schools of Islamic thought that tended to be inward oriented, rather than focusing on legalistic interpretation of the Koran and the Hadiths. Sufism in Islam, which exemplified the inner path to God, found fertile ground in the subcontinent and flourished in part because it was compatible with, and integrated elements of, Hinduism-based Bhakti (elaborated below). Despite attempts by the Hindu right and Islamist radicals today to cite historical animosities and separateness of the two religious communities, the burden of proof lies with them if they are to challenge the notion that Islam's response to the South Asian context was largely inclusivist, based in part on tolerant universalist mysticism.[15] Recognizing this historical situation does not amount to downplaying the competing tendency of Mughal rule which also existed, and which was indeed aggressive and exclusivist, reaching its apogee under Aurangzeb (1658–1707).

Competing impulses

These two competing impulses are captured well in the differences between Aurangzeb and Dara Shikoh, the two sons of Mughal Emperor Jahangir. The elder son, Dara Shikoh, who belonged to the Chishti school of Sufism, was a scholar who is notable for his work on one of the most eminent Sufi female saints, who was his mentor, as well as for promoting the translation of the Hindu religious text, the Upanishads, into Persian. On the other hand, Aurangzeb followed policies that were clearly discriminatory towards non-Muslims, displaying an unprecedented level of religious bigotry. Yet Aurangzeb did not have a smooth path – he faced opposition from a number of family members, including his own son, Akbar (not to be confused with his ancestor Emperor Akbar), who rebelled against his father in 1681 and joined forces with Hindu Rajput princes. Once the Rajputs retreated under Aurengzeb's attacks, Akbar then joined Raja Sambhaji, the son of Shivaji, who fought the Mughals and remains an icon for Hindu activists.[16]

---

[15] Akbar S. Ahmed, Inaugural Address of the Fellowship of Peace, Gandhi Center, Washington, DC, January 8, 2004.

[16] Amartya Sen, "Secularism and Its Discontents," in Kaushik Basu and Sanjay Subrahmanyam (eds.), *Unravelling the Nation: Secular Conflict and India's Secular Identity* (New Delhi: Penguin Books, 1996), pp. 33–35. Sen provides an excellent rebuttal to those who are inclined to view Indian history in terms of Hindu–Muslim contention.

At the peak of Muslim power under Emperor Akbar (1556–1605), who "united" India for only the second time in its history, the empire included today's Afghanistan, Pakistan, India and Bangladesh; but Akbar's achievement of political control may be said to equal his commitment to religious tolerance and the sharing of religious spaces. Indeed, Akbar attempted to create a new religion, the Din Ilahi, which drew upon Islam, Hinduism and Zoroastrianism. (Another outstanding example of the search for a more tolerant religion at the highest political level, comes from Emperor Ashoka, Akbar's only predecessor in uniting India. Although Ashoka converted to Buddhism, he also formulated his own version called Dhamma, a variant of the Sanskrit word meaning 'universal law.' The main principles he articulated were religious tolerance and non-violence.) Akbar's court included a sizeable number of Hindu advisors, intellectuals and artists, equal with Muslim advisors, and Akbar even took a Hindu Rajput princess as his wife. Although Akbar is exceptional in his attempt actively to integrate Hinduism and Islam, there was little effort by others to thwart the process.

What is important to note is that Aurangzeb was the exception, rather than the rule, among Mughal leaders. Although Akbar has been celebrated for attempting to create unprecedented religious openness, during the entire Mughal era there were varying levels of cultural and religious interaction. Even Aurangzeb reportedly had 175 Hindus out of a total strength of 575 higher officials in his court. Although no post-Mughal state eclipsed the openness of Akbar, it was common practice for the Hyderabad court to celebrate Hindu religious festivals (and to make substantial donations to the hospices and shrines of the Sufis).[17] In the waning days of Mughal rule, Bahadur Shah in Delhi continued to maintain religious tolerance. Interestingly, the assessment of earlier Hindu religious leaders, such as Sri Aurobindo, supports the accommodative impulse of Muslim rule. His view is worth quoting at some length: "The Mussulman domination ceased very rapidly to be a foreign rule ... The Mughal empire was a great and magnificent construction and an immense amount of political genius and talent was employed in its creation and maintenance. It was as splendid, powerful and beneficient and, it may be added, in spite of Aurangzeb's fanatical zeal, infinitely more liberal and tolerant in religion than any medieval or contemporary European kingdom or empire."[18]

It should be noted that whether a Muslim leader is characterized as less aggressive or less communal does not necessarily tell us about his behavior regarding the activity that many associate with Islamic religious

[17] Eugenia Vanina, "Communal Relations in Pre-Modern India," in Settar and Kaimal (eds.), *We Lived Together*, p. 182.
[18] Quoted in Sen, "Secularism," p. 33.

intolerance – the destruction of Hindu temples. As some historians have pointed out, despite the accommodative character of the Bahamanis, the expansion of their kingdoms came at the expense of the previous Vijaya-nagar Empire, and the looting of temples for their wealth was allowed. Ironically, while engaging in military campaigns against Vijayanagar or its territories, at times it was the Hindu generals of the Bahamani Adil Shahs or Qutb Shahs who planned the plunder of temples.[19]

There is scant evidence that any Muslim ruler tried to impose a theo-cratic state in India. In spite of the jiziya tax imposed by some Muslim rulers (by and large for economic reasons, or perhaps to appease orthodox clergy), Hindu law was applied in all other matters to decide cases involving Hindus. Episodes of direct religious persecution of Hindus were rare, as were communal riots. As one expert puts it, "No proper count has been made, but on a rough reckoning, armed conflicts between Muslim rulers probably outnumbered those between the Muslim and Hindu rulers in Indian history."[20] At the popular level, the extent of religious tolerance, including shared sacred spaces and mutual exchange epitomized by Sufism and Bhakti worship, was extraordinary, especially from today's perspective.

Tolerance and co-worship at the popular level

To grasp the syncretic traditions in South Asia fully, it is useful to consider Sufism from Islam and the Hindu Bhakti movement together; particular attention will be given here to Sufism. Bhakti is a devotional movement in Hinduism, emphasizing intense emotional attachment to a personal god. The term's origin is Sanskrit, meaning "to share," later taking on the meaning of "love, sharing and devotion." The Bhakti movement was at its height from 800–1700, and had a momentous impact on the Muslims of India, including the Mughal Emperor Akbar. It began as a challenge to the powerful Vedic ritualistic aspects of Hindu religion, abjuring caste hierarchies, gender inequities, and the privileged position of Sanskrit as the language of Hindu religious study. One of the lesser known Bhakti saint-poets was Sant Prannath who lived during Aurangzeb's reign, and propagated the unity of religions through his comparative study of religions.[21] In his congregations, the Bhagavad

[19] Regani, "We Lived Together," p. 221.
[20] Dwijendra Tripathi, "The Crisis of Indian Polity: A Historical Perspective," in Settar and Kaimal (eds.), We Lived Together, p. 300. See also, K. S. Singh, "Diversity, Heterogeneity and Integration: An Ideological Perspective," in Settar and Kaimal (eds.), We Lived Together, p. 244.
[21] P. S. Mukharya, "Contributions of Sant Prannath to the Composite Culture of India," in Settar and Kaimal (eds.), We Lived Together, pp. 120–131.

Gita and the Koran were read together, preceding Mahatma Gandhi's practice of reading from the Bhagavad Gita, Koran and Bible in his anti-colonial meetings by two centuries.

Bhakti worship fitted in well with Sufism, a form of mysticism which attracted a large following among Muslims of South Asia also during the medieval period (1200–1700). Sufis welcomed non-Muslims into their hospices. Both believed in meditation and singing and taking guidance from a saint or pir. The spread of Sufism in spite of the hostility of the ulema or the established clergy to saint worship, underlines its unique attraction at the popular level. The manner in which Hindus, Muslims and Sikhs worship in the subcontinent has been greatly influenced by the Bhakti–Sufi interaction. Gurbani singing at a Sikh gurdwara, qawwali at a dargah (shrine) by Muslims, and kirtan at a Hindu temple all have common roots.

This movement spread across the subcontinent from north to south. During the late fifteenth and early sixteenth centuries, Kabir, conventionally cited as the greatest of all Sufi poets, wrote poems that were accessible to all, seeking to reconcile Hinduism and Islam. Kabir, whose antecedents are not exactly known, is reputed to have been born a Hindu and raised by Muslim weavers. He rejected the idea of choosing between Hinduism and Islam and instead promoted the basic unity of all religions. He abjured the caste system, but accepted the Hindu notions of reincarnation and karma. From Islam, Kabir took the idea of the equality of all men before God, and Sufi mysticism. Sikhism, a reform-oriented religion established in the late fifteenth century, has deep roots in both Sufism and the Bhakti movement; Guru Nanak, the founder of Sikhism, was a disciple of Kabir. Sufism is viewed by some as a critical bridge between "polytheistic Hinduism and monotheistic Islam" as they encountered each other in the subcontinent.[22] The sentiments of Sufi and Bhakti saints are captured well in a popular verse: "Learn from the eyes the way to develop unity and harmony; the two eyes appear different, but their vision is one."[23] The crossing of traditional boundaries between religions came to be a hallmark of pre-British India, as Sufism and Bakhti blended to promote religious harmony without making it a political project.

Sufism tended to remain aloof from political power, and its growth was not dependent on state protection or patronage. For example, Sheikh Daud of Lahore refused to meet Emperor Akbar when he wanted his blessing; others declined to combine missionary activities with

---

[22] Dilip Hiro, *Holy Wars* (New York: Routledge, 1989), p. 35.
[23] K. A. Nizami, "Contributions of Mystics to Amity and Harmony in Indian Society," in Settar and Kaimal (eds.), *We Lived Together*, p. 148.

political expansion, when asked to do so by such rulers as Mohammad Tughlaq. Most rural Muslims, many with Hindu ancestors, continued to perform their earlier religious practices and customs. A good number of Hindus went on pilgrimages to Muslim shrines without fear of being stigmatized or ostracized. Although there were cases of conversions and re-conversions during this period, the state did not become involved or question such practices. It would seem that the Mughal rulers did not allow themselves to be dictated to by the clergy, despite there being a fine line between religion and politics in Islam.[24]

Although the historical context in Afghanistan differed in that the population was almost entirely Muslim, the tradition of Islam there owed much to Sufism, much like India. The large Sunni majority followed the more tolerant and inclusive Hanafi school of jurisprudence. Moreover, orthodox Islam was mediated by the existence of pre-Islamic social structures, particularly the tribal "khan" system in which power resided in tribal leaders or khans, whose preeminent position was recognized by the state. The ulema thus did not have a great deal of opportunity for amassing power in the face of these social realities. The early Durani empire in the mid-eighteenth to the early nineteenth century, for example, did not feel compelled to enforce any particular religious interpretation as the source of their power lay in the (ethnically Pashtun) tribes, rather than in Islam. One well-regarded expert notes that "As individuals, the khans showed considerable piety, but, as a group, they were not keen on yielding their privileged place in the institutions of the state to members of the religious establishment. In their capacity as landlords and leaders of their clans, they saw to it that, like other groups of specialists, such as carpenters, barbers and musicians, ordinary religious practitioners (mullahs) remained subordinate to them. This pattern of relationship between local landlords and mullahs remained in force until 1978."[25]

Afghanistan successfully repulsed colonial forces repeatedly and thus never came directly under colonialism. Once Britain withdrew from the subcontinent in 1947, the dominant discourse of Afghan intellectuals was Afghan nationalism, not Islam. Islam had never penetrated the Afghan state structure as a political ideology. Since the establishment of the Afghan state in 1747, Afghan rulers have relied on tribal alliances to maintain power. The religious establishment was by and large viewed in purely religious and cultural terms, rather than political.

[24] G. P. Sharma, "The State and Religious Identities," *The Hindu*, September 29, 2000.
[25] Ashraf Ghani, "Afghanistan: Islam and Counterrevolutionary Movements," in John L. Esposito (ed.), *Islam in Asia: Religion, Politics and Society* (New York: Oxford University Press, 1987), p. 82.

The greatest impact of Islam in what is now Pakistan, is generally seen as beginning with the arrival of a sizeable number of Chishti and Suhrawardy Sufis in the thirteenth century from Persia. Khwaja Moinuddin Chishti's tomb which is located in north India in Ajmer, Rajasthan, attracts thousands of pilgrims, both Muslim and non-Muslim. (Nearby Hindu shopkeepers begin their day by placing their keys at the steps of the dargah, and the sandalwood paste for the shrine is prepared by a Brahmin whose family have been devotees for centuries.) In the modern era, various political and religious leaders from Bangladesh and Pakistan have been visitors to Ajmer. Examples of this historical legacy of religious tolerance are found across contemporary India, even as Sufism continues to exert a powerful influence in Pakistan, Bangladesh and Afghanistan. There are simply too many cases of co-worship to mention: the Ayyappa temple in Kerala is just one.[26] Located in the Sabari hills in central Kerala, Hindu pilgrims pay respects at the dargah of Vavuruswami (known as a Muslim saint) on their way up to the temple. Over 30 million pilgrims visit the Ayyappa temple each year from all over South India.

It should be pointed out that a more orthodox strain of Sufism did develop on the Indian subcontinent and Afghanistan. It sought to ensure that Islamic mysticism did not somehow become so diffuse so as to disappear into Hindu mysticism.[27] However, the lived traditions continued without being destroyed, and are found in the most unlikely places even today.

Sufism in Kashmir

Ironically, these traditions of co-worship are historically found to an even greater extent in conflict-ridden Kashmir. Despondent over the deterioration of communal relations as partition loomed, Mahatma Gandhi is famously reported to have said "If there is a ray of hope, it is only from Kashmir." Kashmir's particular encounters with Hinduism, Buddhism and Islam produced a socio-cultural and religious fusion that has often been popularly referred to as "kashmiriyat." The roots of this amalgamation are extremely strong, but one of the most poignant questions raised in the context of today's violence is the extent to which it can weather the

---

[26] For examples, see K. R. N. Swamy, "Shrines That Promote Harmony," *The Tribune*, March 24, 2002; Yoginder Sikand, "Where Have We Gone Wrong?" *Deccan Herald*, December 5, 2002; Yoginder Sikand, *Sacred Spaces: Exploring Traditions of Shared Faith in India* (New Delhi: Penguin Books, 2003); and Hasan, "Competing Symbols," pp. 104–105.

[27] Asta Olesen, *Islam and Politics in Afghanistan* (Surrey, England: Curzon Press, 1995), pp. 47–51. The objective of 'orthodox' Sufism was to try and close the gap between religious law or Sharia and the mystical doctrines of Sufism. For example, Deobandism which became known for its traditionalism, was also linked to some Sufi orders.

insurgency and its impact. Kashmiriyat is often used nostalgically to recall a past that is in danger of being buried deeper and deeper by the Kashmir conflict. Beyond the shared cuisine, music and language that it evokes, lies a religio-philosophical tradition of distinct and astonishing convergence between Hinduism and Islam. While the Sufi and Bhakti heritage and shared worship remains strong in different parts of the subcontinent, there is a scattered quality to it, and there are other much more established forms of Islam and Hinduism as rivals. What sets Kashmir apart, is that the syncretic religious form has always been dominant, with the orthodox approaches marginalized. It is impossible to comprehend such a picture without reference to the history of the region.

Kashmir was brought into the Mauryan empire in the third century BC by the Hindu Emperor Ashoka. Ashoka's conversion to Buddhism proved important for Kashmir. Renouncing war after the horror that his army inflicted at Kalinga (present-day Orissa), Ashoka adopted Buddhism and sent Buddhist emissaries to propagate the faith. Several important Buddhist figures settled in Kashmir and Emperor Ashoka established Srinagar as its capital. Buddhism still continues to be dominant in Ladakh, north of the Kashmir Valley. It is mainly from Kashmir that Buddhism and its influence spread to Afghanistan, Central Asia and Tibet. Islam appeared in Kashmir slowly at first, from Central Asia, then with a widespread and more lasting impact through the arrival of Sufi saints, in particular Bulbul Shah from Persia[28] in the early 1300s. He was the first missionary to introduce Islam at the state level when his discussions with the ruling Buddhist monarch Rinchen Shah led to his conversion to Islam. In 1585, the Mughal Emperor Akbar brought Kashmir back under Delhi's control, wresting it away from a widely respected Kashmiri king, Zainal Abedin. But by 1750, Afghan invaders had overpowered the declining Mughal rulers, and captured Kashmir. By then, Islam had already made great inroads into Kashmir, but through the work of Sufi missionaries, rather than under coercion from invaders or warriors.

Being a center for Muslim traders, and other leading figures travelling along the caravan routes in both directions, the Kashmir Valley region was influenced most by Islam. But Islam emerged in Kashmir in an indigenous form, attuned to the traditions and sensibilities of the Kashmiris. The local Sufi order of Silsila-e-Rishiyan (Rishi order) is most closely associated with Sheikh Nooruddin Noorani (popularly known as Nunda Rishi), revered by Muslims and Hindus alike. The concept of rishi (sage or saint) was not

---

[28] Some historians contest this, suggesting either that he came from Turkistan or from Baghdad.

alien to Kashmir given the existence of rishis among Hindus and the Buddhist Sangha. In contrast to the Sufis in Iran and Central Asia, these rishis used the local language for their poems and discourses, thus ending up at the forefront of Kashmiri literature. Kashmiri Sufism also exhibited parallels with tantric Buddhism that had earlier existed in the area.

Most important from our perspective, Nunda Rishi's own spiritual mentor was a Hindu woman mystic, Lal Ded, who is held in high esteem by both communities.[29] She is said to have come under the influence of Sufis, along with local Hindu Shaivaism (a form of worship which aims to achieve union between God and disciple without any priestly inter-mediation). At one level, both were historical expressions of resistance to the religious rigidities of Islamic law and inequalities of the Brahminical code respectively. Nunda Rishi is referred as the "Alamdar-I-Kashmir," or the "Flag Bearer of Kashmir," and even militant Kashmiri leaders like Yasin Malik evoke both Nunda Rishi and Lal Ded, attesting to their continuing powerful hold on the Kashmiri consciousness.[30]

The most popular places of worship in the Kashmir Valley are still shrines rather than conventional mosques. Even in mosques the practice of prayers by singing (taken from the older tradition of Hindu bhajans and kirtans) goes on, only in Kashmir.[31] Neighboring Jammu, whose popu-lation is now predominantly Hindu, shares the Sufi traditions of the Kashmir Valley. Historically, Hindus and Sikhs outnumbered Muslim worshippers at many of the shrines. Yoginder Sikand describes how Hindus and Muslims thronged the shrine of Pir Raushan 'Ali Shah, Jammu's oldest Sufi mystic, just one week after an attack on a crowded bazaar near one of the city's main temples.[32] Even the Amarnath Cave in Jammu, dedicated to the Hindu God Shiva, has a persisting legend which ensures the continuation of a tradition of giving a share of its donations, made by the thousands of pilgrims who come from different parts of India, to a Muslim shrine in the area.

In recent times, Islamists have attempted to persuade or coerce people into giving up the annual practice of Urs, a typical Kashmiri festival held each year at the shrines of Sufi saints on the anniversaries of their deaths and traditionally celebrated by Muslims, Hindus and Sikhs. Indeed, groups of armed militants have reportedly prevented Kashmiri Muslims from participating in their traditional festivals at Sufi

---

[29] Sikand, *Sacred Spaces*, pp. 256–257.
[30] See for example, Yasin Malik, "Kashmiris Yet to be Identified Internationally: Yasin," *Kashmir Times*, March 18, 2004.
[31] Saifuddin Soz, "Kashmiriyat versus Militancy," *Economic Times*, February 28, 2004.
[32] Sikand, *Sacred Spaces*, p. 216.

shrines and even destroyed some of the buildings. Large numbers of Kashmiris have, however, ignored or resisted calls to disengage from these practices.

Antecedents of exclusive identities

In light of all this, it seems paradoxical that South Asia should witness some of the most intractable ethno-religious conflicts and religious extremism. For a full understanding of the emergence and evolution of "communal" identities into their politicized versions, we need to look at two other aspects of the subcontinent's history: the workings of British colonialism on the one hand, and the unstable nature of secularism on the other. This interaction of external geopolitics and internal secular space in producing conditions for religious extremism offers early evidence for the book's central thesis. While the intricacies of the impact of British rule are left to historians of the colonial period, I suggest a political analysis that is useful for extending our study of the contours of extremism today.

Divisions on the subcontinent clearly existed prior to British rule, but they may be better described as communitarian, rather than the more virulent communal, divisions.[33] A key question is how these social distances, that had always existed along with common traditions, were transformed into communal enmities. The answer is intimately, though not exclusively, related to the British colonial enterprise. The British entry into a socio-politically fragmented India was accompanied by the none too surprising deft utilization of classic divide and rule policies. In the beginning, this strategy was aimed at various rulers without regard to religion *per se*, but it was modified over time, laying the groundwork that culminated in the sort of communal carnage that the subcontinent had hitherto managed to avoid. According to the highly respected historian, S. Gopal, "Communalism as a distinct phenomenon emerged only about the middle of the nineteenth century."[34]

Beyond the strategic logic of divide and rule were more underlying prejudices. The British rulers tended to draw on European Orientalism to understand so-called "Hindu society," in the process erroneously homogenizing Hinduism based on selected Brahminical texts as their reference point. The administrative efforts of the British authorities also contributed to the process of sharp differentiations: for example, the

---

[33] G. P. Sharma, professor of history at Jamia Millia Islamia University in New Delhi, makes this distinction, "The State and Religious Identities."

[34] S. Gopal, "Nehru, Religion and Secularism," in R. Champakalakshmi and S. Gopal (eds.) *Tradition, Dissent and Ideology* (Delhi: Oxford University Press, 1986, 208.

decennial census, or more specifically the British notion behind the census that caste and religion were the chief organizing principles of Indian society.[35] In addition, the misperceptions that the British formed about which community was more "seditious" at different points in time (for example, the belief that Muslims were more responsible for the 1857 revolt) and the colonial response to such perceived sedition served to alienate Hindus and Muslims politically.

Ultimately, the chief motivation of all Britain's policies was to consolidate its own geopolitical ambitions on the subcontinent. By the end of the nineteenth century, however, the existence of a distinct Muslim consciousness, if not nationalism, that sought to ensure Muslim rights vis- à-vis the Hindu majority, made that task of consolidation easier for the British. But British intervention had clearly stoked that Muslim alienation in the first place. The overthrow of Mughal rule, the displacement of the Persian language by English and the establishment of the zamindari system which tended to replace the wealthy Muslim classes with newly elevated Hindus, all contributed to Muslim disillusionment. Muslim reaction was expressed most notably by people such as Sir Syed Ahmed Khan and Syed Ameer Ali who called for a Muslim renaissance. Sir Syed Ahmed Khan founded the Aligarh Mohammadan Anglo-Oriental College, in a bid to create educated Muslim classes that could compete on an equal footing. He sought in particular to promote a synthesis of Muslim and western culture. The motivation was to shore up Muslim interests which were viewed as dangerously eroding, rather than launch a separatist movement.[36] However, the transformation of nascent Muslim consciousness into a demand for separate statehood cannot be understood in isolation from the British experience.

Institutionalizing differences

The division of Bengal by Governor-General Lord Curzon in 1905 provides a striking example of how the British wittingly and unwittingly furthered communal antipathies. The division was justified by the need for greater administrative efficiency in the province (the area covering Bengal, Bihar and Orissa and having 78 million people). After the split into Eastern and Western Bengal, the majority of the population ended up, respectively, Muslim and Hindu. The reaction of Indians and, in particular, Hindu Bengalis was one of shock and outrage, believing that

---

[35] For a detailed discussion of how the needs of the census began to overwhelm existing fragmented identities, see G. Balachandran, "Religion and Nationalism in Modern India," in Basu and Subrahmanyam (eds.), Unravelling the Nation, pp. 92–97.

[36] Md. Abdul Wadud Bhuiyan, Emergence of Bangladesh and Role of Awami League (New Delhi: Vikas Publishing House, 1982), pp. 2–5.

it was a deliberate blow to the growing solidarity and self-consciousness of Bengali speakers.[37] It is hard to refute the claim that Curzon's action was dictated as much, if not more, by the objective of blunting Bengali nationalism, as by administrative concerns. Although the partition of Bengal was rescinded in 1911 in the face of tremendous opposition, it had left its imprint on communal feelings. By then, the Muslim leadership deeply resented the annulment of a decision that had served to create new opportunities for them in Muslim-majority Eastern Bengal. Once established in this fashion, new vested interests would prove difficult to dislodge, despite the reunification. Important sections of Muslim opinion had also interpreted the vehement opposition by many Hindu political leaders to Bengal's partition as evidence that Hindus were against Muslim political advancement.

Perhaps the single most important stimulus to Hindu–Muslim polarization was the Minto–Morley Reform Act of 1909, introducing the notion of separate electorates based on religion. This provision has been roundly criticized for fostering a separate *political* identity for Indian Muslims, thereby creating the potential for politicizing communal feelings as never before. The 1918 Report on Indian Constitutional Reforms declared that "It [the system of communal electorates] was opposed to the teachings of history. It perpetuated division of creeds and classes which meant the creating of camps organized against each other and taught them to think as partisans and not as citizens. It stereotyped existing relations and was a very serious hindrance to the development of self-governing principals."[38] At independence, the architects of India's constitution eliminated this feature and substituted general electorates in which members of all castes, religions, and communities could vote. By then, however, religious triumphalism had taken dangerous root on Indian soil.

Still, it may be noted that the idea of Pakistan came late from Muslims in India, and when it came, it was far from unanimous.[39] Several ironies existed: the largest support for Pakistan came from the provinces with Muslim minorities, not from the Muslim majority provinces located in northwest and northeast India; the future prime minister of Pakistan, Jinnah, was himself a secular Muslim, whereas Maulana Azad, a top-ranking Indian National Congress leader, who once held the presidency of the party,

---

[37] See S. C. Raychoudhary, *History of Modern India: A Detailed Study of Political, Economic, Social and Cultural Aspects* (Delhi: Surjeet Publications, 1992), p. 45.

[38] Quoted in Raychoudhary, *History of Modern India*, pp. 261–262.

[39] Jinnah declared his support for the idea of Pakistan only in 1940 at the Lahore Session. The Jamaat-i-Islami was formed in 1941. Prior to that, the Pakistan idea was only raised seriously by the poet–politician Mohammad Iqbal in 1930 even though the Muslim League had been established in 1906.

was a deeply religious Muslim. In other words, Muslims, like other Indians, were diverse. The idea of Pakistan may have met their religious identity, but not their regional identity, a situation that has contributed to ongoing instability in Pakistan itself.[40]

It is an interesting counter-factual exercise to ponder India's political pathways in the absence of British colonialism: categorical statements are difficult to make except to reiterate that communalism of the sort that emerged was not historically inevitable nor even the most likely outcome. The Indian context did provide the British with opportunities that they exploited; they did not shape India exactly as they pleased. But it was British geopolitical compulsions and their privileged state position that allowed competing tendencies of the domestic situation to be utilized in this way. The spread of tension between Hindus and Muslims in turn, became a key legitimating factor for continuing British power in India. From the well-worn argument of colonialism's "civilizing mission," the new justification became one of "defense of the minorities." In reality, however, minority interests were protected only to the extent that they served imperial power.[41] To quote Lord Olivier in 1926 "No one with a close acquaintance with Indian affairs will be prepared to deny that, on the whole, there is a predominant bias in British officialdom in India in favor of the Muslim community, partly on the ground of closer sympathy, but more largely as a make-weight against Hindu nationalism."[42] The successful consolidation by the British of politicized religious sentiment has left a legacy for post-colonial elites to utilize as well. The potential for constructing the ethno-religious or socio-cultural "other" in oppositional politics and geopolitics has remained a critical feature in contemporary South Asia. This brings us to what I suggest is the *instability* of secularism that permeates post-colonial secularism in the region, and its accompanying challenges.

Unstable secularism in South Asia

Despite the scale of communal violence accompanying India's partition, the initial post-colonial leadership across the region was by and large characterized by "secular" outlooks. Maulana Maududi, the founder of

---

[40] Ayesha Jalal's discussion of pre-partition politics in India takes up these issues in great detail. See *The Sole Spokesman: Jinnah, the Muslim League and the Demand for Pakistan* (New York: Cambridge University Press, 1994) and *Democracy and Authoritarianism in South Asia: A Comparative and Historical Perspective* (New York: Cambridge University Press, 1995).

[41] Deepa Ollapally, "South Asia's Politics of Paranoia," *The World & I* (May 2003), p. 57.

[42] A. R. Desai, *Social Background of Indian Nationalism* (Bombay: Popular Prakashan, 1991), p. 399.

Jamaat-i-Islami, stated with disappointment no doubt that "From the League's Quaid-i-Azam down to the humblest leader, there was no one who would be credited with an Islamic outlook and who looked at the various problems from an Islamic point of view."[43] Jinnah stood opposed to what he called a "Mullah Raj," and at the outset of Pakistan's independence, there were even high level recommendations pointing to the difficulties of creating an Islamic state, and advocating the separation of religion and politics.[44] Within Pakistan, secular sentiment was also found in the regional nationalisms of Sind, Baluchistan and East Pakistan, that emerged in short order.

At a practical level, it is not difficult to understand the choice of some version of secularism as an initial guiding political principal: the heterogeneity of the populations in each country demanded no less. Moreover, it could not have been lost on the immediate post-independence leadership that, in order to guard against external interference based on ethno-religious grounds, secularism would best serve state security, even for Pakistan. Since each of the states was externally vulnerable on this count, such a framework would have been of common interest. No doubt, the long-shared historical tradition of co-existence and lack of sharp differentiation also predisposed most of the top leaders at a personal level towards secularism. It is not surprising that, at the outset, state leadership in the region tacitly or otherwise essentially subscribed to secularism in statecraft. But in none of the South Asian states did such logic adhere completely (India comes remarkably close), and secularism waxed and waned in the public sphere, influenced by both internal and external factors.

Competing historical tendencies

The instability of secularism in South Asia may be traced back to the different tendencies that had emerged in India by the late medieval period. These have been referred to in simplified form as "proto-communalism and proto-secularism," though there is no exact correspondence to their current manifestations. Proto-communalism has been described as "a complex of ideas insisting upon the superiority of a certain religious community over all others and projecting the state as the defender and advocate of those who profess the 'true' religion." This stands in contrast to the proto-secularist belief in composite culture, and an attitude of "all creeds as equally rightful and all communities as equal co-sharers of the

[43] Quoted in K. B. Sayeed, *Pakistan: The Formative Phase* (Karachi: Pakistan Publishing House, 1960), p. 120.
[44] Bhuiyan, *Emergence of Bangladesh*, p. 19.

Indian identity."[45] In its historically-dominant, non-extreme form, even proto-communalism was not incompatible with a tolerant approach towards others, including a measure of autonomy of belief and social life. For example, the attempt by orthodox ulema to force the Delhi Sultan Shamsuddin Iltutmish to threaten his Hindu subjects with the ultimatum "death or Islam," was derailed, and such an appeal from the clergy was never seriously entertained, even by the most religiously fanatical Muslim rulers. None of the offshoots or smaller replicas of the Mughal empire, like Hyderabad or Awadh, perpetuated the bigoted policies of Aurangzeb. Confrontation did not characterize the policy of Hindu kings either, under whom lived minorities of Jains, Buddhists and, later, Muslims. Similarly, their intense struggle against the Mughals did not translate into the Sikhs, Marathas or Rajputs becoming enemies of Islam as a faith or Muslims as a community.[46]

However, within the proto-communal approach lay the potential for extremism: the notion of "true faith" and the need for others to accept a level of subservience; the possibility of the state throwing its weight behind the purveyors of this view; and the temptation by the state to mobilize religious opinion, especially under conditions of domestic crisis or external threats. The scope for minority insecurity was evident, and the challenge for South Asian politics would be to keep this tendency in check or on the margins. The challenge would also be to resist intrusion by ethno-religious movements or ideologies, as well as for the state itself to refrain from utilizing those very forces for political or geopolitical purposes.

In the late nineteenth century, Hindu revivalism, spearheaded by the Arya Samaj and the cow protection efforts, was symptomatic of a new and more assertive consciousness but stayed limited. Islamization in Bengal and sections of northern India inspired by Shah Waliullah and successors, as well as the rise of pan-Islamic feelings in the wake of the Greco–Turkish war of 1897, was also a powerful new force.[47] Islamic revivalism had begun in the nineteenth century in Bengal as a reaction to western colonialism, and the core message of various movements had come to be identified with external, that is Arab, culture and tradition. For example, the Faraidi movement led by Shariat Ullah who had studied Islam for ten years in Mecca was influenced by Wahabism of Saudi Arabia. This movement even denounced the concept of saints, so integral to Sufi Islam. As Imtiaz Ahmed notes, this shift towards a more formalist and

---

[45] Vanina, "Communal Relations in Pre-Modern India," in Settar and Kaimal (eds.), *We Lived Together*, pp. 174–178. Vanina offers one of the best analyses of the development of these divergent strands of thought, and I rely heavily on her account for this section.
[46] *Ibid.* pp.174–175.   [47] Hasan, "Competing Symbols," p. 103.

rigid interpretation was critically aided by the British colonialists: their own particular understanding and promotion of Islam went directly against Sufism and legitimized a narrower and ultimately more intolerant redefinition.[48] This redefinition fitted the British Orientalist discourse much more neatly, and it also provided more structure to the Islamic context within which the colonial authorities had to operate.

By the beginning of the twentieth century, there were essentially two competing tendencies among the Muslims: a liberal trend epitomized by the Aligargh Muslim University, and the orthodox religious seminaries and clergy at Deoband.[49] Against this backdrop, it is clear that the long proto-secular tradition would rub up against proto-communalism in the region's historical trajectory. Whatever the current contentions are, however, secularism was neither a foreign nor transplanted concept; it arose in the sub-continental context for specific historical reasons and according to historical predelictions.

Political secularism

The debate on secularism in South Asia has been sharp and acrimonious in part because its detractors dismiss it as non-indigenous or unsuitable to the socio-cultural realities of the region. Part of the problem arises from the tendency to equate secularism in the subcontinent with its counterpart in the western world. The western notion emerged out of its own historical struggles, and has, by and large, been resolved to the satisfaction of its populations; in South Asia, the concept is still undergoing definition. The intricate polemics on secularism are not needed here and I will not be taking up detailed questions related to the particular values underlying secularism or its normative content. Nor will I consider deeper objections that a distinction between "comprehensive" and "political" secularism is untenable. For the purposes of this work, I will assume that political secularism is a meaningful concept, and also hope to explain the concept further.[50]

As noted in the introductory chapter, the concept of "political secularism" seems especially suited for South Asia's socio-cultural and political realities. Briefly, this type of secularism may be distinguished from the

---

[48] Imtiaz Ahmed, "The Role of Education."

[49] Kemal A. Faruki, "Pakistan: Islamic Government and Society," in John L. Esposito (ed.) *Islam in Asia: Religion, Politics and Society* (New York: Oxford University Press, 1987), pp. 53–55.

[50] See Rajeev Bhargava, "What is Secularism For?" in Rajeev Bhargava (ed.) *Secularism and Its Critics* (Delhi: Oxford University Press, 1998), pp. 486–542.

western approach whose ideal practice calls for the strict separation of religion from politics, and for the state to function completely outside the religious sphere. There is near-consensus among South Asia analysts that it is extremely difficult to disentangle religious and non-religious practices in the subcontinent; it is the response to this consensus that sets apart those who see themselves as opponents or proponents of a secular model in the region. The opponents stretch across a wide spectrum, from Ashis Nandy who calls for the abandonment of the secular project entirely, to T. N. Madan who surmises that the secularists also stoke religious extremism and fanaticism by not accepting the value of religion in human society, to others who are simply skeptical.[51] (The debate over secularism has evolved most comprehensively in India.)

As the adherents of political secularism see it, it is not necessary to make an air-tight case for separating the religious and non-religious spheres fully. Rajeev Bhargava articulates their position well: "Rather than espouse the untenable thesis of the separation of all religious and non-religious practices, it is possible to argue instead for the separation of some religious and non-religious institutions ... What distinguishes it [political secularism] is its advocacy of the value of separating *some* of these actions in their institutionalized forms, largely because it finds the alternative option less satisfactory. It follows that secularism is compatible with the view that the complete secularization of society is neither possible nor desirable."[52] Nobel laureate Amartya Sen's argument regarding secularism and the position of the state is relevant here: "The requirement is not that the state must stay clear of any association with any religious matter whatsoever. Rather, what is needed is to make sure that insofar as the state has to deal with different religions and members of religious communities, there must be a basic symmetry of treatment. Therefore, to be secular in the political sense, the state does not have to withdraw from dealing with religions and religious communities altogether ... The important point to note here is that the requirement of symmetric treatment still leaves open the question of what *form* that symmetry should take."[53] He suggests, for example, that a state deciding to provide no financial assistance to any religiously affiliated hospital might appear

---

[51] See, for example, Ashis Nandy, "The Politics of Secularism and the Recovery of Religious Tolerance," *Alternatives* 13 (April 1998) and T. N. Madan, "Secularism in its Place," *Journal of Asian Studies*, 46.4 (November 1987).

[52] Bhargava, "What is Secularism For?" p. 488.

[53] Amartya Sen, "Secularism and its Discontents." Sen also notes that secularism does not rise or fall if other principles, such as fairness or justice, have to supercede it (strictly speaking) under particular circumstances; it only points out that the domain of secularism is also circumscribed (p. 24).

more secular than a state that provides financial assistance to all hospitals irrespective of religious connections, but that the latter is, in fact, politically secular. This state is able to claim a "principled distance" between the political and religious sphere, a critical component of political secularism.[54]

The assumption is that perfect secularism is simply not possible for any given state in the South Asian context. What needs to be evaluated is the extent of so-called "principled distance" aspired to, and achieved by, the state *from all religious and non-religious polarizing ultimate ideals.*[55] Political secularism allows us to fully capture (and guard against) potential faultlines in the multi-dimensional societies of South Asia, and hold the state to a standard of "principled distance" from religious, ethnic or other exclusionary or chauvinistic tendencies. The sentiment underlying this conception of secularism seems to be what most secular post-independence leaders in South Asia (especially India) believed was necessary to fashion a workable state and, in turn, a stable region. The various domestic and international pressures and temptations to diverge from this path, however, have assured that this extraordinarily complex enterprise would not be smooth or easy.

State construction and identity conflict

Political representation according to religious community was becoming a key to power by the nineteenth century, with strong implications for the type of state that would succeed British colonialism. The emergence of a broad and powerful national movement in India that was either indifferent to, tolerant of or even willing to embrace ethno-religious differences, was something that British rulers deeply wanted to avoid. British requirements and objectives significantly undercut the prospects for strengthening political secularism. In other words, the previously-latent competition between ethnic, religious and secular identities was mediated by the geopolitical identity needs of the British state in India. It succeeded because British geopolitical needs were largely perceived to be better met with a divisive, religion-based system. The rise and decline of Abdul Gaffar Khan's movement in the North-West Frontier Province (NWFP) is a classic illustration.

---

[54] This does not mean that the state has to be absolutely neutral: one task is to protect places of worship and peoples' right to worship which might require state intervention, such as the imposition of president's rule in four states after the Babri Masjid destruction.
[55] Bhargava, "What is Secularism For?" pp. 492–494.

The legacy of Abdul Gaffar Khan

Abdul Gaffar Khan's non-violent Khudai Khidmatgar (Servants of God) movement for resisting British rule was in response to Mahatma Gandhi's call for a non-violent struggle against the colonialists.[56] The followers of Gaffar Khan (popularly known as the Frontier Gandhi) had to swear that "I shall never use violence. I shall not retaliate or take revenge, and shall forgive anyone who indulges in oppression and excesses against me."[57] Interestingly, Gaffar Khan's non-violence was also rooted in his concept of "jihad," or holy war, because, in his view, non-violent resistance provided the opportunity for "martyrdom in the purest form, since putting one's life conspicuously in one's enemy's hands was itself the key act."[58] Gaffar Khan and his Pathan (or Pashtun) followers dominated the NWFP for two decades despite eschewing violence, and he became a valued partner of the openly secular Indian National Congress.

Indeed, the unexpected success of Gaffar Khan's non-violent movement in the North-West Frontier Province between 1930–1947, and its alliance with the Indian National Congress, proved to be its death knell. The British (later in concert with the Muslim League) relied on a divide and rule strategy, and employed an astonishing level of repression to destroy Khan's movement. There was fear that the movement could provide the basis for a dangerous pan-Indian nationalism, and that it could spread to the Tribal Areas, seen as the frontline of the British Raj.[59] Britain's (and then Pakistan's) geopolitical interests were clearly defined against a credible and innovative nationalist movement that managed to bring together Islam, non-violence, Pashtun cultural autonomy and ethno-religious tolerance. It was this very combination that posed a threat first to British imperial rule, and then to the politics of state centralism in the newly created Pakistan. In the build-up to partition, the Muslim League, with the support of the colonial authorities, deliberately used anti-Hindu rhetoric to try to discredit Gaffar Khan's electoral alliance with the Indian National Congress in the NWFP. Together, their strategy was to project the Congress as a Hindu party. For example, British Governor Cunningham wrote in a 1942 policy memo "Continuously preach the danger to Muslims of connivance with the revolutionary Hindu body.

---

[56] The most well-researched study of Gaffar Khan's movement is by Mukulika Banerjee, *The Pathan Unarmed: Opposition & Memory in the North West Frontier* (Karachi: Oxford University Press, 2000).

[57] Quoted in Karl E. Meyer, "The Peacemaker of the Pashtun Past," *New York Times*, December 7, 2001.

[58] Quoted in *Ibid.*   [59] Banerjee, *The Pathan Unarmed*, pp. 167–191.

Most tribesmen seem to respond to this."[60] In the referendum which gave the NWFP only a choice between joining Pakistan or India, Khan urged a boycott. The Muslim League exhorted people to vote for Pakistan "as their religious duty," stoking communal sentiments and, amid charges of vote rigging, managed to win convincingly.[61]

Gaffar Khan's movement could not ultimately withstand the weight of British and Pakistani geopolitical identity needs that went squarely against the secular compromise that Khan envisioned. But it was also susceptible to the unstable secularism of South Asia: the Congress defeat of 1947 in Pashtun areas was in part made possible due to the communal riots that broke out in India, making it difficult to insulate the region from the Islamic emotionalism of the Muslim League. Khan's legacy is lost in part because his goal of autonomy for NWFP within a united, secular India never materialized. Indeed, Gaffar Khan could not reconcile himself to a purely Muslim state, and Pakistan's new government arrested him on charges of sedition, later banishing him from the NWFP. Allowed to return during the last years of his life, he died in Peshawar aged 98 in 1988; his funeral procession was said to have stretched for miles across the border into Jalalabad in Afghanistan. As we will see in the next chapter, Khan's historical legacy lingered, but again suffered a near-fatal blow under a new geopolitical thrust, this time from a combination of the US and Pakistan – leading to nothing less than "Talibanization," with a Pashtun social base at its core.

The Nehruvian vision

The composite secular identity in India that ultimately survived the colonial intrusions, was basically a compromise between the conceptions of Jawaharlal Nehru and Mahatma Gandhi, but tilting towards the former. Gandhi's pithy comment that "Those who want to separate religion and politics in India understand neither religion or politics," underscored his particular beliefs. Nehru's anathema to religion put him on something of a collision course with his mentor, and as the recognized candidate for Prime

[60] Quoted in Adeel Khan, *Politics of Identity: Ethnic Nationalism and the State in Pakistan* (New Delhi: Sage Publications, 2005), p. 95. The author again quotes another note by Cunningham about 1939–1943: "Our propaganda since the beginning of the war had been most successful. It had played throughout on the Islamic theme." Khan also points to payments promised by the British to various big khans to meet and urge religious leaders to serve the "cause of Islam."

[61] *Ibid.* pp. 95–100. Khan provides a detailed account of the British and Muslim League attempts to break the political hold of Gaffar Khan. Still, the League could not gain the support of the Pashtuns as late as 1946, with the Congress winning 16 out of 22 seats in the Pashtun areas in elections of that year.

Minister, Nehru's views also carried tremendous weight but even he did not harbor any illusions about Indians discarding their religious identities. Rather, it was a recognition of the deep-seated religiosity of the Indians and the plurality of India's religions that prompted Nehru to work against the use of religion for political purposes, and avoid the dangers of communalism. The resulting construction was something that oscillated between a rather strict secularism and a looser version, reflecting the difficult environment that had been inherited. This flexibility has proved to be politically indispensable. As a leading scholar of Nehru argues, it is precisely Jawaharlal Nehru's improvised and elusive notion of secularism regarding "Indianness" that has allowed the country to remain a single political entity despite huge internal differences. India's political self-definition neither monopolized nor simplified the definition of Indianness.[62]

In theory at least, this strain of secularism left little need or room for the development of exclusive identities that could foster anti-state or other extremist movements. The Nehruvian approach served the particular geopolitical identity needs of the Indian state well. India shares a border with every other state in South Asia save Afghanistan; apart from Afghanistan and Pakistan, no other state shares a border with any other in the region. Non-secular identity-based ideologies or movements clearly posed a threat to India's multi-faceted polity. Thus both geopolitical identity needs and the political compromises reached after independence worked in the same direction, and have been perceived as desirable by India's state managers, almost uninterruptedly since the beginning.

In spite of this, India has become the location for numerous ethnoreligious challenges, from within and without. The rise of Hindutva forces in the 1980s at the national level also pointed to the creeping weakness of the Nehruvian model. As the most potent political purveyor of Hindu nationalism, the Bharatiya Janata Party (BJP) tapped into the legacy of V. D. Savarkar who constructed Hindus and a Hindu nation as political categories in 1923, and M. S. Golwalker who narrowly conceptualized Hindustan as the land of the Hindus.[63] Remarkably, this vision of India has been successfully marginalized. No South Asian state has escaped these challenges, and all have seen the ebb and flow of political secularism over time. South Asia does not present an easy picture: only India is a declared secular state. All the others have formally defined state identity in terms of Buddhism, Hinduism and Islam (Sri Lanka and Nepal respectively for the

---

[62] Sunil Khilnani, *The Idea of India* (London: Hamish Hamilton, 1997), p. 179.
[63] For a good discussion, see Neera Chandhoke, *Beyond Secularism: The Rights of Religious Minorities* (New Delhi: Oxford University Press, 1999), pp. 70–71.

former two, and for the latter, Pakistan, Afghanistan and Bangladesh). The political and geopolitical impulses and implications of this development need to be reckoned with in understanding an environment that invites extremist thinking of different types.

Extremist challenges to secular traditions

The decline of relatively secular and open politics since the 1970s and 1980s occurred across the South Asian region, but it was also a global phenomenon. Many see it as a reaction to the continued inability of secular-oriented states to meet economic and political expectations, combined with instability due to the challenges of insecure and competing identities that have not been resolved by post-colonial states. The result has been a sharpening of exclusionary identities, in which states hardly acquit themselves well. Evidence presented in this book shows that we may make this point even more forcefully: state elites have repeatedly dismantled secular institutions that had stood the test of time, leading to a polarizing of identities.[64] To draw a comparison with South Asian medieval society, we may cite Mushurul Hasan's view of how religious or communal sentiment was held in check, especially at the level of the state. According to him "Admittedly, there existed a fragmented and differen-tiated form of religious consciousness, which may have led Sultans and their ideologues to offend religious sensibilities. But religious solidarity was not the basis of collective socio-economic experiences. *The ideology of the State, trimmed to suit the interests of the ruling elites, accommodated religious concerns. Yet, it did not rest on the notion of a unified 'community,' with iden-tifiable interests, which forms the main pillar of modern day 'communalism.'"* (emphasis added).[65]

In contemporary South Asia, apart from India, examples of the state promoting religious or communal identities that increase its hold over society are fairly common. What is often not recognized is the geopolitical content of these identities. For example, in the post-1971 period, Pakistan's leadership attempted to turn away from a "South Asian" cultural orientation and embrace a Middle Eastern, specifically Saudi Arabian, religious identification and connection. It served a dual purpose: legitimacy for a Pakistani army that was reeling from the country's loss of its eastern wing in a war with India, and underscoring an affiliation with a

---

[64] This shifts the onus for extremism from perceived failed secularist projects. See, for example, Ali Riaz who picks apart the argument that places the blame on secularists for the rise of Islamization in *God Willing: The Politics of Islamism in Bangladesh* (Lanham, MD: Rowman & Littlefield, 2004), pp. 18–22.

[65] Hasan, "Competing Symbols," p. 103.

wealthy patron that increased its regional influence. In this case, domestic needs and a new geopolitical identity were seen as meshing well. In Afghanistan too, the turn towards the Middle East by different groups came rather late in the country's history as did the adoption of Wahabism, with its vicious anti-Shiite, anti-Sufi beliefs.[66] Once again, the potential of politico-economic support and patronage against Soviet forces played a huge role. The popular justification in both instances was common religious purpose, something which was to prove a double-edged sword for the South Asian region, most seriously for Pakistan and Afghanistan themselves, in the years to come. It is no accident that the suspected hijackers of 9/11 happened to spend time in both Afghanistan and Pakistan.

In Sri Lanka, Sinhala majoritarianism and Buddhist communal elements became incorporated into the state's conceptions of national identity. This was influenced to a considerable degree by Sri Lanka's geopolitical position, not just India's lopsided strength, but more specifically, 60 million Indian Tamils. On the part of the Sri Lankan state, we see at once two contradictory tendencies: one that is threatened by the Tamil equation from India, and another that attempts to reconcile with the reality of India. Bangladesh has been the most surprising – going from alignment with India at the time of its independence, to a continued struggle between two sections of state leadership regarding the appropriate distance to keep from India, to the extent that competing state identities in Bangladesh currently owe much to how regional geopolitics is viewed. Indian leadership on the other hand, has refrained from constructing state identities that have religious connotations. Even so, the drive for overweening state power under Indira Gandhi and Rajiv Gandhi alienated Kashmiri Muslims, an alienation that happened to fit well with Pakistan's geopolitical identity. India's increasingly unstable secularism in the 1980s also probably made it easier for state action in Kashmir to be perceived in politicized religious terms; for the Indian state, Kashmir's position on the periphery of the border with Pakistan, combined identity and security in a particularly aggressive way. As we will see, the intertwining of identity and security perceptions, mediated by the state, has been a persistent factor in the way extremism has evolved in the region.

---

[66] To counter the minority view that argues Wahabism was imported to the subcontinent in the early nineteenth century by Syed Ahmed of Rae Bareili, see the historian Charles Allen, "The Hidden Roots of Wahhabism in British India," *World Policy Journal*, 22.2 (Summer 2005), p. 87. Allen's argument is strained: the so-called adherents of Wahabism in British India never called themselves Wahabi, and most of their religio-political actions could be equally explained as anti-colonial. Even Allen describes the hardliners as "Wahabis in all but name," begging the question of why they did not adopt the name.

Conclusion

From direct colonial intervention of the past, to geopolitical pressures and threat perceptions in the contemporary period, external forces have exerted a good deal of influence on domestic structures and orientations in South Asia, much as Peter Gourevitch has suggested in his particular take on international relations theory. But the character and intensity of the impact is strongly conditioned by the nature of the domestic environment encountered, particularly the existence of exclusive or inclusive identity constructions. The presence of secularist legacies (although unstable) is important in this regard. The pre-colonial history of the region offers a fairly convincing counterpoint to the current dominant thinking on ethnic and religious extremism in South Asia. Close attention to the shared history and persistence of common traditions in South Asia of a liberal kind, tends to throw into serious question the stereotypes underlying post-9/11 discourses. Thus, it poses a significant puzzle for the conventional approaches which give preponderance to internal impulses for extremist violence.

India's stunning election result of May 2004, confounding nearly every political pundit's prediction, provides a glimpse into the limits of exclusionary identity formation. After an uncharacteristic climb for the forces of Hindutva since 1998 with the victories of the Bharatiya Janata Party (BJP), the Indian electorate voted for a coalition whose major plank was secularism. The victory of stronger secular parties had a perceptible impact in neighboring Pakistan and Bangladesh, where liberal and moderate Muslims found additional legitimacy for their own stands.[67]

In contrast, the strong showing of religious parties in the Pakistani elections of 2002 requires explanation since their share of the vote had been hovering at around only 4 percent. This development cannot be explained, as Chapter Three shows, without an understanding of the "military–mullah" tacit alliance and the US's war on terrorism. Afghanistan's 2005 elections and the role of the US in them reveal how geopolitical identity needs do not remain static: in 2005, the US preferred the victory of secular elements, whereas in the 1980s, it was the religious groups that it had pinned its hopes to. It remains to be seen just how far this type of geopolitical conversion on the part of the US can go within a fractured Afghanistan, since many view the US's new involvement as part of a unilateral assertiveness that is not just grating but also untrustworthy.

---

[67] Personal observations to the author by Bangladeshi and Pakistani analysts after the May 2004 elections.

What we find regularly in South Asia are different forms of a three-way contest between ethno-religious, secular and geopolitical identity constructions. The North-West Frontier Province example discussed above illustrates the confluence of these identities, and their enormous implications. The privileged position of the state gives it particular leeway to balance these different strands: each offers something to the state, but takes something else away. Underlying these three forces, are the broader political and international pressures. In the succeeding chapters, we turn to the manner in which these factors have interacted, and their specific impact on the contours of extremism in Afghanistan, Pakistan, Kashmir, Sri Lanka and Bangladesh.

3 Afghanistan's changing fortunes

After September 11, Afghanistan became almost synonymous in the popular mind with terrorism and religious extremism. The image of a wild ungovernable region shot through with warlordism and ethnic warfare became established and, along with it, an underlying assumption that such a state of affairs had been a historical inevitability. The curious absence of any Afghans among the 19 suspected hijackers of September 11 went unnoticed by most commentators. With the fall of the Taliban and the rise of Hamid Karzai's government, however, there is now a new image of an Afghanistan transformed into a "success story," thanks to international intervention.

Neither perception – of the historical inevitability of the preceding violence or of a country about to be saved from itself – is wholly accurate. Much like its neighbors in South Asia, the Afghan identity is made up of diverging secular, religious and geopolitical identities. To understand the rise of extremism in Afghanistan and forecast its future, it is necessary to see how these different tendencies have interacted to produce religious militancy and the excesses of the Taliban and beyond. The US invasion of Afghanistan in October 2001 turned the spotlight on the key political and military actors in Afghanistan who had long been shielded from international sight: first during the covert anti-Soviet war; then through the dizzying civil wars; and finally under the Taliban's self-inflicted isolation. Understanding the emergence and evolution of these key figures over time gives us a way of tracking the trajectory of extremism in Afghanistan.

This chapter begins with a number of conventional explanations for extremism and why we need to go beyond them. It then turns to the internal environment and the degree of political secularism, keeping in mind the historical patterns laid out in Chapter Two. We ask the critical question of how competing identities evolved and impacted the orientations and responses of different groups, and why the more extremist notions took hold in Afghanistan over time. Finally, we look at the prospects of more moderate identity conceptions emerging and enduring.

Attempts to explain extremism

Normal politics as we know it has not existed in Afghanistan since the late 1970s, making it difficult for standard political analysis. However, some observations about the four commonly-cited factors in the emergence of extremism outlined in Chapter One may be made.

For example, the *relative deprivation* explanation of extremism does not stand up well in this context: militancy and extremist sentiment has permeated different classes and social levels, covering both rural and urban areas in Afghanistan. Furthermore, staggering poverty levels have been a fixture in Afghanistan for generations, without it falling into a cycle of extremist violence until now. Even if we look at this according to the economic status of various ethnic groups, as postulated by Ted Gurr, the Hazaras who have historically been the poorest, have not been at the forefront of violent movements as might be expected. It is also difficult to make the case that the rise or fall in the economic fortunes of the different ethnic groups, and changes in relative economic standing, directly led to the militancy. During the years of war against the Soviet Union from 1979–1988, it is easy to find cooperation between ethnic groups in the war effort. However, the manner of distribution of *outside* money and weapons to the different militant groups did lead to internal social cleavages. This points to an indirect link between relative economic standing and group rivalry, but certainly not in the way that the relative deprivation model anticipates.

The notion of *elites* manipulating groups towards extremist religious identities is more plausible, but even at the height of the war against the Soviets, we find variation among the militant leaderships themselves on religious conceptions of identity, in addition to the views of royalists, traditional tribal heads and liberals. Burhanuddin Rabbani, Mohammad Qasim Fahim, Abdul Rashid Dostum, Ismail Khan and Gulbuddin Hekmatyar are good examples of this lack of consensus on identity as well as strategy among the mujahideen. As we see later in this chapter, such variation characterizes the entire contemporary period. What seems more significant is outside manipulation on identity formation, and the way that Afghan elites have responded to those pressures and incentives. Thus we need to go beyond internal elites.

The explanations that cite *lack of political access* and *state repression* for the emergence of extremist groups face the anomaly that a "state" as we generally know it did not function in Afghanistan for extended periods of time between 1979 and 1996. (In contrast to some of the other militant movements in South Asia, such as in Sri Lanka and India, that are anti-state and secessionist, the different groups in Afghanistan ultimately fought *for the establishment of a state.*) In the early 1970s, we do find that Mohammed Daoud's government was hostile to the Islamists, leading several, including Rabbani, his close associate Ahmed Shah Massoud, and Hekmatyar, to go into self-exile in Pakistan. The denial of political rights, followed by outright suppression by the state, reached its height with the imposition of communist rule in 1978. The emergence of religious opposition during the early 1970s was important, but it was largely inchoate and lacked muscle.[1] The extreme direction it would take was not at all clear at the outset. In 1970, when a protest was held in Kandahar against modern expressions such as western garb and higher education for women, more than 5,000 women staged a public demonstration with widespread sympathy. The US embassy report on this noted that the failure of the Islamist protest to spark a "major fire" showed the weakness of Islamic fundamentalists.[2]

In fact, the very absence of an effective central state in Afghanistan and its fragmentation, however, was what made it extremely vulnerable to outside influences. Afghanistan was sliding towards the status of a failing state. So we need to look beyond the conventional political access and state repression arguments for an explanation of the rise of extremism.

The religious explanation

The apparent irrelevance of these three factors, and the emergence of the Taliban, with its Islamic puritanism and support for al-Qaeda, could be cited as *prima facie* evidence that the culprit to be blamed for extremism is *religion*. Remnants of the Taliban and al-Qaeda, together with groups like Gulbuddin Hekmatyar's Hizb-e-Islami, have been waging a low-level insurgency since 2001. They have persisted in the face of new presidential elections in 2004 and parliamentary elections one year later, calling into question the future governance and stability of Afghanistan. Thus an understanding of the religious sources of extremism continues to be important for the making of any prognosis for the country.

The widely held view of Afghanistan's religious intolerance is, however, historically unwarranted, with radical Islam a surprisingly new

---

[1] Rasul Bakhsh Rais, *War Without Winners: Afghanistan's Uncertain Transition After the Cold War* (Karachi: Oxford University Press, 1994), p. 174. See also Olesen, *Islam and Politics*, p. 168.

[2] William Burr (ed.) *The September 11th Sourcebooks, Volume IV: The Once and Future King? From the Secret Files on King Zahir's Reign in Afghanistan, 1970–1973,* National Security Archive Electronic Briefing Book No. 59, October 26, 2001. See also M. H. Kakar, "The Fall of the Afghan Monarchy in 1973," *International Journal of Middle East Studies* 9.2 (1978), pp. 195–214.

phenomenon. The Taliban's religious orientation, methods and strategic objectives, were significantly alien to the country. The same point could be made about the most extreme Islamist groups within the anti-Soviet mujahideen. Religiously speaking, Afghanistan's traditions are not as distinct from its South Asian neighbors as it might appear at first glance. The hold of Sufi Islam in South Asia, with its lack of dogma or political aspirations, as described in Chapter Two, extended to Afghanistan as well. In addition, tribal structures in the Pashtun areas served as a check against totalizing forms of Islam. The ethnic differentiation among major Afghan groups and their particular cultural mores, practices and beliefs also competed against the definition of a monolithic national identification based on a single "official" version of Islam. Louis Dupree, well-known anthropologist of Afghanistan, has claimed that "Islam practiced in villages and nomad camps, would be almost unrecognizable to a sophisticated Muslim scholar. Aside from faith in Allah and Muhammad as the messenger of Allah, most beliefs related to localized, pre-Muslim customs."[3]

Worship of Sufi "saints," which is theoretically forbidden according to strict interpretations of Islam, was commonplace in Afghanistan. Hundreds of tombs of saintly men and thousands of small shrines dot the Afghan landscape, just as they do in India, Pakistan and Bangladesh. Sufism commanded the largest following, cutting across ethnic, social and regional groups. The majority of traditional ulema in Afghanistan who are trained as Islamic scholars are linked to Sufi networks and view Sufism as the true representative of Afghan Islam.[4] Most importantly, from today's perspective, it is remarkable to note one expert's assessment: "In the Afghan tradition, the state and religion remained two separate and mutually exclusive domains."[5] This is in stark contrast to the politically charged strict Wahabism that crept into Afghanistan, an unwelcome development in the view of most local ulema. As we will see, Wahabist influence came to Afghanistan not through religious institutions, but by a more circuitous political route.

Those who would make a religious argument could point out that the anti-Soviet struggle had a decidedly Islamic tone from the beginning, and that the war spontaneously radicalized religious sentiment, even leading to messianic terrorism. This is a plausible, but deceptively simple argument. It suggests determinism, and an absence of important mediating factors, neither of which stands up to evidence. A purely religion-based argument

---

[3] Louis Dupree, *Afghanistan* (Princeton, NJ: Princeton University Press, 1973), p. 104.
[4] Rais, *War Without Winners*, pp. 175–176. See also David B. Edwards, *Before Taliban: Genealogies of the Afghan Jihad* (Berkeley, CA: University of California Press, 2002), pp. 252–260.
[5] Rais, *War Without Winners*, p. 174. See also Olesen, *Islam and Politics*, pp. 44–48 on the importance of Sufi centers spread throughout the country.

would have to explain several anomalies: longstanding religious traditions that were counter to the Taliban's ideological orientations; the split in the mujahideen movement itself on issues of pan-Islam and Afghan nationalism; the ethnic group differentiation that often overwhelmed the religious bonds during more than 20 years of warfare and beyond; and the range of strategies and religo-political positions that has emerged for former warlords and commanders vis-à-vis the new government after October 2001. A key question, then, is how these traditions were challenged and transformed. This takes us to the central argument that goes beyond religion – from the *politics* of religion, all the way to the *geopolitics* of religion.

The evolution of the Afghan state

Afghanistan emerged as an independent entity in 1747 when the Durrani clan unified the splintered Pashtun tribes under a confederacy. As they derived their power from the tribes, the Durrani rulers were not committed to enforcing a particular form of religious interpretation through the state.[6] The Afghan state has never been strong, with little ability to raise revenues or exert its powers unchallenged, especially in the northern areas. It was further weakened when, in 1893, the British divided the Pashtuns, for the first time, between British India and Afghanistan. Durrani leaders maintained their rule in Afghanistan until King Zahir Shah was overthrown in a bloodless coup by his cousin Mohammed Daoud in 1973. The establishment of a republic under Daoud proved unstable and short lived. With the imposition of communist rule in 1978 and Soviet intervention to back it up in December 1979, Afghanistan plunged into a prolonged political, military and ideological crisis from which it is still recovering. The collapse of the Afghan state was one casualty.

Current day "warlords," or commanders as they are commonly referred to in the country, are a legacy of the Afghan wars, but powerful regional leaders and regionalism have always been part of the political landscape.[7] As the largest ethnic group, Pashtuns have been politically dominant and have tended to view the Afghan state as a "Pashtun" state. Yet, without a commanding majority, other minority groups could not be ignored. The *modus vivendi* has been a political compact between the Pashtun and Tajik leaders in Kabul, giving the latter a substantial role in the affairs of the state. Once the Soviets withdrew in 1988, however, the furious internal wars

---

[6] Ghani, "Afghanistan," pp. 82–83.

[7] On the link between regionalism, warlordism and Afghanistan's historical weak center, see the author's "Combating Warlordism and Regionalism in Afghanistan," US Institute of Peace, Washington, DC, November 1, 2002.

produced an unprecedented situation that placed the minority leaders in control of the state between 1992 and 1996, until it was wrested back by the Pashtun Taliban. Since 2001, the dilemma for the US and international community's "nation builders" has been how to put the Afghan state back together in a way that recognizes the dominance of the Pashtuns, without alienating other minority groups. This has been particularly delicate because the initial success of the US invasion was heavily dependent on the Northern Alliance of minority guerrilla commanders who despised the Taliban. Ethnic and religious identities that have become much more politicized in recent years have been a major obstacle. One missing link has been the lack of a sufficiently "moderate" Pashtun leadership with a pan-Afghan national identity.

As we will see, the decline of moderate Pashtun groups can be traced to the geopolitical needs of neighbors and outsiders, and this explains much about the character of the alternative identities and state structures that culminated with the Taliban regime. Indeed, it would be fair to say that the nature of the Afghan state has come to be determined almost entirely by outside intrusion, needs and preferences. Whether we agree with the direction it has taken since 2001, and disagree with the earlier trend, or not, it is hard to deny the geopolitical content in the definition of state structures and identity. The "outside-in" effects of the international system as posited by Gourvitch and outlined in Chapter One, is strongly reflected in the evolution of the Afghan state. Any current restructuring of the state that does not bear this in mind is bound to fail.

Political secularism

Beneath Afghanistan's overwhelming Muslim population lies other identities that have been equally, if not more, important: ethnic, sectarian, regional and tribal. The Hazaras and Uzbeks who have historically had the least say in Kabul, were forcibly integrated during the reign of Amir Abdul Rehman in 1880–1901 with the help of the British. The Shiite Hazaras, whom the Taliban regarded as infidels, were at the receiving end of the Taliban's stringent Sunni Islamist assault in 1998. Remarkably, however, modern Afghan history has not involved nationalist or secessionist efforts by the various ethnic groups that extend across political boundaries in northern, western and southern Afghanistan.[8]

---

[8] This somewhat unique situation in South Asia is pointed out in Donald Wilber, *Afghanistan* (New Haven: HRAF Press, 1962), pp. 53–55. There were even a number of Hindus in eastern and northern Afghanistan and around Kabul. Small Jewish colonies existed for centuries as well, especially in Herat without evidence of any persecution of these groups.

Even during the pitched battles of 1992–1996, ethnic groups were fighting for control of *Kabul*, the symbolic Afghan state. Notionally, at least, a pan-Afghan identity existed. This was possible not just because of the fragmented and non-threatening state structure, but also because dominant identities were loose and fairly open. Until the Taliban's takeover, the state could even be described as "politically secular" as defined in Chapter One: it tended to maintain a principled distance from sectarian and chauvinistic tendencies, and avoided directly propagating such conceptions.

The rise of Islamism

The first rumblings of modern Islamic assertiveness in Afghanistan came in the early twentieth century, in response to King Amanullah Khan's modernization drive. The downfall of King Amanullah, who had been inspired by Mustafa Kemal in Turkey, was not, however, brought about by religious opposition alone; he retained the support of important Afghan religious pirs until the end. Competitive tribal politics played a strong part, with the King's fate sealed in the face of covert British assistance to his successor, Nadir Shah in 1929.[9] The overthrow of the King cannot be viewed as a unified attempt to stem secularization. According to one close expert, "during the next forty years ... subsequent attempts at modernization, democratization and liberalization have been influenced by plain secularist ideas while making concessions to Islam."[10] For example, the Ministry of Education operated the Ulum-i-Sharia, the largest religious school, from the early 1940s, with the aim of producing "modernist" scholars. Students were exposed to both religious instruction as well as a regular academic curriculum.[11] Efforts by the state to introduce greater freedoms for women from the late 1950s never led to any noteworthy popular opposition.

As described in Chapter Two, Abdul Gaffar Khan's anti-colonial movement in the Pashtun region of Pakistan that allied with the secular Indian National Congress, and sought to utilize Gandhi's non-violent methods, met with huge success for nearly 20 years. On both sides of the border, Pashtuns historically supported fairly secular, "nationalist" parties in large numbers. The Afghan Millat Party, which represented the most important of the latter groups, enjoyed widespread backing until the emergence and dominance of Islamist groups during the

---

[9] The British did not trust King Amanullah's anti-imperial stand and potential flirtation with Russian ideology (Olesen, *Islam and Politics*, pp. 172–175). For an argument that religious factors were not paramount against the King, see L. B. Poullada, *Reform and Rebellion in Afghanistan, 1919–1929* (Ithaca: Cornell University Press, 1973).
[10] Olesen, *Islam and Politics*, p. 166.   [11] Wilber, *Afghanistan*, pp. 69–70.

Afghan wars. The Durranis, who controlled the Afghan state, based largely in the south and in Kandahar, were never fully enamored with ideological jihadism. When the revolt against the Soviets began, it was based on tribal networks of Durranis, clan chiefs and ulema. These leaders were more tolerant of ethnic minorities and Shiites, did not challenge tribal structures like the Loya Jirga (a traditional gathering to select and legitimize new rulers), and espoused more tolerant religious views than newer Islamists.[12] The 1964 Constitution of Afghanistan under King Zahir Shah, passed by a Loya Jirga, remained relatively secular and liberal into the 1970s. It created the framework for a democratic state, ensuring free speech and equal rights for all citizens, including women. Afghanistan also had a policy of two official languages: Pashto and Dari.

The Islamist movement emerged at Kabul University in the 1960s in opposition to increasing foreign, especially communist, influence. The distinction drawn out between Islamists and traditionalists by one expert of Afghan Islam is instructive: "Islamist thought, compared to the traditional outlook, is revolutionary in the sense that it projects a unified notion of both state and society as well as the spiritual and material. They have tended to raise political action to the level of religious duty ... Party concepts such as cadre, indoctrination, political work and quest for political power have been equally Islamicized in content and motivation. These are radical departures from the traditional Islam of Sufis and ulema, who paid little attention to the politics of Islam."[13] Prior to the war against the Soviets, the Islamist base in Afghanistan has been described as "tiny." The precipitous melting away of the Taliban regime under US attack and its inability to deny or negate the political evolution under the Karzai government suggests that the radical Islamic roots were not firmly planted.[14] Why were the traditionalists then unable to resist encroachment by newer groups? The internal dimension is only one, minor part of the answer.

Challenges to secularism

Internally, while a relatively open outlook was dominant, as in much of South Asia, secular traditions were never fully stable and did remain vulnerable to narrower sectarian or chauvinistic challenges. For example, Afghanistan's Sufi traditions could not fully withstand attacks that it was

---

[12] Ahmed Rashid, *Taliban: Militant Islam, Oil and Fundamentalism in Central Asia* (New Haven: Yale University Press, 2000) makes this point throughout his book.

[13] Rais, *War Without Winners*, pp. 177–178. For a similar characterization, see Olesen, *Islam and Politics*, pp. 236–252.

[14] William Maley makes a similar point in *The Afghanistan Wars* (New York: Palgrave Macmillan, 2002), pp. 266–267.

un-Islamic when assaulted by self-proclaimed protectors of the "true" faith. Sufism had always been susceptible to charges that it was a Hinduized form. However, there had never been much space for religious zealots making such assertions, and they would have been seen as rash in the Afghan context. It is not surprising that the battle between the moderate traditionalists and the extremists was not won on theological grounds. It was the *geopolitical* role of religion that proved decisive. The Soviet invasion was clearly the catalyst, but in 1979 hardly anyone familiar with Afghan society would have predicted the religious extremism and terrorism that would evolve.

The Deoband, Quttabist and Wahabi influences that ended up leaving such deep marks on Afghanistan had earlier been denounced by the traditional Afghan ulema. In part due to the geographic isolation of the Khyber Pass, the country had been minimally influenced by pan-Islamic movements historically. The work of Maulana Maududi, the founder of the Jamat-i-Islami party, as well as the Pakistani state next door in 1947, did have a strong impact on Afghan Islamists. Maududi's argument that Muslims should strive towards an Islamic state caught the imagination of early Afghan Islamists who were based at the Faculty of Theology at Kabul University. They were also heavily influenced by the Ikhwan-ul-Muslimeen (Muslim Brotherhood)'s Sayyid Quttab whose politicized Islam was well-known.

Saudi Wahabism has its roots in the seventeenth century as a conservative Islamic movement dedicated to eliminating innovations like mysticism, pre-Islamic practices, saint worship and Shiism.[15] Thus Wahabism was particularly at odds with the Islam of South Asia. It needed the critical intercession of individuals such as the influential Abdul Rabb Rasul Sayyaf, a Pashtun Afghan religious scholar who received Saudi funding to propagate Wahabism and reject Shiism.[16] In Afghanistan's early history, Amir Abdul Rahman Khan had actually fought against the influence of Wahabism, and during the mujahideen period, attempts by radical Arabs to change Afghan Islamic practices, such as the manner of prayer, led to local antagonisms.[17]

---

[15] Andrew McGregor, "Jihad and the Rifle Alone: Abdullah Azzam and the Islamist Revolution," *The Journal of Conflict Studies*, 23.2 (Fall 2003), p. 94.

[16] *Ibid.*, p. 102. Sayyaf was associated with the Islamist movement in Kabul, but he was better known as a "Wahabi" in Afghan circles (Rais, *War Without Winners*, p. 186). On the global export of a new mix of Saudi Wahabism and Egyptian revival of jihadism, see Mohammed Ayoob, "Political Islam: Image and Reality," *World Policy Journal*, 21.3 (Fall 2004); Brian Glyn Williams, "Jihad and Ethnicity," p. 8; Edwards, *Before Taliban*, pp. 269–270; and International Crisis Group, *Afghanistan: Judicial Reform and Transitional Justice*, Asia Report No. 45, Kabul/Brussels, 28 January 2003, p. 4.

[17] See Maley, *The Afghanistan Wars*, p. 82.

A spectrum of nationalisms

During the initial period of insurgency, despite the battles being waged loosely under the banner of Islam against an alien ideology, the dominant groups could be characterizing more as "nationalist" than hard core Islamist. There was no single conception of Islamic identity that fused the various anti-Soviet groups.[18]

By the early 1980s, Gulbuddin Hekmatyar and radical Islamism were at one extreme. At the other was a group comprising of liberal modernists led by Abdul Rahman Pazhwak, who had been president of the UN General Assembly in 1966.[19] Others included parties with substantial followings among Pashtun tribes led by Sufi elites such as Sibghatullah Mujaddedi and Sayyid Ahmad Gailani. Ideologically, the National Islamic Front, led by Gailani, advocated a fairly open democracy for an Afghanistan free of Soviet control. Another similar party was Harakat-i-Inqilab-i-Islami of Maulvi Muhammad Nabi Muhammadi, a traditional religious scholar with large popular support especially in the South. This was a liberal party and accommodated different viewpoints. The so-called traditionalist religious groups were attacked and marginalized not by secularists, but by Islamist extremists.

Under the direction of Hekmatyar, the Hizb-e-Islami was one of the earliest and most centralized political parties, which was unusual given Afghanistan's decentralized, localized structure. While Rabbani, head of the dominant Jamat-i-Islami of Afghnistan, and Hekmatyar, were both resolved to implement Sharia in a new Afghanistan, Rabbani favored a multi-party system and gradualism while Hekmatyar wanted a single-party Islamic state. The objectives of most parties related to ousting the Soviets and restoring Afghan independence, whereas Hekmatyar envisaged taking the war into Soviet Central Asia to free Muslims there of Soviet rule.[20]

---

[18] William Maley, a noted expert on the groups, describes the initial resistance as "basically a grassroots movement. This is frequently overlooked, especially by those whose focus of interest is skewed towards radical groups supported indirectly by the United States." See *The Afghanistan Wars*, p. 60. Even a former member of Pakistan's Ministry of Foreign Affairs who was active at the time, notes the lack of a unified agenda among groups. See Riaz M. Khan, *Untying the Knot: Negotiating Soviet Withdrawal* (Durham, NC: Duke University Press, 1991), pp. 68–72.

[19] Henry S. Bradsher, *Afghanistan and the Soviet Union* (Durham, NC: Duke University Press, 1983), pp. 218–220. An insider's account of the cleavages is provided by a former member of the ISI. See Mohammad Yousaf and Mark Adkin, *The Bear Trap: Afghanistan's Untold Story* (London: Leo Cooper, 1992), pp. 38–43. According to Yousaf, "75 percent" of ISI General Akhtar's time on Afghanistan was spent "in trying to achieve some sort of harmony between factious leaders," p. 39.

[20] Dilip Hiro, *War Without End: The Rise of Islamist Terrorism and Global Response* (London: Routledge, 2002), p. 212.

Beyond a commitment to fighting Soviets and their Afghan protégés, and establishing a government with some Islamic elements that would provide peace, there was little understanding or concern on the part of local commanders about the ideologies of the external political allies. The need for weapons, ammunitions and assistance tended to dictate these relationships.[21] According to highly respected Afghan scholar and policymaker, Ashraf Ghani, "the self appointed leadership of the resistance has kept aloof from the Afghan population inside and outside Afghanistan, relying on the religious discourse to ensure a following. But speaking in the name of Islam has neither brought unity of ranks nor unconditional popular support."[22]

The "mujahideen" today

Not surprisingly, in the post-9/11 era, there is a fairly wide spectrum of religious and political preferences in Afghanistan. This is not just because of opportunistic revisions in terms of cost and benefit by particular groups, but also a reflection of their longstanding tendencies.

Marshal Mohammad Qasim Fahim, the most powerful of Afghanistan's ethnic Tajik commanders and a former warlord with control over his own militia, had been viewed as the principal political rival to President Hamid Karzai. He became the Afghan defense minister after Taliban rule until 2004. Others have remained on the outside. Gulbuddin Hekmatyar, the dominant Islamist warlord during the mujahideen's battles, still poses a serious challenge to the Karzai government and US anti-terrorism efforts. As a Sunni Muslim Pashtun, he operates out of the Pashtun tribal belt between Afghanistan and Pakistan. Together with elements of al-Qaeda and the Taliban, his group poses a longer-term threat.

Between these two ends of the spectrum stands Ismail Khan, whose politico-military evolution has been no less notable than Fahim's. Ismail Khan was made governor of Herat under Karzai's transitional government, but he boasted a provincial army of 25,000 men. He operated as a law unto himself, maintaining his own militias and levying taxes and customs. His allegiance to the Kabul government was minimal, and he posed a different type of challenge to Karzai from Fahim and Hekmatyar. Yet after the presidential elections of 2004, Khan was persuaded to give up his gover-norship and join the central government as the energy minister.

---

[21] Neamat Nojumi, *The Rise of the Taliban in Afghanistan: Mass Mobilization, Civil War, and the Future of the Region* (New York: Palgrave, 2002), p. 89.
[22] Ghani, "Afghanistan," p. 94.

Like Khan, Abdul Rashid Dostum, the key Uzbek commander, preferred to function as an insider/outsider of the Karzai regime initially. Dostum, too, had his private milita giving him a level of autonomy from the central government, but was successfully shifted into the specially created post of chief of staff of the armed forces in 2005. All four have their roots in the mujahideen movement, representing major ethnic factions. Their political evolution may be seen as a strong indicator of the longstanding diversity and flexibility of Afghan political culture.

The choice between a more open Afghan nationalism and pan-Islamic internationalism has yet to be resolved under Karzai's government. The past continues to throw a long shadow. Among the various groups of the pre-Taliban mujahideen, the most united were the Northern Tajiks under Rabbani and his military commander, Ahmed Shah Massoud. In contrast, the Pashtun leadership in the south became increasingly fragmented, with the more liberal and Sufi-influenced parties growing weaker. The downward slide of these groups cannot be explained without turning to the regional and international geopolitics swirling around Afghanistan.

The convergence of external interests

During the anti-Soviet war, Afghanistan's conflict-ridden environment, and the competing mujahideen groups that emerged, offered a potent combination for outside meddling. There was an unprecedented convergence of geopolitical interest – between Saudi Arabia, Pakistan and the US – in privileging the more extreme Sunni Wahabi Islamism, an onslaught that a weak country like Afghanistan could hardly withstand. Like the rest of South Asia, Afghanistan could never construct strong, stable central government institutions. Even more than in other South Asian states, the national government managed to reign over a fragmented political structure by not demanding too much from the provinces. Unlike the others, the absence of formal colonialism meant that there was no single moment of British exit and so no immediate need to construct a legitimizing ideology for a post-colonial state. On the other hand, the creation of Pakistan in 1947, dividing the Pashtuns, stimulated a state response that brought together Pashtun nationalism and geopolitical identity.

The Pakistani agenda

Pashtuns from both sides have long interacted with one another across the borders; their location in border areas of Baluchistan and the North-West

Frontier Province (NWFP) has allowed them to monopolize these critical trading (and smuggling) routes.[23] When Pakistan merged all the provinces in West Pakistan into a single administrative unit in 1955 in an attempt to offset the power of East Pakistan, the Kabul government saw this as a measure to dilute the clout of the NWFP's Pashtuns, even leading to military clashes in 1960 and 1961.[24] Pakistan's predominantly Punjabi military has harbored suspicions about Pashtun intentions, with the result that having a pliable government in Kabul has been a top priority. Pakistan's geopolitical interest in Afghanistan has frequently been attributed to the military's interest in gaining "strategic depth" on the western border to balance the strategic vulnerability on the eastern border with India. However, the need to counter potential moves towards cross-border Pashtun nationalism has been a strong factor. During the anti-Soviet war, pan-Islamic ideology played an extremely useful role in deflecting whatever support there was for Pashtun nationalism which an overcentralized Pakistan state would not accomodate. In the process, an ideology that was for all practical purposes alien to Afghan culture and historical traditions was ushered in.

As the Islamists began operating out of Pakistan in the early 1970s, they received support from the avowedly secular Zulfiqar Ali Bhutto government in Islamabad. Why would Bhutto follow such a policy, especially when the Islamists were linked with his opponents in the Jamat-i-Islami party of Pakistan? The answer is that his geopolitical interests dictated it. The ebb and flow of Pakistan's support for the Islamists would suggest geopolitical, not religious motivations, whether under ostensibly religious or secular leadership.

The Saudi agenda

From the late 1970s, Afghanistan was at the receiving end of ideological and geopolitical dictates from Saudi Arabia and the US, as well as Pakistan. This particular three-way combination was to prove lethal in shaping the character of the resistance movement. Saudi Arabia's close involvement in the Afghan conflict arose from two motivations: a way of dealing with its own radicals, who were threatening to become a menace

---

[23] Paul Titus, "Routes to Ethnicity," in Paul Titus (ed.) *Marginality and Modernity: Ethnicity and Change in Post-Colonial Baluchistan* (Karachi: Oxford University Press, 1997), p. 291.

[24] On the hostile Afghan–Pakistan border relations, see Michael Rubin, "Who is Responsible for the Taliban?" *Middle East Review of International Affairs*, 6.1 (March 2002); and Michael Griffin, *Reaping the Whirlwind: Afghanistan, Al Qa'ida and the Holy War* (London: Pluto Press, 2003, p. 16.

to the monarchy, by exporting them, while proving the monarchy's Islamic credentials; and promoting Saudi-style Wahabism in the rivalry with Iran's new Shiite clergy led by Ayatollah Khomeini. Saudi Arabia had emerged as the central player in support of international Islamism by 1965.[25] The Saudis tended to fund the most conservative individuals, charities and religious seminaries in Pakistan and Afghanistan. Saudi funding was huge, with the Saudis widely believed to have matched the US contribution dollar for dollar. In part to avoid any friction with their critical Saudi patrons, the Pakistanis avoided bringing Shiia groups into the mujahideen coalition made up of Sunni organizations based in Peshawar.[26]

Groups came to be known informally as internal and external fronts, with the latter referring to those Sunni parties whose leadership was stationed mostly in Peshawar, working closely with the Inter-Services Intelligence (ISI), the military intelligence wing of the Pakistan government.[27] In 1990, mujahideen commanders based inside Afghanistan organized a short-lived National Commanders Shura, ostensibly to coordinate military strategy. Their real intent was to create an alternative leadership to the exiled top brass and the alliance between Hekmatyar and the ISI.[28]

One of the most damaging outside intrusions came in the form of a new generation of textbooks for Afghan children, underwritten by US grants in the mid-1980s. Violent and radically religious-based, these textbooks were developed in Peshawar by a committee of anti-Soviet Afghan educators under the direction of the seven-party coalition that enjoyed US–Pakistan support, and American experts on Afghanistan. Over 13 million books (printed mostly in Pakistan), were distributed at refugee camps and Pakistani madrassas.[29] In the post-9/11 period, there has been a major campaign to revise the inflammatory material of the 1980s. From 2004 onwards, new textbooks have been introduced by the Afghan Ministry of Education, with technical assistance from the Teachers College at Columbia University, funded by UNICEF and the Danish development agency DANIDA.

---

[25] John Cooley, *Unholy Wars: Afghanistan, America and International Terrorism* (London: Pluto Press, 2002), p. xv.
[26] Hamid Hussain, "Afghanistan – Not So Great Games," *Defence Journal (Pakistan)*, April 2002, p. 6. Available at www.defencejournal.com.
[27] Interview with a former Afghan commander, June 2005, Washington, DC.
[28] Barnett Rubin, *The Fragmentation of Afghanistan*, p. 182.
[29] International Crisis Group, *Pakistan: Madrasas, Extremism and the Military*, ICG Asia Report No. 36, July 29, 2002, p. 13. Craig Davis provides a detailed account based on fieldwork conducted. See " 'A' Is For Allah, 'J' Is For Jihad," *World Policy Journal*, 19.1 (Spring 2002). See also Hafizullah Emadi, *Culture and Customs of Afghanistan* (Westport, CT: Greenwood Press, 2005), p. 73.

Consolidation of Islamist groups in Pakistan

In 1981, there were more than 100 small parties with offices in Peshwar, representing numerous orientations from nationalist to tribalist, but in 1985 the Commissioner of Afghan Refugees for the Pakistan government announced that only seven Islamist parties would be allowed to remain in operation.[30] Both the Pashtun nationalist Afghan Millat party and members of the Afghan royal family were prevented from operating legally in Pakistan.[31] Gailani and Mujadeddi's armed groups remained small, largely due to the lack of external funding and patronage.[32]

Pakistan's narrow definition of acceptable parties meant that only the designated Islamist parties would have access to funds from international donors, almost all of which was disbursed by Pakistan. These seven were given rights to issue party membership cards to the swelling number of refugees, who could not register to live in refugee camps, or receive tents, foodstuff and other rations without them. As the major conduit for weapons and funds from the US, Pakistan was given pretty much free rein, but the US was not ignorant nor averse to the direction of its policies.

Among the Islamists, Hekmatyar's Hizb-e-Islami's strong ties to Jamat-i-Islami in Pakistan, a political ally of Pakistani president Zia ul-Haq, helped to consolidate his position. But Hekmatyar's attraction for the ISI also derived from his lack of notable grassroots support inside Afghanistan, which made him more beholden to his patrons.[33] The Hizb-e-Islami was also allowed to run its own security service, thus arrogating even more power over the fleeing Afghans. All the major mujahideen parties recognized by Pakistan were non-Durrani. Ghilzai tribal groups, located in the east and around Kabul, who had been in some competition with the dominant Durranis, benefited from Pakistan's patronage.[34] The more politically independent Durranis, who formed the nucleus of traditional Afghan power, found themselves being eclipsed by Ghilzai and Pashtun "upstarts" like Hekmatyar. Exploiting tribal differences in this fashion would ensure that a strong unified Afghanistan, with the potential to challenge Pakistan, would not emerge after the overthrow of the Soviets.

---

[30] For detailed descriptions of these events based on extensive field work, see Edwards, *Before Taliban*, pp. 267–268.

[31] Michael Rubin, "Who is Responsible for the Taliban?" p. 7.

[32] Michael Griffin, *Reaping the Whirlwind*, p. 420.

[33] Robert Kaplan, "The Taliban," *The Atlantic Monthly*, September 2000. Available at www.theatlantic.com.

[34] This is a major theme in Rashid, *Taliban*. For a description of these two major divisions among Pashtuns, see for example, Olesen, *Islam and Politics*, p. x.; Wilber, *Afghanistan*, pp. 41–44.

Although Pakistani military leaders involved in the operation contend that "battlefield competence" was the only criterion for providing funds, the way that some highly skilled groups were marginalized calls this into serious question.[35] The most obvious case is that of Ahmed Shah Massoud whose group was regularly ignored by Pakistan and the US even though it had repeatedly proven itself on the battlefield, and managed to cover six northern provinces that were located on vulnerable Soviet borders through which ran the Soviets' main lines of communication and energy supplies. Tellingly, Massoud had criticized the US and Pakistan and, most importantly, continued to reject the oversight of the ISI. Moreover, as an ethnic Tajik, Massoud was not seen as a viable candidate for an ISI that wished to control Afghanistan through its Pashtun clients.[36]

Internal fragmentation

Following Soviet defeat, between 1992 and 1996, Kabul was ruled by a loose coalition of commanders mostly from northern minority ethnic groups, with Rabbani as the nominal head, repeatedly kept off-balance by Hekmatyar whose "spoiler" capacity could not be overcome. Competition between the different mujahideen groups that had barely been checked during the anti-Soviet war, came out in full force in the race to control Kabul. The dizzying flip flops of allegiances and break ups, and Hekmatyar's ruthlessness nearly destroyed the capital city and claimed tens of thousands of lives.

Most independent observers have praised Rabbani and his defense minister Ahmed Shah Massoud for attempting to create a state structure that would deliver a modicum of security and stability. In Herat in the west, Ismail Khan managed to govern between 1992 and 1995 under relatively stable conditions.[37] In the north in Mazar-i-Sharif, Dostum ran a fairly efficient administration, ostensibly liberal in character. Whatever the different opinions held about these non-Pashtun factions, it could be safely concluded that none of them was aiming to establish a radical Islamist form of governance.[38] They also exhibited a good deal of independence from outside patrons.

---

[35] Steve Coll offers convincing evidence in this regard. See *Ghost Wars: The Secret History of the CIA, Afghanistan and bin Laden, from the Soviet Invasion to September 10, 2001* (New York: Penguin, 2004), pp. 11–13 and pp. 63–68. Brigadier Mohammad Yousaf puts forward the non-ideological argument. See Yousaf and Adkin, *The Bear Trap*, pp. 104–105.

[36] Coll, *Ghost Wars*, p. 10.

[37] "As Good as It Gets," *The Economist*, November 1, 2001.

[38] William Maley gives an excellent account of the events leading up to the Taliban takeover, describing the positions of the various commanders. See *The Afghanistan Wars*, pp. 197–217. See also Griffin, *Reaping the Whirlwind*, p. 21 on Massoud's independence.

However, no similar well-established rebel networks existed in the Pashtun-dominated south, which became the bastion of Taliban support. While the non-Pashtun areas continued to exhibit scope for moderate leadership even into the mid-1990s, such groups had now been destroyed.

The rise of the Taliban

Soviet withdrawal from Afghanistan led to a drying up of US funds, but a different form of support led by the ISI took hold: new recruits from Algeria, Egypt and other Arab states were increasingly financed by private sponsors such as Osama bin Laden, Islamic banks and charities, as well as by the enormous funds flowing from the drug trade that the US Central Intelligence Agency had encouraged during the war.[39] Saudi Arabia replaced the US as the largest patron, and Pakistan–Saudi relations became cemented in a common cause, particularly during their bid to support the Taliban. The connection between the Taliban and al-Qaeda, and other terrorist supporters, was made in the 1980s with the arrival of Arab fighters. The continuation of Pakistani logistical and military support after the Soviets left has been well documented.[40] Soviet collapse in 1991 also opened a strategic opportunity in newly independent Central Asian states for Pakistan – to reach critical new markets and energy resources via a weak and dependent government in Kabul.

Under the Taliban, Afghanistan experienced a transition from "an accidental to a mature terrorist state."[41] In an interview with *Le Nouvel Observateur*, Zbigniew Brzezinski was asked whether he regretted having armed extremist Islamists and future terrorists. His response was: "Which is more important in world history? The Taliban or the fall of the Soviet empire? A few over-excited Islamists or the liberation of Central Europe and the end of the Cold War?"[42] More than anything else, the decimation of the moderate traditional Pashtun leadership and Pakistani interference allowed the Taliban to explode onto the scene in 1996 and hold onto power until 2001. This goes a long way to explain Hamid Karzai's current frustration

---

[39] Cooley, *Unholy Wars*, pp. xvi–xvii.
[40] Declassified State Department cables are a good source: US Embassy (Islamabad) Cable, "Afghanistan: [Excised] Briefs the Ambassador on his Activities. Pleads for Greater Activism by UN" August 27, 1997, Confidential, 5pp., released through the Freedom of Information Act to the National Security Archives and cited in Sajit Gandhi (ed.) *The Taliban File Part II*, The National Security Archive, March 19, 2004; US Embassy (Islamabad) Cable, "Bad News on Pak Afghan Policy: GOP Support for the Taliban Appears to be Getting Stronger," July 1, 1998, Confidential, 2pp., released through the Freedom of Information Act to the National Security Archives and cited in Gandhi (ed.) *The Taliban File Part II*.
[41] This characterization is by Griffin, *Reaping the Whirlwind*, p. 111.
[42] Quoted in Cooley, *Unholy Wars*, p. 11.

vis-à-vis the Pakistan government. It is not enough for Afghan identity to shift; Pakistan's geopolitical identity needs have to change as well.

The post-Taliban environment

The new terrorism

In the post-Taliban, post-9/11 environment, a prevailing line of analysis in the US has been to see extremist Islamist threats as loose transnational networks, without central political authority. The view is that terrorist cells function in a stateless environment, linked together by loose ties, but often acting spontaneously and independently. Transnational, non-state actors, using the internet, informal hawala economic structures and messianic ideologies, are posited to have overwhelmed state capacities. (One implication for military strategy would be to "keep the terrorists on the run" given their fragmented nature, and some Pentagon strategists have suggested this.) This would be consistent with the argument considered in Chapter One on the impact of transnational factors on the rise of extremism.

The idea that the new form of stateless cells of terrorists are the biggest threat needs to be taken seriously because this suggests that we cannot simply use a state-oriented geopolitical analysis. On the face of it, it would seem a plausible idea given an increasingly random appearance of suicide bombers and the use of improvised explosive devices targeting a variety of soft targets in numerous countries. However, careful analysis by Dan Byman in *Deadly Connections* and others has thrown into question the idea that these fragmented groups can exist without state sponsorship.[43] Byman's evidence from the Middle East and South Asia strongly indicates that groups posing threats we see as unconventional can rarely, if ever, exist without some form of support by conventional states. Going one step further, he shows why states and these groups need each other. Among the states that are identified (at minimum) as enablers of terrorism, Pakistan is prominent.

With the new American policy of combating not just terrorist groups, but also their sponsors and those who provide safe havens, such ties may become even more hidden, and will have to be vigorously investigated. United Nations Security Council Resolution 1373 passed unanimously on September 28, 2001 also makes it clear that states will be breaking

---

[43] Dan Byman, *Deadly Connections: States that Sponsor Terrorism* (New York: Cambridge University Press, 2005). See also Ahmed Rashid's authoritative account continuing to implicate the Pakistan military well after 9/11 in *Descent into Chaos: The United States and the Failure of Nation Building in Pakistan, Afghanistan and Central Asia* (New York: Viking Penguin, 2008).

international norms if they do not extradite or prosecute terrorists, and deny them safe haven.

Thus the so-called "new terrorism" that Daniel Benjamin and Steven Simon posit, does not represent a major break with the past. Many factors are responsible for their integration (or rather insinuation) into South Asia, but none is as important as the *manner* in which the geo-political interests of the US and Pakistan have played out. To suggest that these extremists and terrorists are part of a shifting coalition of amorphous groups is only one minor part of the story.

The impact of the US military campaign

American military intervention has led to even greater fragmentation of the social order, almost along the lines prior to the emergence of the Taliban.[44] According to senior Afghan officials, the huge reliance of US forces on factional commanders or warlords to defeat the Taliban in 2001 and thereafter, led to a strengthening of these figures while fragmenting national power and frustrating the reform process.[45] Along with fear of warlords, the threat of American military action is seen as one of the two major sources of insecurity for Afghans, especially in the south and east.[46] The US has a fairly low public opinion rating among Afghans: in 2004, polls showed the US getting only 13 percent "very favorable" ratings, whereas the UN received "very favorable" ratings from 51 percent of those polled. Jihadi leaders did even worse, with only 7 percent being given as "very favorable" assessment.[47] The post-Taliban round of fighting has brought in even greater numbers of weapons into the area. Afghan officials frequently complain that short-term US military requirements are taking precedence over demilitarizing Afghanistan. Even top leaders close to Karzai note that "the US has made them [warlords] re-emerge" even though they are "extremely unpopular in Afghanistan."[48] UN officials have consistently complained that American military priorities undercut the development of Afghan state institutions.

One highly touted response by the US has been to create a new military-cum-development unit made up of Provisional Reconstruction Teams (PRTs) based in major provinces. The idea was to provide a secure structure for development outside Kabul. Assessments of these

---

[44] "International Crisis Group, Afghanistan: The Problem of Pashtun Alienation," ICG Asia Report No. 62, Kabul/Brussels, August 5, 2003, pp. 14–15.
[45] Ali A. Jalali, "The Future of Afghanistan," *Parameters*, US Army War College Quarterly, 36.1 (Spring 2006), p. 5.
[46] Interview with senior researcher from Afghanistan, May 2003.
[47] The Asia Foundation, *Voter Education Planning Survey: Afghanistan 2004 National Elections*, A Report Based on a Public Opinion Poll, New York, July 2004, pp. 107–108.
[48] Discussion with a high level advisor to Hamid Karzai, Washington DC, November 20, 2002.

units show that they have been plagued by a variety of shortcomings, including aid workers being too closely identified with the military, the breakdown of civil–military cooperation and an inability to penetrate the most needy areas due to continuing threats. All this has led to the "co-location" of some PRTs in coalition forces, challenging its very rationale.[49] The admission by Major General Eric Olson, the operational commander of US forces in late 2004 that his troops were "not even close" to defeating the militants, is no less accurate in 2008.[50]

The Karzai government has walked a tightrope politically on the issue of combating or co-opting warlords and commanders. The need to disconnect regional commanders from their independent sources of income and control of private militias is widely recognized. The government's main strategy in dealing with potentially renegade commanders has been simultaneously to incorporate the highest level commanders into the administration and to diminish their regional power.[51] One incentive for regional warlords to throw their support behind the government is the classic government monopoly of the national exchequer. In the case of the Afghan government, however, only a small percentage of international assistance – 10 to 16 percent – actually comes through the government, with the remaining being funneled in through international non-governmental organizations, the UN and aid agencies.[52]

In the months leading up to the presidential elections in 2004, Karzai, as president of the transitional government, stepped up efforts to appease powerful regional leaders, especially Ismail Khan and Abdul Rashid Dostum. The government retreated from potential armed conflict with these two powerful militia bosses, with Karzai paying a personal visit to Khan in Herat and negotiating with Dostum.[53] Both Dostum and Khan were reportedly willing to consider giving up their troops and arms only in exchange for top government posts. Likewise, Fahim was persuaded to give up his position as defense minister prior to the 2004 presidential elections, and was subsequently neither re-appointed nor given another cabinet post. Instead, he received the

---

[49] See for example, Robert Perito, *The US Experience with Provincial Reconstruction Teams in Afghanistan: Lessons Identified*, US Institute of Peace Special Report No. 152, October 2005.

[50] *The Hindu*, September 15, 2004.

[51] International Crisis Group, *The Afghanistan Transitional Administration: Prospects and Perils*, Afghanistan Briefing, July 30, 2002, pp. 9–10.

[52] Barnett R. Rubin, Humayun Hamidzada and Abby Stoddard, *Through the Fog of Peace Building: Evaluating the Reconstruction of Afghanistan* (New York University: Center on International Cooperation, June 2003), p. 5; and the author's *Combatting Warlordism*.

[53] Pamela Constable, "Karzai Attempts Diplomacy With Afghan Warlords," *The Washington Post*, May 19, 2004.

special lifetime privileges of a "marshal," the highest military rank in the country. Ismail Khan was made energy minister, and Dostum accepted the position of chief of staff to the Commander-in-Chief. So far, this strategy of "civilianization" shows some signs of producing results – with the important exception of the south and east. Thus, in the post-Taliban period, former warlords have posed two distinct challenges, with those in the north and west fairly successfully accommodated into the new political structures, and those in the Pashtun east and south remaining a potent threat to Kabul and Washington.

The balance between extremists and moderates

As the Taliban's base is among the Pashtuns, there is clearly a dilemma about how to increase support for the regime in Kabul among the Pashtuns while, at the same time, the US and Afghan government fight the Taliban. Likewise, the US is caught between Pakistan's interests in cultivating Pashtun support and maintaining sway over the Taliban and its aim of getting the Pakistanis to be serious about fighting the remnants of al-Qaeda and Taliban who continue to launch attacks from the border. American policymakers have been split on the appropriate policy.[54] A major task for Karzai is to mobilize Afghan sentiments towards the earlier inclusive, gradualist approaches regarding national identity and Islam. In the light of past history, the aim would be to insulate the country from external extremist elements and marginalize sectarian, religious radicalism domestically. The biggest threat to the new Afghan project continues to come from across its border in Pakistan.

America's dependence on the Pakistani military will continue to exert pressure to accommodate Pakistani interests in Afghanistan. After the death of the first UN international staff member in November 2003, Afghan Foreign Minister Abdullah Abdullah stated that the perpetrators belonged to the "Taliban-al-Qaeda network" who "found refuge among their mentors along our eastern and southern borders," a reference to strong belief in Afghanistan that militias are attacking unhindered from Pakistan.[55] Even among the Afghan Pashtuns, there is ambivalence at best; cross-border Pashtun nationalism would seem to have certain limits when it clashes with Afghan nationalism.

[54] *Dawn*, April 20, 2004. The Pakistani newspaper identified the US envoy to Afghanistan, Zalmay Khalilzad, as the "chief representative of the Pakistan-bashers in the US administration while the State Department often advocates the views of those who see Pakistan as a partner in the war against terror."

[55] Sayed Salahuddin and Mike Collett-White, "French UN Worker in Afghanistan Shot Dead," World-Reuters, November 16, 2003.

Resurgent cross-border Islamism?

While Pakistani Pashtuns may feel sympathy for their Afghan brethren in the US campaign, Afghan Pashtuns remain suspicious that Pakistan seeks to control events in Afghanistan. Over time, Pashtun nationalism has weakened within Pakistan, as they have gained a greater stake within the state. There are a variety of reasons for this, not least that Pashtuns over time have become better represented in Pakistan's military services, the dominant state institution.[56] The Afghan wars, in which Peshawar was the vortex of the pan-Islamic mujahideen, also undercut ethnic identification in the political realm. The eclipse of the nationalist National Awami Party (renamed Awami National Party) in the NWFP by others such as the Jamiat Ulema-e-Islami (JUI) was cemented thanks to the latter's active participation in the Afghan conflicts. The biggest difference between Afghan Pashtuns and Pakistani Pashtuns concerns the Afghan state: Pashtun Pakistanis do not have a stake in a consolidated Afghan state, thus a weakening of the "Pashtun" Afghan state hardly worries them as it would Afghan Pashtuns. If anything as one analyst puts it, "Afghan Pashtuns are suspicious that Pakistan has been undermining the Afghan Pashtun state."[57]

This sentiment is found at the highest levels of Afghan politics. After a lengthy interview with President Hamid Karzai, well-known journalist Ahmed Rashid wrote: "he made it clear to me that Pakistan's policy is giving him sleepless nights ... Mr. Karzai says he cannot understand why General Musharraf is allowing these extremists, who have been living in Pakistan since the defeat of the Taliban, to undermine his government and the Pashtun belt; nor can he comprehend why these rogue elements have not been arrested or handed over to the Afghan government."[58] There is concern that the ISI's modified strategy revolves around the development of "a new Pashtun Islamist formation drawing on both the Taliban and Hekmatyar's Hizb-e-Islami party."[59] Once again, it is the geopolitical interests of outsiders that could dictate the direction of identity politics in Afghanistan.

Recasting the Afghan identity

Pitted against this potential resurgence of Taliban-influenced ideology, is the recasting of Afghan state identity. Ostensibly, geopolitical pressures

---

[56] On the declining levels of Pashtun nationalism in Pakistan see Adeel Khan, *Politics of Identity*, pp. 100–104.
[57] Interview with a senior International Crisis Group representative, Washington, DC, November 26, 2002.
[58] Ahmed Rashid, "The Other Front," *The Wall Street Journal*, February 11, 2003.
[59] Quoting a leading Pakistani analyst in the International Crisis Group, "Afghanistan: The Problem of Pashtun Alienation."

are all working together in a benign manner towards a geopolitical identity which is most consistent with an open, more cosmopolitan identity domestically. In this case, a closer look at popular internal orientations suggests that a moderate outcome has a significant chance. The most ardent keepers of a pan-Afghan ethos are often viewed as the urban, educated minority, but that does not capture the full picture. As a senior Afghan leader put it, "people inside Afghanistan are actually united despite outsiders such as Iran, Pakistan and the Taliban trying to split people along ethnic and religious lines, showing the extent of nationalism that exists in the country today."[60]

Others close to the ground agree, and see a surprising resilience in the Afghan identity. There is no secession fever despite the past bloody civil conflicts: *the Afghan state is more a failure in the institutional sense than in an ethnic sense.* The utter fragmentation of the state has not led to a parallel fragmentation of national identity as many assume it must. Across the border in the North-West Frontier Province, Asfandyar Wali Khan, a leader of the Awami National Party, asserts that, "If you have studied Afghan history, then you would know that their struggles have always been based on nationalism and not on religion. It is the US which brought in religion and used it in the recent wars. This phase has been like a curse for the people of Afghanistan."[61] According to Ahmed Rashid, "there is a strong sense of national Afghan identity, even among the most marginalized minorities like the Shia Hazaras."[62] Furthermore, a recent survey reveals that "Afghan respondents universally disputed the importance of ethnicity as a divisive factor among the general population. Instead, blame for ethnic tensions was attributed to military factions and their foreign sponsors."[63]

If we consider outside factors contributing to Afghan national identity, it is hard to miss that a fragmented Afghanistan has worked much more in favor of both Pakistan's and America's national security objectives in the past. For Pakistan, a weak and disunited Afghanistan pre-occupied with internal conflict offered the best insurance against revanchist Afghan nationalism spilling over the Durand Line. Thus Pakistan's use

---

[60] Discussion with high level advisor to Hamid Karzai, Washington, DC, November 20, 2002.

[61] Interview with Asfandyar Wali Khan by Humra Quraishi, "Gandhi's Khan-daan," *The Times of India*, July 29, 2004.

[62] Ahmed Rashid, "Inside the Jihad," The Atlantic Online, Atlantic Unbound Interviews, August 10, 2000, p. 7.

[63] Center for Economic and Social Rights, *Human Rights and Reconstruction in Afghanistan*, New York, May 2002, pp. 3, 15. In contrast, some other observers suggest that Afghan nationalism is too weak to support a cohesive state and point to the recurrent political instability of the past two decades as the major obstacle to reconstruction. See, for example, Hussain, "Afghanistan – Not So Great Games," p. 7.

of pan-Islamic solidarity introduced during the anti-Soviet war, undercut Afghan nationalism. For the US the twin mobilizing forces of anti-communism and pan-Islamism were useful tools, with the latter in particular being effective in recruiting both fighters and sponsors from the Islamic world. Pan-Islamism then served the interests of the US and Pakistan, though for entirely different reasons. The disarray in Afghanistan's mujahideen movement also tended to suit both Pakistan and America's search for groups that would be more malleable than the nationalists. This process allowed more extremist factions to emerge and prosper.

History repeating

In a parallel with the past, the continuing war on terrorism provides a convenient excuse to various parties to remain armed and prevents a return to normal politics. Attempts at disarmament, demobilization and reintegration (DDR) have shown dismal results. The DDR component of Afghanistan's military reform does not have any real jurisdiction over groups such as the Afghan Militia Force and Afghan Guard Force, drawn from local militias, which are financed and equipped directly by the US.

The ongoing war is providing the climate for new, deadly tactics: the stepped-up suicide attacks since 2005. All analysts agree that this comes from al-Qaeda; suicide attacks are traditionally alien to Afghans. In 2006, after the worst day of suicide bombings in Afghanistan since the Taliban was overthrown, President Karzai publicly stated that he had intelligence reports months ago that suicide attackers were being trained in frontier areas and most attacks were being carried out by "foreigners."[64]

The weakness of the Afghan state calls into question its ability to execute its avowed liberal, cosmopolitan project. The minority leaders in particular have a strong preference for a decentralized, even federal system. Prior to the elections, Abdul Rashid Dostum's Junbish Party was the most important group pressing the Constitutional Commission for extensive devolution of governmental power. Ismail Khan's position was supportive of a less-defined federalism.[65]

Whatever the ideal may be regarding the Afghan state set-up, historically it has never had a successful centralized system. The natural point of equilibrium has been one of decentralization along provincial lines, resulting in more or less ethnically homogenous units, except for

---

[64] *Dawn*, January 17, 2006.
[65] International Crisis Group, *Afghanistan's Flawed Constitutuional Process*, ICG Asia Report No. 56, Kabul/Brussels, 12 June 2003, p. 7.

the highly diverse Kabul. If past experience here and elsewhere is any guide, a multi-ethnic state such as Afghanistan is unlikely to be stable without a critical degree of provincial autonomy. Ironically, the greater the level of a pan-Afghan nationalism, the more likely that the interests of its diverse constituencies would be met through a truly federal system.[66] Election results in 2004 and 2005 that revealed voting along ethnic lines has not translated into major impediments to government action.

Ethnic politics do not invariably have to deteriorate into violent competition as long as political structures do not threaten minority power or identity. Although the voting patterns do suggest that the pull of regionalism has to be accommodated, there is no danger of this translating into secessionism. Thus those who fear that a federal system is a first step towards ultimate state disintegration, will find evidence to the contrary in the Afghan context. It does, however, mean that it will be difficult to isolate regional commanders fully in the future. True to Afghan history, the center is likely to remain fairly weak.

Undercutting extremism

Karzai's victory at the polls in the presidential race in 2004, and the holding of parliamentary elections one year later, has laid the groundwork for a transition to normal politics after a gap of over 25 years. New domestic structures have been fashioned since 2001 to meet the more open identity conceptions of the Karzai government. But as we have seen, domestic institutions do not exist independently of outside influences and, once again, the looming question is the impact of regional and global geopolitics, namely the US and Pakistan, in shaping outcomes within Afghanistan.

The major disjuncture between the current period and the pre-2001 era, is that the geopolitical identities required by Pakistan and the US this time around are not necessarily consistent. For Afghanistan, this could mean the difference between moderate and extremist outcomes, and a stable or unstable polity. The Afghanistan Compact of January 2006 calls for a commitment that all US-led "counter-terrorism operations will be conducted in close coordination with the Afghan government and ISAF," the NATO-led International Security Assistance Force.[67] This is partly to

---

[66] An example may be drawn from India. During the mid-1990s when coalition politics emerged with a fury representing diverse regional and sub-regional tendencies, there was fear that the government would be unstable at best, and that the country could begin to fall apart at worst. A decade later, these fears have proved unfounded.

[67] Andrew North, "Why Afghanistan Remains a Work in Progress," BBC News, January 30, 2006. Available at http://news.bbc.co.uk.

correct the method by which the war against the Taliban and al-Qaeda was initially prosecuted, resembling the 1980s pattern – US weapons, money and other resources distributed to a variety of commanders rather than to any centralized political authority.

In 2004, the Constitutional Loya Jirga (Grand Council) of 502 members approved the country's new constitution, the sixth since the first one in 1923. During the Loya Jirga, accusations of intimidation were regularly leveled at radical Islamists.[68] But in an unprecedented bow to inclusiveness, the new constitution institutionalized the civil law system; the jurisprudence of Islamic law would only be applied if there were no existing laws that dealt with the matter.[69] Shiite jurisprudence now has near-equal status with Sunni law, in a spirit of pluralism. The constitution does not grant preferential status to the Hanafi school, nor does it make specific references to Sharia law.[70] There had been pressure by some Islamic scholars and jihadi party members who advocated that Sharia be the sole source of law.[71]

The country's cultural diversity was further reflected in the language policy. Pushtu and Dari were kept as official languages, but five other languages were also acknowledged, together with the freedom to publish or broadcast in any of them. Hamid Karzai's selection of two Vice Presidents, one a Tajik and the other a Shiite Hazara, following the presidential elections in 2004, also demonstrates a clear desire to move beyond sectarian and ethnic chauvinism from the very top, and reassert broad national unity and, in the process, promote "political secularism."

Attempts to reshape regional geopolitics

The geopolitical conception of the new Afghan state is one in which foreign and security policy is not driven by ethno-religious factors. In other words, its worldview is conditioned by broader, pragmatic elements. But Afghanistan is still fragile and its domestic structures cannot be expected to be insulated from outside pressures. Indeed, it is commonly believed that Karzai has less influence over certain sections of the country

---

[68] Barnett Rubin, "Crafting a Constitution for Afghanistan," *Journal of Democracy* 15.3 (2004), p. 10.

[69] Said Tayeb Jawad, Afghanistan's Ambassador to the US, "New Constitution of Afghanistan," paper presented at *Political Transition in Afghanistan: The State, Islam and Civil Society*, Woodrow Wilson International Center for Scholars, Washington, DC, April 20, 2004, p. 2.

[70] US Department of State, *International Religious Freedom Report 2005*, Bureau of Democracy, Human Rights and Labor, Washington, DC, November 8, 2005.

[71] International Crisis Group, *Afghanistan's Flawed Constitutional Process*, p. 9. On the other hand, Dostom's party had rejected any need to include a reference to Sharia.

than do Iran, Pakistan and Uzbekistan. The six countries that border Afghanistan, however, did sign a "Good Neighbor Declaration" in December 2002, promising to respect Afghanistan's territorial integrity and independence.

Pakistan and Iran would be the most likely to attempt to sustain extremist Islam in Afghanistan, although Iran's distaste for the Taliban and its troubled historical relations assures that it will not extend support for the ongoing insurgency. A key factor will be the creation of a moderate and forward-looking Pashtun leadership that can be a viable alternative to the Taliban or the Islamist extremists from the Pashtun belt.

Almost all the extremist and terrorist elements threatening the Afghan state are found on the border areas with Pakistan. The Pakistan government is suspected of having a "dual policy" towards Afghanistan in which President Musharraf promises cooperation to curb extremism but turns a blind eye in practice. Top Afghan officials have lambasted the Pakistan government about this. Even the former Taliban ambassador to Pakistan, Abdul Salam Zaieef, has stated his belief that Pakistan is supporting cross-border militant attacks to try to exert influence over the government in Kabul.[72] Some Afghans describe the Pakistani leadership as playing "both fireman and arsonist."[73]

This has produced deep frustration in Afghanistan, and reactions have ranged from diplomatic objections to outright condemnation at the highest levels. According to Ali Jalali, former Afghan interior minister, Pakistan's 70,000-strong military force along the border region has been focusing on al-Qaeda and non-Pakistanis, but has done little to contain the Taliban, the biggest challenge to Kabul.[74] He accuses Pakistan of having safe havens, recruiting centers in madrassas, staging areas and training camps for the Taliban. His successor, Zarar Ahmad Muqbil, while speaking at the lower house of parliament on the increasing clashes in 2006, declared that "Helmand, Kandahar, Paktia, Paktika, Kunar and Nuristan are those provinces which are insecure and restive. I must say clearly that these are the provinces which have joint borders with Pakistan." He claimed that "the eastern neighbor" to Afghanistan has equipped and sent the Taliban to fight.[75] The US State Department's 2006 Country Reports on Terrorism states that "it [Pakistan] remains a

---

[72] Ron Synovitz, "Afghanistan: Upsurge Of Violence Reflects New Taliban Tactics," Radio Free Europe/Radio Liberty, Wednesday, May 24, 2006. Available at http://rfe.frerl.org.

[73] Neamat Nojumi, "Remember Afghanistan?" *Los Angeles Times*, October 9, 2005.

[74] See for example, Jalali, "The Future of Afghanistan," p. 8.

[75] Waliullah Rahmani, "Helmand Province and the Afghan Insurgency." *Terrorism Monitor*, 4.6 (March 23, 2006), p. 4.

major source of Islamic extremism and a safe haven for some top terrorist leaders."[76]

Karzai and Musharraf themselves became embroiled in a war of wards about who was responsible for increased Taliban attacks in 2006.[77] The animosity between Afghanistan and Pakistan has shown up in unpredictable ways. For example, a formal complaint was lodged by the Afghan foreign ministry against naming Pakistani ballistic missiles after Afghan historical figures. According to the Afghan information minister, "We asked them [Pakistan] not to use the names of great elders of Afghanistan on weapons of mass destruction or other war equipment. These great elders played a major part in building national solidarity and in transferring science and knowledge from the homeland across southwest Asia."[78] It is well-known that Pakistan deliberately named its India-specific missiles after Afghan invaders who successfully attacked India in the past: Ghauri, Ghaznavi and Abdali. Thus the Afghan demand hit a particularly raw nerve in Pakistan's military establishment. (This is also a dramatic illustration of how identity factors may be used to serve geopolitical purposes.)

Regional bridge building and diversification

The Afghan government's strategy for protecting its independence has been to slowly diversify and deepen its relations with other neighboring countries, especially India and Iran. For example, Karzai has made four visits to India in the four years since 2002.[79] He received the prestigious Indira Gandhi Peace Prize during his fourth visit. Since 2001, Pakistan has seen its influence waning and its adversary India's rising.[80] By 2004, India was providing relief or reconstruction work in 27 out of 29

[76] Office of the Coordinator for Counterterrorism, The Department of State, April 30, 2006.

[77] Tensions between Afghanistan and Pakistan over whether the latter is doing enough against terrorism have refused to die down. See *Dawn*, April 24, 2003 and November 24, 2003. In 2006, one of the most open rifts occurred with Karzai publicly declaring that "In Pakistan, they train people to go to Afghanistan, conduct jihad, burn schools and clinics. What kind of Islam is this?" *The Washington Post*, May 19, 2006.

[78] *Dawn*, February 23, 2006. These controversies have been widely reported in the press. See, for example, Rahimullah Yusufzai, "What's in a Name?" *The Jang*, February 24, 2006.

[79] Karzai obtained his Masters degree in Political Science from SDA College in Shimla, India in 1984 and thus has longstanding personal ties with India.

[80] India has been steady in its contribution to reconstruction work in Afghanistan, focusing especially on transport infrastructure. One of the Indian projects is the Zaranj-Dilaram road which is an indirect link to the Chabahar port in Iran (*The Hindu*, March 6, 2003). This could provide an important outlet for landlocked Afghanistan (and possibly reduce its dependence on Pakistan and the port of Karachi).

provinces, and had made a commitment of $400 million until 2008.[81] In the regional geopolitical contest with India, however, Pakistan has the option of making life difficult for Afghanistan. This is a major source of frustration in Kabul's bilateral relations with India.

Afghanistan has also attempted to play the role of a regional bridge – naturally, one of its biggest attractions. Its geographical location makes it an excellent transit route, and with the natural gas and oil reserves of the post-Soviet Central Asia, and India's enormous demand for energy supplies, the economic stars seem favorably aligned for Afghanistan. The payoffs could be huge – up to $135 million a year in transit fees for a pipeline that would run from Turkmenistan via Afghanistan through Pakistan to India. Kabul realises that maintaining independent growth and development over the long term will require a regional focus. For India, reaching the Central Asian markets through Afghanistan is the best route, but it remains deadlocked due to Pakistan's denial of transit privileges. The induction of Afghanistan into the South Asian Regional Association for Cooperation (SARAC) as its eighth member in 2007 (backed most strongly by India), is a step in the right direction. During his visit to India in 2006, Karzai announced his idea of "a tri-polar structure of cooperation" with India and Pakistan.[82] He specifically singled out curbing terrorism as a priority, and his remarks could be seen as an attempt to bring together the two traditional adversaries to fight terrorism in the region.

From the perspective of promoting stability in Afghanistan, good relations between Kabul and Tehran is also a necessity, not a luxury. Iranian investment in bordering Herat is boosting the local economy. The projected energy demand from India indicates that both the pipeline option from Turkmenistan and the proposed Iran–Pakistan–India pipeline could be financially viable and not competitive. However, American policy, stemming from its global geopolitical concerns, has been to isolate Iran diplomatically (especially to circumvent Iran in any energy supply scheme in the region). There is little likelihood that the US will modify its policy towards Iran, and Afghanistan will have to live with that reality, even if it is at the expense of its own national and regional interests.

Conclusion

The winners and losers of the long-running Afghan conflicts have ultimately determined the outcome in the underlying competition

---

[81] *The Hindu*, October 8, 2004.
[82] Radio Free Europe/Radio Liberty, April 11, 2006. Available at www.rferl.org.

between the religious, politically secular, and geopolitically conditioned identities in Afghanistan. In a break with the country's traditional orientation, the winners represented the most polarized and radicalized Islam, culminating with the Taliban. The triumph of such radical forces could not have occurred without the critical intercession of external actors, most notably Pakistan, the US and Saudi Arabia. Regional and international geopolitics reshaped domestic structures and orientations, privileged the most radical groups as foreign policy instruments and, in the process, tipped the balance towards extremism.

Even with a new government in Kabul espousing a politically secular orientation, and important changes at the domestic level supporting it, external factors continue to be significant. This time, Afghanistan is caught between divided regional geopolitics: the US and international community espousing moderate politics; and the remnants of the Taliban, and al-Qaeda espousing extremism and continuing to find support in Pakistan. Observers from the region do not pin much hope that America's second intervention in Afghanistan will produce the desired results either. The conclusion from a meeting of experts from Afghanistan and neighboring countries is eye opening: "no one in the region felt confident that either US commitment or the internationally sponsored government and reconstruction effort would last. Hence both states and a range of other actors are seeking to benefit from the war on terrorism as well as Afghan relief and reconstruction efforts, while quietly maintaining ties that would enable them to revert to the previous mode of competition and conflict, if necessary."[83]

A worst case scenario for Afghanistan after US withdrawal would be a re-run of the 1990s, emboldening militants and leading to destructive regional interference. Speaking in 2005, Afghanistan's former interior minister concluded that although the insurgents did not "yet have the capacity to pose strategic threats to the government, they create a sense of insecurity, hinder economic reconstruction, and weaken government influence in remote areas. They may eventually lead to a much stronger insurgency capable of challenging the government."[84] One disturbing new feature has been the spate of suicide attacks, suggesting a different approach on the part of the militants although there is no history of martyrdom acts in Afghanistan. Indeed, some of the deadliest violence occurred in 2006, five years after the Taliban was driven from power by the American invasion.[85]

---

[83] Center on International Cooperation, "Conference Summary: Regional Approaches to the Reconstruction of Afghanistan," Istanbul, Turkey, June 3–5, 2002, p. 9.
[84] Jalali, "The Future of Afghanistan," p. 9.
[85] Pamela Constable, "Afghanistan Rocked as 105 Die in Violence," *The Washington Post*, May 19, 2006.

The Taliban rule demonstrated that the exercise of power by a single ethnic group, divorced from Afghanistan's historical moderate culture of accommodation, is unstable. The lack of traditional, moderate Pashtun leadership is proving to be a major obstacle for consolidating the state, and resurrecting submerged identities under Karzai is proving difficult. This may be directly traced to the legacy of the marginalization and decimation of traditional tribal and Sufi leadership among the Pashtuns during the anti-Soviet war. At this stage, Afghanistan's domestic structures and dominant state identity are poised such that its geopolitical identity needs are consistent with a more open, politically secular version. The vulnerability to external geopolitical identity needs, however, has only declined, not disappeared. In this context, the future role of Pakistan as Afghanistan inches towards a multi-ethnic plural and democratic polity remains critical. The chapter on Pakistan that follows throws further light on how the geopolitics of religion there is unfolding, with serious consequences for the future of Afghanistan.

4   Pakistan at the crossroads

The surprising electoral success of a number of religious parties in the 2002 national elections in Pakistan brought the question of religion and politics to the forefront in an unprecedented fashion. The main issues are: the extent to which this demonstrates a break with the past; the relationship between violent extremism, terrorism and politico-religious groups; and the implications for regional and international relations. The subsequent victory of more secular mainstream political parties in the elections of 2008, following the dramatic assassination of former Prime Minister Benazir Bhutto, holds the promise of reversing Pakistan's slide towards extremist politics.[1] But at the same time jihadi groups are redoubling their efforts inside Pakistan[2] and in the border areas with Afghanistan. The two main political parties have only a tenuous power-sharing agreement at the center, the resurgent secular Pashtun National Awami Party (NAP) in the North-West Frontier Province has been a prime target for intimidation and attacks by religious radicals and remains highly vulnerable, and the prime minister and parliament are having to "co-habit" with a hostile President Pervez Musharraf. Pakistan is at a critical juncture.

None of these trends can be understood without a deeper analysis of the evolution of politicized Islam in Pakistan. In Pakistan, as in neighboring countries, we find a wide spectrum of general political sentiment, from secularism to religious extremism. Most importantly, within the context of religio-political groups in Pakistan, we find notable variations even among groups with common origins and overlapping sympathies.

---

[1] Official results of the 2008 parliamentary elections for the major parties were: Pakistan People's Party 120 seats (up from 80 in 2002); Pakistan Muslim League (Nawaz) 90 (up from 18); Pakistan Muslim League backed by Pervez Musharraf 51 (down from 118); Muttahida Majilis-i-Amal (MMA) 6 (down from 59) and National Awami Party (NAP) 13 (up from 0). See the website of the Election Commission of Pakistan, www.ecp.gov.pk. The MMA still has a strong presence in the Senate with 15 members.

[2] The deadly bombings in Lahore, Pakistan's cultural capital, which had largely escaped the fate of other cities, in March 2008, were noteworthy.

How can we understand these divergences? What has determined the balance between extremist and moderate political outcomes in Pakistan?

In Pakistan, as in Afghanistan and Kashmir, Islamist politics is represented by a wide range of groups. The six-party Muttahida Majlis-i-Amal (MMA) coalition, which was a partner of the ruling alliance under President Pervez Musharraf until 2008, is the most important in the political arena. It is dominated by Jamaat-i-Islami (JI) and Jamiat Ulema-e-Islami (JUI), the two largest religious parties in Pakistan. Violent extremist groups represented by Harakat ul-Mujahideen (HuM), Jaish-e-Mohammed (JeM), Lashkar-e-Toiba (LeT) and various sectarian groups operate outside the political realm, but have covert political links.

Since their victory in the North-West Frontier Province and Baluchistan in 2002, the MMA has been making trade-offs between exercising political power through the Assemblies and militancy on the street. The association of MMA with more violent extremist leaders and groups has been a point of contention, especially with regard to those involved in Afghanistan and Kashmir. Even more than in Afghanistan, the impact and political reach of Islamist groups from MMA to HuM is often out of all proportion to their measurable power.

This chapter shows that this perplexing situation cannot be understood without factoring in the overweening role of the Pakistani state, particularly in its militarized form. As in Afghanistan, the influence of particular geopolitical identity constructions has played a significant role in marginalizing secular versions of identity and privileging Islamist conceptions.

The chapter begins by assessing alternative explanations for the rise of extremism in Pakistan, looking most closely at dominant ethno-religious explanations which I argue can neither account for the variations between the groups nor their emergence at different points in time. Next, an overview is provided of the internal "secular" context, based on the historical background set out in Chapter Two. The state and its relationship to political secularism is clarified. The chapter looks at the pivotal role of the military-led state and the development of geopolitical identities, strongly correlated to regional and international forces. Finally, I suggest how secular, religious and geopolitical identities have operated in such a way as to tip the balance of power towards extremism.

Attempts to explain extremism

The religious factor

Chapter One gave a systematic critique of the most common explanations for ethno-religious extremism; evidence from Pakistan offers little to the contrary. The ethno-religious (or primordial) school that has regained considerable currency in recent times tends to an "Orientalist" discourse regarding South Asians.[3] For example, from today's vantage point, many analysts of terrorism perpetuate the dominant images of the Pashtuns as violent religious extremists, almost as formulated by the British during their failed attempts to conquer them. But the historical events of the North-West Frontier Province (NWFP) and the posture of the Pashtuns (or Pathans) prior to British withdrawal from India, belie this characterization. The non-violent anti-colonial movement led by Gaffar Khan, described in Chapter Two, reveals an important and entirely different tendency among the Pashtuns which is overlooked or ignored.

The common knowledge that the Pashtuns are the ethnic base of the Taliban is clearly not matched by a general understanding of the region's non-violent, anti-imperialist past, or that the Pashtuns "used to revere Gandhi and Abdul Ghaffar Khan."[4] The history of the NWFP poses a strong challenge to the notion of religion as a driving force for extremism in Pakistan. We can also point to the experience of Baluchistan to question the role of religion. The 1973–1977 Baluch separatist movement, its relative quiescence during the Afghan conflicts, and its re-emergence since 2000, suggest that the role of religion is at best a contingent factor that can be directed and re-directed.

Within Pakistan generally, the rise of the religious parties and other extremist Islamist groups was not pre-ordained. Pakistan's political landscape is dotted with ethnic, sectarian, paramilitary and Islamist groups (some of whom are prone to violent methods) along with conventional secular-oriented political parties, all competing in formal and informal political spaces. Over the course of post-independence history, "political Islam" has never been very significant in Pakistan, which is particularly telling considering that Islam is cited as the basis for the state's foundation.

In terms of election results, the performance of religious parties has been uniformly unimpressive. Until the MMA's victory in 2002, no Islamic party had been able to capture more than five percent of the vote. Even in 2002, the MMA was only the third largest party with 11.3 percent of the vote, behind the Pakistan People's Party (PPP) at 25.8 percent and the Pakistan Muslim League (PML-Q) at 25.7 percent.[5] The

---

[3] The classic work on this topic is Edward W. Said's *Orientalism* (New York: Vintage Books, 1978).

[4] Balraj Puri, "India, Kashmir and the War Against Terrorism," *EPW Commentary*, October 27, 2001.

[5] These are based on figures reported by the Election Commission of Pakistan for the October 10, 2002 elections. See www.electionguide.org.

existence of the Islamist terrorist HuM, LeT and JeM outside the formal political system is arguably *prima facie* evidence for religion driving extremism. Likewise, the presence of the violent sectarian groups, the Sunni Sipah-i-Sahaba Pakistan (SSP) and Shia Sipah-e-Mohammed Pakistan (SMP), are further examples of religiously motivated extremism. But it is important to note the absence of these groups before the 1980s and look for explanations outside the religious sphere.

Other factors

Popular explanations for extremism do not hold up well in Pakistan, although some do better than others. Economic arguments based on relative deprivation seem plausible if we consider the ranks of extremist groups in Pakistan, especially those drawn from radical madrasas (religious seminaries) with large impoverished populations. Yet, the first Pakistani "martyr" in Afghanistan was an undergraduate from a government college in Karachi, not a madrasa student.[6] The largest Islamic party in Pakistan, the Jamaat-i-Islami, has not been madrasa-based, although members of its student wing have been recruited for violent jihad. In any event, madrasas have existed for centuries across South Asia as centres of learning for Muslim students; historically, they were the main sources of education for them. So even if we do find a large number of madrasa graduates in extremist groups, the poverty of many students at the madrasas cannot explain the recent rise in extremism on its own.

Arguments based on elite manipulation are also problematic. Pakistani elites have promoted a wide variety of policies regarding religion and the use of violence. Moreover, many leaders have switched positions over time or have not made their positions clear. Changes in position are often connected to whether such leaders are in or out of political office. For example, Benazir Bhutto repeatedly stated her opposition to cultivating extremist groups for foreign policy purposes, but many would question her own government's conduct during the 1990s. Likewise, there is no categorical way of ascertaining President Pervez Musharraf's own stand towards home-grown militants. The same may be said for some of the leaders of the JI and JUI. With the large diversity of elite voices in Pakistan, the question arises as to whose voice is heard and why. In practice, proximity to state officials seems crucial. This leads us to two aspects of the state-level explanation of terrorism: political access and state repression.

---

[6] See International Crisis Group, *Pakistan: Madrasas, Extremism and the Military*, p. 12.

Unlike in other cases, such as in Algeria and to some extent Egypt, Islamist forces have not had to wage a struggle with the Pakistani state in order to carry on their activities. Indeed, Islamist leaders and parties have maintained a comfortable working relationship with the state, even a privileged one. As for groups being motivated by a lack of political access, it has been the mainstream democratic elements that have been shut out one way or the other in Pakistan, rather than the religious parties. Likewise, repression by the Pakistani state has been reserved mostly for irredentist or regionalist forces such as the Bengalis in East Pakistan, Baluchis in Baluchistan and Sindhis in Sind, not the Islamist groups engaged in extremism. As this chapter will demonstrate, the state in Pakistan has had a decisive role indeed, but not in the manner that Hafez and others have described.[7]

Political secularism and its decline

Contrary to what we might have expected, the movement for the establishment of Pakistan was led by relatively secular leadership, rather than the Muslim clergy. As outlined in Chapter Two, the dominant form of Islam at the mass level was Sufism, even in the areas that formed the new state of Pakistan, and even the more institutionalized Islam in South Asia did not follow the same path as the Middle East.

For example, the Egyptian Sayyid Qutb is regarded by many as the most important of the modern-day proponents of orthodox militant Islam, someone who has inspired violent extremists, including individuals like Ayman Zawahiri, the second in command in al-Qaeda.[8] Although Qutb used the writings of Maulana Abul Ala Maududi, a figure with widespread influence in South Asia as the founder of the Jamaat-i-Islami, Maududi is viewed as having been more reluctant to mix religion with politics than Qutb. Such a stance made it easier for religious and secular identities to share the domestic space from the outset in South Asia.

As has been repeatedly noted, Mohammed Ali Jinnah, the champion of Pakistan, was largely secular-minded, and did not believe in combining politics and religion. For example, he had been relatively cool towards the Khilafat movement during the 1920s in which the Muslim

---

[7] Hafez, *Why Muslims Rebel* gives one of the best expositions about the lack of political access leading to Islamist activism and extremism.

[8] Sayyid Qutb was sentenced to death by Egyptian president Gamal Abdel Nasser. As a secularist, Nasser had been a key target of Qutb. Qutb's death transformed him into a martyr for a new generation of militants.

clergy in India had a dominant role.[9] He was more influenced by the reformist sentiment at India's Aligarh Muslim University than the orthodox institutions at Deoband. Jinnah's landmark speech of August 11, 1947, outlined a democratic and "secular" polity, one in which the state in Pakistan had little concern with people's religion. In Pakistan's first cabinet, the law minister was a Hindu and the foreign minister an Ahmedi. At independence, Islamic law pertained largely to personal or family law such as marriage, divorce, inheritance and guardianship, a situation that remained relatively undisturbed for 30 years.[10] While Muslim majoritarianism at the symbolic and idiomatic level clearly existed, it did not occupy a central place in officialdom; the state could be termed more or less "politically secular." Such a situation, alongside the unfettered activities of religious groups, calls for deeper investigation into the path of religious-based political extremism in Pakistan.

The political evolution of the JI and the JUI

Although both were longstanding religious parties, the Jamaat-i-Islami (JI) and the Jamiat Ulema-e-Islami (JUI) had little hope of political power before 2002. The JI is the biggest and most potent religious party in Pakistan, established in 1941 by Maulana Abul Ala Maududi in northern India. It initially opposed the Pakistan movement and stood for a united India, arguing that Islam was a universal religion not confined to national boundaries, but once partition occurred, Maududi migrated to Pakistan and the JI shifted its position.

The JI has fairly strong international exposure, with independent units in the region. It served as the voice of the clergy or ulema during the debates surrounding the adoption of Pakistan's first constitution in 1956. It retained the more incremental approach of Maududi (rather than that of Sayyid Qutb) over the years, and gained a large middle class following, but less support among the masses, unlike Qutb and the Muslim Brotherhood in Egypt.[11] Despite substantial student cadres and a base of support in society, the JI has never been able to translate its

---

[9] Asghar Ali Engineer, "Hindu–Muslim Relations Before and After 1947," in Sarvepalli Gopal (ed.) *Anatomy of a Confrontation* (Delhi: Penguin Books, 1991), pp. 186–187. None other than L. K. Advani of the Bharatiya Janata Party cited Jinnah's secularism in a speech in Pakistan. See *Deccan Herald*, January 6, 2006.

[10] For a detailed discussion of the shifts initiated by President Zia ul-Haq, see Martin Lau, "The Fifteenth Constitutional Amendment in Pakistan and its Implications," paper presented at The South Asia Forum Seminar, Department of Law, School of Oriental and African Studies, London, October 26, 1998.

[11] Kristin Mendoza, "Islam and Islamism in Afghanistan," available at http://www.law.harvard.edu.

support into electoral success. It won just 4 out of 300 seats in the first national elections in Pakistan, with no improvement over the years. In the 1993 and 1997 parliamentary elections, it won only two seats.

The JI's strength beyond Punjab has been tenuous, with regional and linguistic identity crowding out the religious one; for example, it lost a good deal of support in the 1980s to the secular and regionalist Sindhi group Muttahida Quami Movement (MQM), and only managed to regain a better footing as part of the religious coalition in 2002. The Jamaat has, however, stayed in the spotlight with such high profile activities as spearheading the protest movement in 1989 against Salman Rushdie's book *The Satanic Verses*. Following the military coup that overthrew the democratically elected Nawaz Sharif in 1999, the JI saw greater opportunity for political power. Qazi Hussain Ahmed, the leader of the Jamaat, declared in 2000 that "With the failure of all the secular parties and military, Pakistan is now in a liberation period. It may take five or ten years to fully liberate the masses. But there's no alternative for Pakistan now but Islam."[12] This has proven to be an overstatement, but the MMA's political success placed the Islamist parties in a better position to work towards such a goal than ever before.

The smaller JUI has fared better than the JI in elections, but its support base has been restricted to the NWFP and Pashtun areas of northern Baluchistan. Within the MMA, Pashtun nationalism is an undercurrent that does not always mesh with the common bond of religion. The NWFP was one of the least economically developed areas of the colonial empire, and post-independence Pakistani leaders recognized that it would be difficult to get the NWFP to conform to the political identities that had been crafted. This point had been clearly driven home by the support for Gaffar Khan's objective of a secular, united India and, failing that, as a minimum, a fully autonomous, secular Pashtun region. Gaffar Khan's main aim was to protect the Pashtun identity, which he feared would be marginalized within a unitary Punjabi-dominated Pakistan. Sections of the NWFP were termed special administrative areas by Pakistan's central government and split into "tribal" and "settled" areas, reinforcing the detachment from the state. A peripheral status for the NWFP and the so-called Federally Administered Tribal Areas (FATA) was established from the beginning.

Regional identity is also wrapped up in Deobandi religious thought, a branch of Sunni Hanafi Islam that emerged in British India with the establishment of a madrasa in Deoband, a village 80 miles from Delhi, in 1867. The clergy at Deoband were conservative and revivalist, seeking to

---

[12] Quoted in Robin Wright, "The Chilling Goal of Islam's New Warriors," *The Los Angeles Times*, December 28, 2000.

reassert Islamic values and thought within the colonial context.[13] The Deoband movement was strongly anti-Shia and saw a restrictive role for women, influences that the Taliban was later to take to an extreme.

Post-partition, the JUI became the most active group in Pakistan to set up madrasas for orthodox religious education, especially in the NWFP and Baluchistan. These madrasas, whose agenda hardly resembled the original reformist thinking at Deoband, and were run by poorly trained mullahs, were strategically placed to become radical training grounds when the Afghan conflict broke out. From the mainstream JUI, dozens of breakaway, extremist factions emerged, and together provided a vast support system for young Afghan refugee men and boys, who became the backbone of religious extremism across the border.[14] The Afghan jihad and the funding that flowed in substantially enhanced the prestige and power of these groups and institutions. It also fostered close links between the religious groups and armed groups whose recruits for the Afghan war were now coming out of these Pakistani madrasas.[15]

The JI–JUI divide

Despite their religious affinity, the JUI and JI have not always seen eye to eye, and the 2002 electoral coalition was a historic anomaly. The biggest difference has surfaced over the military's political intervention: for example, shortly after popularly elected Zulfiqir Ali Bhutto was executed in 1979, following the military coup by General Zia ul-Haq, an alliance of parties joined forces as an anti-military group – the Movement for the Restoration of Democracy (MRD). The JUI joined the MRD coalition but the JI joined the government of General Zia, even accepting cabinet posts despite popular condemnation.

The JUI itself then split on the question of joining General Zia ul-Haq's military government in 1980, with the main group staying with Maulana Fazlur Rehman and refusing to cooperate with the military, and a breakaway faction going with Maulana Sami ul-Haq (JUI-S) to support Zia. In contrast to the JI, Fazlur Rehman was closer to Benazir Bhutto's democratically elected government in the mid-1990s, and governed in coalition from 1993 to 1996. Rehman even supported her right to become prime minister and opposed the JI campaign in the 1990s to prevent a woman from becoming the head of government of a Muslim country. In 2004, as the Pakistan National Assembly threatened to remain deadlocked over the selection of the opposition leader, Fazlur

---

[13] Rashid, *Taliban*, p. 88.   [14] Rashid, *Taliban*, pp. 89–90.
[15] Benjamin and Simon, *The Age of Sacred Terror*, p. 201.

Rehman aligned with Benazir's PPP. It was only at the eleventh hour that his party switched, after Rehman himself was allowed to become the leader of the opposition, in an apparent deal with the military and Pervez Musharraf.[16]

Another distinction between the JI and the JUI is their differing involvement in the Afghan and Kashmir conflicts. The JI has been much more preoccupied with Kashmir than the JUI while the JUI has been much more so with Afghanistan, something that is not widely understood. In Kashmir, the JI has exerted its influence by supporting the largest violent militant group, the Hizb-ul-Mujahideen.

The JUI's position stems mostly from shared Pashtun identity in Afghanistan, and on Kashmir and India, its somewhat less militant stand comes from its history. The regional identity in the NWFP has been represented most strongly by the moderate and secular oriented National Awami Party (NAP), the successor to Abdul Gaffar Khan's Frontier Congress. In the past, the JUI aligned with the NAP in an effort to resist central control more effectively. For example, the two parties collaborated to form coalitional provincial governments in both the NWFP and Baluchistan following their victory at the polls shortly after martial law was lifted in 1972.[17] Underlying the JUI's approach to the central government is the belief that a democratic set-up holds the best promise for protecting regional Pashtun and Baluch identity.

The JI on the other hand, with its largely Punjabi base, has remained close to the Punjabi-dominated military.[18] Within the religious sector, the JI may be described loosely as the main conveyor of "official Islam," most amenable to military-statist versions, whereas the JUI has been more aloof from the military. Pakistan as a geopolitical entity is not necessarily integral to JUI's identity.

Some observers have noted that the JUI was not entirely in favor of jihad in Jammu and Kashmir, and that its line on Kashmir has been materially different from that of the JI's; Kashmir was conspicuously absent from the main document of the JUI's convention held in 2000. This omission apparently did not go down well with the ISI and others

---

[16] Rehman was made opposition leader by the PML-Q speaker of the house, Chaudhry Amir Hussain, reportedly in exchange for the MMA supporting Musharraf's army chief status until at least 2007.

[17] M. Rafique Afzal, *Pakistan: History and Politics 1947–1971* (Karachi: Oxford University Press, 2001). In the 1970 elections, the JUI won 6 of the NWFP's 18 seats.

[18] In 1984, Punjabis made up approximately 55.8 percent of the higher ranks of Pakistan's federal bureaucracy, compared with 2.7 percent of civil servants from rural Sindh, 3.1 percent from Baluchistan and 11.6 percent from the NWFP. Punjabis make up about 65 percent of the army's officer corps and 70 percent of other ranks in the army. Bushra Asif, CSIS Project, "Pakistan's Future and US Policy Options," December 1, 2003.

in Pakistan who view India with almost compulsive hostility.[19] The JUI's anti-imperialist legacy seems also to have conditioned its stance on Kashmir and India. Its parent body, the Jamiat-ul-Ulema-e-Hind (the original organization of the Muslim clerics of the Deoband school) is based in India, and continues to have fraternal links with the JUI through mutual visits, athough the two groups are independent, without any organizational ties or common mandate. Prior to partition, the Jamiat-ul-Ulema-e-Hind made the struggle against colonialism its top priority and was opposed to the creation of Pakistan. Indeed, it was quite close to Mahatma Gandhi and the Congress Party (a relationship it has continued since partition). For such stands, the organization was strongly criticized by the Muslim League.[20]

Hints of some differences on regional geopolitics surfaced between the JI and JUI in 2003, reflecting the JUI's historical anti-imperial tendencies as well as its lower priority for Kashmir. Fazlur Rehman's repeated calls for better Indo-Pakistan relations shortly after the 2002 elections were on the grounds that they were necessary to keep the US out of the region. In this context, he even stated that the Kashmir issue should be resolved through dialogue, as envisaged under the Simla Agreement, and that he did not favor third-party mediation between India and Pakistan (a coded reference to America).[21]

In July 2003, Rehman made a nine-day visit to India during which he met with many politicians, media people and other high profile leaders, and, most notably, talked at some length with Prime Minister Atal Bihari Vajpayee. His main theme in India was the need to work together to end "American expansionism."[22] The religious connotations of the Kashmir

---

[19] K. K. Katyal, "A Forward Looking Visit?" *The Hindu*, July 21, 2003. Questions were, however, raised about Fazlur Rehman's sincerity given his alleged links with the Harkat-ul-Mujahideen. According to some, although the JUI supports the Harkat, these connections were developed in Afghanistan, not the Kashmir Valley. Mohammad Amir Rana, an expert on Islamist groups in Pakistan, notes that the Maulana has been reluctant to call the Kashmir conflict a jihad, rather, "The battle in Kashmir is only for land, so we prefer the jihad in Afghanistan." See Praveen Swami, "A Peacemaker From Pakistan," *Frontline* 20.16, August 2–15, 2003.

[20] On the JUI's early Congress links, see for example, B. G. Verghese, *An End to Confrontation: Restructuring the Sub-Continent* (New Delhi: S. Chand & Co. 1972), pp. 122–123.

[21] *Daily Times*, March 28, 2004 and Amit Baruah, "Shimla Pact Still Relevant: Fazlur," *The Hindu*, July 18, 2003.

[22] M. J. Akbar, "Fazlur Rehman's India Trip is a Harbinger of Good Intentions," *Gulf News*, July 21, 2003. Opinions differed on how to interpret the new gesture by the so-called "Father of the Taliban." In India, M. J. Akbar and B. Raman provide two opposing views, the latter warning observers not to be taken in by the Maulana's rhetoric, the former suggesting that the Maulana is part of a "new space in the Pakistani consciousness" gaining ground after Iraq. Raman suggests that Rehman's role in promoting the Taliban to power and alleged ties with the HuM and its earlier incarnation cannot be dismissed. At the same time, even Raman acknowledges Fazlur Rehman's flexibility in politics and ideology. B. Raman, "Beware the Maulana," July 23, 2003. Available at www.rediff.com.

conflict were played down.[23] Upon his return to Pakistan, Fazlur Rehman denied creating a rift with coalition partner Qazi Hussain Ahmed of the JI by his conciliatory tone in India and stance on Kashmir. The Pakistani press, however, reported that the JI leader only kept quiet to save the MMA from falling apart.[24] The point is that their disagreement had more to do with divergent notions of geopolitical interests, than with religious or sectarian differences. And, despite their disagreements, there is little doubt that the JI and the JUI have contributed significantly to the radicalization of Pakistan's Islamist politics.

Beyond the political arena to violent extremism

As we have seen, the rise to prominence of narrow puritanical movements and Islamic revivalism is relatively new in Pakistan, and against local Sufi traditions. However, both the JI and JUI strongly disapprove of Sufi practices, and have sought to impose more stringent interpretations of Islam, and it is out of these tendencies that violent jihadi groups have emerged.[25] Although the JUI and JI have both projected an image of gradualism and tended to work as political "insiders," their links to more radical groups outside the formal political arena remain a large question. At the very least, the ascendancy of the JI and JUI as influential political insiders created a climate conducive for religious extremism.

In the context of violent Islamism globally, reports before and after 9/11 have shown how important Pakistan had become as a base or hideout. Ramzi Youssef, a key culprit in the 1993 attack on the World Trade Center, was arrested in Pakistan. Mir Aimal Kansi, who fired an assault rifle at the entrance to the CIA headquarters in 1993 killing two CIA employees, was captured in a Pakistani hotel two years later. In early 2002, senior al-Qaeda operative Abu Zubaidah was captured in Pakistan and later, in September 2002, Ramzi Binalshibh, another suspect in the 9/11 operation, was arrested, again in Pakistan. One of the most important figures who was allegedly a key planner of 9/11, Khalid Sheikh Mohammaed, was found in Rawalpindi in 2003. At one time, out of the 620 suspects detained at the US military base in Guantanamo Bay, 540 were said to have been arrested in Pakistan, which suggests that extremists must

---

[23] Interview with Maulana Fazlur Rehman by Onkar Singh in New Delhi, July 18, 2003. Available at www. rediff.com.

[24] See for example *The News*, August 3, 2003.

[25] For a good description of the rise of jihadi groups, see Hillel Fradkin, Husain Haqqani and Eric Brown, *Current Trends in Islamist Ideology* Vol. I. (Washington, DC: Hudson Institute, 2005) pp. 12–27.

have considered Pakistan a safe haven.[26] In April 2007, the US State Department's annual report on counterterrorism concluded that new terrorist safe havens were being set up in Pakistan's northwest region.

If the JI and JUI are at the more "moderate" end of the politico-religious spectrum, the HuM, JeM and LeT stand at the other end. Yet, they are not easily distinguishable because the madrasas of the JUI and its offshoots served as recruiting grounds for some of these same jihadis. In addition to military training camps set up during the Afghan war, the meeting ground for Islamist radicals has been the madrasa. Although the vast majority of madrasas across South Asia continue to function as traditional centers of Islamic learning for young boys, the enormous growth of schools that promote a violent form of jihad has severely distorted the earlier picture.

HuM was reportedly created in 1985 with US funds during the Afghan war, but later declared a foreign terrorist group by the US in 1997 following indications that it had kidnapped western tourists in Kashmir.[27] (HuM was previously known as Harakat ul-Ansar until the US declaration. Many groups were renamed after the post-9/11 clampdowns.) Mauana Fazlur Rehman of the JUI, as well as championing the Taliban, has provided, at the very least, ideological inspiration to groups like the HuM.[28] Maulana Sami ul Haq, a parliamentary leader of the JUI, is believed to have ties to both al-Qaeda and the Taliban through his madrasa, as well as being more closely associated with the HuM and Jaish-e-Mohammed.[29] Although the JI is not identified with a madrasa tradition to the extent that the JUI is, the JI has also increasingly made forays into religious schools as a result of its involvement in the Afghan and Kashmir conflicts. The JI's widespread social service network, laid down soon after partition, has given it a presence in Pakistan belied by its electoral numbers. This social network, along with its well-organized cadres, has been activated for radical political purposes in Afghanistan, Kashmir and Bangladesh.

Violent sectarian groups from the Sunni and Shiite schools occupy the extremist end of the political spectrum. Within Pakistan, Sunnis constitute approximately 77 percent of the population, and Shias make up about 20 percent. It is difficult to establish with certainty the specific links that exist among extremist groups, but there seem to be a good deal of informal ties and associations.[30] The most powerful sectarian militant

---

[26] Erich Follath, "The Masters of Jihad," *Der Spiegel*, Spiegel Online, April 5, 2004. Available at http://www.spiegel.de.

[27] Praveen Swami, "Jihadi Groups: Alive and Killing," *The Hindu*, August 29, 2004.

[28] *The News*, August 8, 2003.

[29] "The Masters of Jihad" available at www.spiegel.de.

[30] For discussions on some of the most important radical Islamist groups in Pakistan and their broader contacts, see C. Christine Fair, "Militant Recruitment in Pakistan:

group in Pakistan is the Sipah-i-Sahaba Pakistan (SSP), formed in 1985 by a number of radical Sunni clerics. In 1996, the most extreme elements of the SSP broke ranks and formed the Lashkar-i-Jhangvi (LiJ), but many view the latter as the armed wing of the SSP. It has been reported that the HuM and the former Taliban regime provided arms training to SSP extremists. The SSP has also been linked to Jaish-e-Mohammed (JeM), a Pakistan-based group accused of carrying out terrorist attacks in Kashmir. Pakistani extremists from the SSP, LiJ, HuM and JeM are reported to have shared training camps in Afghanistan where they came into contact with al-Qaeda. The most important of the Shia militant groups is the Sipah-e-Mohammed Pakistan (SMP); others include the Tehrik-e-Jafria Pakistan (TJP) and the Imamia Students Organization. In recent years, Pakistan has been repeatedly hit with virulent Sunni–Shia sectarian violence, in which hundreds of people have died. The attack and counter-attacks have also revealed the increasingly complex relationship between sectarian wars and the "war on terrorism."[31]

Without the sympathy and support of the JI and JUI for Islamist groups waging war in the neighbourhood and for sectarian groups, it is unlikely that violent extremist groups could have mushroomed and made inroads in Pakistan to the extent that they have. But what is often missed is that it has been the Pakistan military's foreign policy aims that have provided the critical link between the political arena and religion-based politics in the first place. As shown in succeeding sections, the military has done this in two ways: by seriously constraining the secular mainstream parties; and by actively favoring religious groups and stimulating religious sentiment. This goes directly against the perception of many external analysts, especially in the west, who see the Pakistani military as the most professional and secular institution in the country.[32]

Implications for Al-Qaeda and Other Organizations," *Studies in Conflict & Terrorism*, 27 (2004); Rodney Jones, "The Prospects for State Failure in Pakistan: Ethnic, Regional and Sectarian Fissures," paper for session on "The Future of Pakistan: Prospects for State Failure," Lawrence Livermore National Laboratory, May 1, 2001; Ayaz Amir, "A Glimpse of the Future," *The Dawn*, January 26, 2001; and Ali Chaudhry, "In the Spotlight: Sipah-i-Sahaba Pakistan (SSP)," Center for Defense Information, July 9, 2004, available at www.cdi.org.

[31] For example, in October 2004, events surrounding operations by Pakistani security forces against a reported al-Qaeda operative who was a member of a radical Sunni sectarian group, followed by a suicide bombing at a Shia mosque, in turn followed by an attack against the Sunni group SSP, suggested increasingly complex links. See for coverage, *The Asian Age*, October 3, 8 and 9, 2004.

[32] Noted South Asia expert Stephen Cohen largely adheres to this view of the military. See *The Idea of Pakistan* (Washington, DC: Brookings Institution Press, 2004).

Shifting political structures and the role of the military

The military's success in weakening mainstream parties lies partly in the unstable character of secularism. This has allowed the military, sitting at the helm, to bend key domestic structures in the legal and educational sectors in Pakistan in a manner that has bolstered its own position through the construction of a particular geopolitical identity. Strategic conceptions in Pakistan became heavily dependent on religiously informed identities. Stoked by the military, this combination has proved to be a powerful block to the political sustenance of mainstream secular parties; at the same time, it has been critical in facilitating radicalism across the region, especially in Afghanistan and Kashmir.

Constraints on the mainstream political parties

Writers on democratic development in Pakistan tend to divide into those who see it as a self-made failure of mainstream parties and party officials, and those who argue that authoritarian elements in the socio-political order, the military in particular, have worked to suppress mainstream politics.[33] Without getting into the intricacies of this much-debated issue, the evidence presented here is significantly supportive of the latter viewpoint. Indeed, what it shows is a distortion of domestic political structural development that cannot be explained away as simply self-inflicted on the part of the politicians.

Pakistan's democratic interlude between 1989 and 1999, during which many believed democracy had become permanently estalished, proved to be short lived. The military coup of October 1999 by General Pervez Musharraf and certain developments since then – most notably the banning of the country's two most important national political parties and standard bearers of Pakistani democracy (the PPP and the PML) and the holding of local elections on a party-less basis – bear striking similarities to previous military regimes. Despite the formal shift back to parliamentary politics since the national elections of 2002 and 2008, two features suggest that there might be less of a break with Pakistan's non-democratic legacy than some believe.

First, the military has been successful in establishing a permanent high-level role in national political decision-making through the adoption of the

---

[33] Stephen P. Cohen at the Brookings Institution and Marvin Weinbaum at the Middle East Institute may be seen for the most part as representing the first school, whereas Husain Haqqani of Boston University and Frederic Grare at the Carnegie Endowment for International Peace are strong proponents of the second line of argument.

Legal Framework Order which set up the National Security Council in 2004. This has given the military a constitutional role, something which no previous military government was able to achieve. Second, during almost ten years (1999-2008) of the marginalization of mainstream parties, religious parties in the MMA have gained greater legitimacy as political actors than ever before. Whether in or out of power, the political ambition and agenda of religious groups will now be a greater force to be reckoned with.

Of the two major secular parties, the PPP has been targeted the most by military regimes. From the military's point of view, the PPP, with its mass base and relatively greater hostility to the army, as well as its Sindhi leadership, posed the bigger threat. The Musharraf regime, too, showed greater willingness to work with the PML than the PPP. In the post-2002 election maneuvering, the PML-Q was created from the conservative sections of the PML as a loyalist party for the regime. A common thread in Pakistan's checkered democratic past has been that no democratically elected government has ever been allowed to complete its term by the military. The military, on the other hand, has enjoyed long spells of unchallenged political rule since 1958.

Even during periods of civilian rule, the critical areas of defense and foreign policy have been in the hands of the military, in particular, Afghanistan, Kashmir and nuclear policy. For example, in early 1998, Prime Minister Nawaz Sharif tried to convene talks between the Taliban and the opposition in Afghanistan. He was unsuccessful despite his consolidation of power and his improved ties with the military. Hardliners within the military were able to retain support for the Taliban as official foreign policy.[34] Likewise, it has been suggested that Benazir Bhutto was allowed to form a government in 1988 only after army chief of staff General Mirza Aslam Beg secured an agreement that she would let the military control policy in these crucial arenas.[35] In her second term in office, recognizing the futility of opposing the military, Bhutto claimed that her government decided to "take the generals' hard line on security plus focus on reducing poverty" in order to mollify the military, but she concluded, "neither worked."[36]

---

[34] Ameen Jan, "Prospects for Peace in Afghanistan: The Role of Pakistan," IPA Trip Report, International Peace Academy, February 1999.

[35] International Crisis Group, *Authoritarianism and Political Party Reform in Pakistan*, Asia Report No. 102 (September 28, 2005), p.5.

[36] Discussion with former prime minister Benazir Bhutto, Washington DC, May 14, 2000. Bhutto reiterated the same point in a talk at the Woodrow Wilson International Center for Scholars, Washington, DC, February 9, 2004.

One line of argument often heard regarding obstacles to democracy in Pakistan is the independent growth of religious groups, and their attraction politically. JI leader Qazi Hussain Ahmed used General Musharraf's military coup to argue that there was a political vacuum in Pakistan and that his was the most organized and broadest socio-political party. Likewise, Hamid Gul, the powerful former chief of the ISI in 2000, predicted the rise of Islam at the political center. According to Gul, "Pakistan will go through its own version of an Islamic revolution. The army is the last hope. And if the army fails – and it probably will – then people will realize they have to do it themselves, revolt against the system. Everyone sees this on the wall. Because everything else in this country has failed, Islam will have to lead the way."[37] But such comments gloss over the extent to which it is the military's political activism which has kept the mainstream parties out of power and religious groups close to power. The question remains how this has been accomplished in the face of considerable popular support for non-religious political parties. The answer brings us closer to the central argument of this book – the construction of a geopolitical identity as a driver for religious extremism.

The military and religious parties

One of the redeeming features that many western analysts see in Pakistan's military is its avowedly secular nature. The Pakistani military has successfully presented itself to the outside as the strongest bulwark against the encroachment of radical religious elements into politics. What is often lost in the military's rhetoric and external preconceptions is the influence of the military in the politics of religion.[38] On closer examination it is clear that, in and out of power, the military has consistently failed to meet the requirements of political secularism, as defined in Chapter One, and this has been particularly true since the mid-1960s.

What the Islamic parties could not gain through the electoral process was achieved mainly under military tutelage, beginning in earnest with Zia ul-Haq.[39] The JI has had close relations with the military since Field Marshal Ayub Khan's regime in the 1960s. During General Yahya

---

[37] Quoted in Robin Wright, "The Chilling Goal of Islam's New Warriors."

[38] For an early critic of the military's role, see Faruki, "Pakistan: Islamic Government and Society."

[39] Husain Haqqani's work makes this argument most convincingly. See *Pakistan: Between Mosque and Military* (Washington, DC: Carnegie Endowment, 2005). See also International Crisis Group, *Authoritarianism*, p. 13

Khan's subsequent rule, the JI was accused of viciously targeting Bengali opposition for the military through various front organizations, a legacy that the JeI of Bangladesh has yet to live down. The strongest opposition to Zulfiqir Ali Bhutto, Pakistan's first popularly elected leader, came from the Pakistan National Alliance (PNA), an eclectic group under the aegis of the military, including the JI and JUI. The PNA ostensibly stood for democratic reform but its agitation in the late 1970s plunged the country into crisis and ended up ushering in an extended period of military rule imposed on the grounds of national security and democracy. Similarly, prior to the 1988 elections in which the PPP appeared to be destined to win an absolute majority, the military and its intelligence wing, the ISI, reportedly helped to create the countervailing Islami Jamhoori Ittehad alliance.

More recently, there was persuasive evidence of Musharraf's regime providing unfair electoral advantages to the religious groups in the 2002 elections. First, it was declared that in order to contest an election, a candidate had to possess a college education, thereby raising the bar unusually high. Then it was deemed that a madrasa degree could qualify as meeting the "college" requirement, clearly giving the religious parties an edge. The MMA was also granted a book as its electoral symbol, which among a poor, largely illiterate population, could stand for voting for or against the Koran. It also benefited from exemptions to curbs placed on other non-religious parties such as not being allowed to hold any public rallies.[40] The military also overlooked the extremism of certain candidates: Azam Tariq, who was accused of involvement in terrorism in 20 pending lawsuits, was allowed to run for a seat in parliament. After his victory, he threw his support behind the Musharraf administration.

The state and geopolitical identities

We cannot understand the rise of Islamist groups and religious sentiment without examining the military's national security needs. As pointed out in Chapter One, high levels of perceived threat or, conversely, good opportunities for external competitive gain, leave greater room for geopolitical national identity conceptions. As such, the promotion of religious groups by the military in Pakistan has been intimately linked to the national security realm. Charles Tilly, in his seminal work on state formation, argues that war or crisis tends to concentrate power in the state, which in turn disposes the

---

[40] See Barry Bearak, "Is Pakistan Coming Apart?" *New York Times Magazine*, December 7, 2003, p. 72. See also Ashutosh Misra, "Rise of Religious Parties in Pakistan: Causes and Prospects," *Strategic Analysis*, 27.2, (April–June 2003), p. 6.

state to maintain power by stimulating such an environment. It is no accident that military governments have been much more obsessed with India than their civilian counterparts. Repeated bouts of direct military rule in Pakistan (1958–1971, 1977–1988, 1999–2008) have provided ample opportunity for the military to bend domestic structures, create political coalitions and foster national identity in a way that meshes with military interests. With this success has come a heavy cost: the rise of religious militancy, regional militarism, political authoritarianism and instability.

The weak popular support for the military-led state in Pakistan has continually created pressures for the construction of legitimizing identities. The military's turn to support from religious sources has set off a mutually beneficial cycle. In such circumstances, whether the military as an institution is secular or not is a moot point. This book suggests that the intense geopolitical identity needs of the Pakistani military have been best nurtured by the marriage of national security and religious sentiment under conditions of weak secularism, contested sovereignty and competitive external politics. In looking at the rise of violent extremist groups, a pattern that is notable is their external orientations – specifically, Kashmir and Afghanistan. External factors cannot on their own explain the ability and success of radical religious groups, however – a mediating actor was needed. In subsequent sections, we find that the Pakistani military is strongly implicated in fostering geopolitical identities which facilitated the type of rapid shifts in Pakistani political culture towards extremism that might not otherwise have taken place.

Legitimizing identities

The regional agitation by Bengalis for greater cultural rights in East Pakistan was the first stimulus for the Pakistani leaders to conflate Pakistani identity with Islamic identity. Pakistan's humiliating military defeat in 1971 and the resulting geopolitical and existential angst turned the military decisively to Islam as a legitimizing force, combined with anti-Indian nationalism. Pakistan's shift towards the Middle East after 1971 was another component of a new worldview that emphasized Islam and, at the same time, put greater ideological distance between Pakistan and an India-dominant South Asia.

Although pressures for new identity constructions became most acute after 1971, the military had already begun turning to religion to gain legitimacy after the defeat in the 1965 war with India. For instance, the transitional military government of General Yahya Khan (1969–1971) is seen as the first to emphasize Islam within the education system, something which was then further consolidated under Zia ul-Haq.

The military has used religion in politics both directly and indirectly. Despite Pakistan's genesis in the Hindu–Muslim two nation theory, Islamic law had remained confined largely to the personal sphere until changes ushered in by General Zia ul-Haq.[41] The extended military spell of Zia came to an end after increasing political pressure, but before holding elections (on a non-party basis) he carried out a referendum in December 1984 seeking a "mandate" to continue in office as president for a new five-year term. The referendum was structured in a way that religion, not politics, was paramount. The electorate was asked whether it believed the government was doing a creditable job of the Islamization of domestic structures, and 98 percent said that it was. Earlier, in 1982, Zia had tried to stave off pressure to hold elections by appointing a Majlis-i-Shoora (Council of Advisors), citing its basis in Islamic law as a legislative body. His slogan was "Islamization of Pakistan." It was under Zia that the Hudood ordinances were passed, laying out Islamic punishment for various offenses such as drinking alcohol, theft, prostitution and adultery, including legislating physical punishment in criminal cases.

The educational sector is a critical area in which the imprint of the state, and especially the military, is visible in crafting an identity that brought security and religious factors together.[42] During General Zia's regime, the highest degree of a madrasa was made equivalent to a masters degree from a university in order to enable a madrasa graduate to compete for jobs.[43] This made a huge difference in career opportunities: previously, only students interested in becoming religious clerics tended to attend madrasas.

The madrasa system has come under enormous scrutiny since September 11. However, independent studies focusing on the status of education in Pakistan are increasingly concluding that distortions in government education are as, if not more, potent in engendering and inculcating intolerant and extremist views.[44] Religious groups have also managed to impart their ideological biases through officially sanctioned textbooks for use in subjects such as Pakistan Studies and Islamic Studies for school-age children. Religious forces close to the state have often ended

[41] See Lau, "The Fifteenth Constitutional Amendment"; and Ashraf Ghani, "Afghanistan," p. 91.
[42] A. H. Nayyar, "The Making of the Pakistani Mind," in Aall and Ollapally (eds.) *Perspectives*. This section relies considerably on Nayyar's work. Nayyar and colleagues have conducted the most detailed research into the nature of textbooks in Pakistan to date.
[43] *Pakistan Link*, May 17, 2000.
[44] The most extensive and widely hailed report, *The Subtle Subversion: The State of Curricula and Textbooks in Pakistan*, was conducted by the Sustainable Development Policy Institute, as part of a project on "A Civil Society Initiative in Curricula and Texbooks Reform", Islamabad, 2003.

up exerting greater influence on the education system than professional educators or other political parties. Far from being averse to this, the state apparatus has been complicit. The development of educational curricula shows how the military-led state has actively promoted material that legitimizes continued conflict with India in terms of religious intolerance and historical distortions and, in the process, consolidated geopolitical identity conceptions in fundamental ways.

The textbooks of the 1950s and early 1960s have been described as "fairly secular," even mentioning Mahatma Gandhi "in respectful terms as a great leader of independence," according to A. H. Nayyar, a leading expert who has conducted the most detailed research on textbooks in Pakistan to date.[45] With the political agenda of Islamization, a discernible shift is found. Apart from the injection of openly religious material into school curricula, the manner in which particular subjects – Pakistan Studies, Social Studies, History and Civics – began to be taught became ideologically charged such that pre-Islamic history in the territory that constitutes current Pakistan, including that of the early Hindu and Buddhist empires, was even eliminated from textbooks.[46] Pakistani educational material prior to the 1970s did not contain the level of animosity towards India and Hindus represented in later textbooks, despite the bloodshed of partition and outbreak of two wars. From the 1970s onwards, "the objects of hate in Pakistani educational material are Hindus and India, reflecting both the perceived sense of insecurity from an 'enemy,' and an attempt to define one's national identity in relation to the 'other.'"[47] The sectors that gain most from such representation are the military and political Islamists, justifiable in geopolitical terms for the former and in religious terms for the latter. One telling sign of the shift in educational orientation, now simultaneously promoting a geopolitical and religious identity, was the emphasis on jihad and shahadat (martyrdom). This particular curriculum change coincided with the war waged against the Soviets in Afghanistan.[48]

Holding the center

Islamist discourse and foreign policy activism has been useful in containing longstanding secessionist tendencies among Pakistan's

[45] Nayyar, "The Making of the Pakistani Mind."
[46] Ahmed Salim, "Historical Falsehoods and Inaccuracies," in Nayyar and Salim (eds.) *The Subtle Subversion*, p. 83.
[47] A. H. Nayyar and Ahmed Salim, "Glorification of War and the Military," in Nayyar and Salim (eds.) *The Subtle Subversion*, p. 97.
[48] Nayyar, "The Making of the Pakistani Mind."

provinces.[49] The potential for such instability was seen from the very beginning, and it is instructive to quote at some length Maulana Azad, an anti-colonial leader in British India who resisted partition and warned his co-religionists leaving India in 1947: "You are leaving your motherland. Do you know what the consequences will be? Your frequent exoduses, such as this, will weaken the Muslims of India. A time may come when the various Pakistani regions start asserting their separate identities: Bengali, Punjabi, Sindhi, Baloch may declare themselves separate qaums. Will your position in Pakistan at that time be better than uninvited guests? The Hindu can be your religious opponent, but not your regional and national opponent. You can deal with this situation. But in Pakistan, at any time you may have to face regional and national opposition; before this kind of opposition you will be helpless."[50]

His words have proven to be prescient in important respects; ethnic and regional agitation in Pakistan continues to ebb and flow. The latest round of ethnic unrest was set off after General Musharraf geared up to increase the exploration of oil and gas, and step up work on the Gwador port off Baluchistan with the help of the Chinese. These internal agitations, as well as continuing regional and international conflicts, are held up as demanding a strong military role.

Impact of regional and extra-regional geopolitics

Pakistan's geopolitical role as the "frontline state" for the US-led war against the Soviets directly and fundamentally affected critical domestic institutions in lasting ways. Changes in the public education domain dovetailed with the teachings in madrasas during this time, focusing on jihad as an instrument of war in Afghanistan. As discussed in the previous chapter, the geopolitical interests of the US and Pakistan dictated the support of an extremist version of Islam relying on madrasa settings in many cases. While it would be unfair to view all madrasas in the same light, the unprecedented mushrooming of madrasas in this era speaks for itself. For the religious groups in Pakistan, one of the advantages of links to the state has been the accumulation of resources to spend on the expansion of madrasas.[51] By 2004, figures for the numbers of such schools

---

[49] For a good discussion of Pakistan's national identity problems, see Mahnaz Ispahani, "Can Pakistan Be Saved?" *The New Republic*, June 16, 2003.

[50] Quoted in Singh, "Diversity, Heterogeneity and Integration," pp. 245–246.

[51] Hassan N. Gardezi, "Jihadi Islam: The Last Straw on the Camel of Pakistan's National Unity," paper presented at the World Sindhi Institute conference, Washington, DC, May 20, 2000.

varied between 10,000 and 20,000 and the number of students attending ranged between 1.5 and 2 million.[52] The World Bank has estimated that 15 to 20 percent of madrasas in Pakistan are involved in military-related teachings and training.[53] Even if only a small percentage of these students are implicated in militant jihadism, there is considerable room for concern.

Policy towards Afghanistan was under the control of the Inter-Services Intelligence (ISI), the military intelligence agency established by General Zia ul-Haq at the beginning of the Afghan war. The involvement of the ISI in encouraging and supporting jihadi groups is discussed in the chapters on Afghanistan and Kashmir. One of the effects of the military's geopolitically determined education policy was to enhance certain strands of Islamic thinking and practice over others. Making Islam more "official" through state policy, and elevating the position of organized Islamic groups politically, worked to the detriment of popular Sufi traditions which operated outside the state domain. Thus within Islam, the balance of power shifted with the weight of the state behind the official ulema. For example, there have been increasing signs that the Sufi worship of saints and celebration of urs festivals are being attacked as "un-Islamic" in parts of Pakistan, especially in the NWFP and Baluchistan, where the political power of the MMA is growing.

Some analysts have made a distinction between "new" and "old" Islamists in Pakistan, diverging on the degree to which Islam was "political," and of its willingness to co-exist with secular politics.[54] The new Islamists are viewed as recognizing, and capitalizing on, the weakness of the state and secular elite, and pursuing a strategy to gain effective control of or "capture" civil institutions like schools and colleges. Their ultimate objective is to gain control of the state itself. The problem with this type of analysis is that Islamists are accorded too much autonomy in Pakistan's political life; political Islam would have been difficult to nurture and translate into political influence without the patronage or dispensation of the Pakistani military.

Under President Musharraf's announced commitment to "enlightened moderation," the promised education reforms have not materialized. Given the vast revamping that would be required, not just of madrasas, but of public sector education, and the vested interests that would be

---

[52] Alan Kronstadt and Bruce Vaughn of the Congressional Research Service use the higher figure, while the International Crisis Group offers the lower number. See K. Alan Kronstadt and Bruce Vaughn, "Terrorism in South Asia", Congressional Research Service, Library of Congress, August 9, 2004, p. 7; and International Crisis Group, *Pakistan: Madrasas, Extremism and the Military*.

[53] *The News*, August 2, 2002.

[54] Pasha, "Islamic Extremists: How Do They Mobilize Support?"

disturbed, reforms are likely to remain piecemeal and ad hoc at best. Dismantling the infrastructure of extremism is a formidable task. As a report by the International Crisis Group puts it, "The madrasa phenomenon cannot be reduced to terrorism nor understood in isolation from civil-military relations, Pakistan-India conflicts, and the larger question of separation of state and religion ... To initiate radical reforms and bring religious education closer to mainstream education requires redefining the military's internal policies and external preferences. It is unclear whether the Musharraf government is willing to do either."[55] Indeed, Musharraf's former Prime Minister Jamali went so far as to assure the MMA and other religious groups that his government " 'would not repeal the ordinance [Hudooth] or effect any changes in the law.' "[56]

The Afghanistan war and its succession battles (discussed in the previous chapter) have been critical in shaping religious militancy in Pakistan. The Kashmir issue has also played a part, to be examined in the next chapter. Indeed, the Pakistan military's *link* role between the wars in Afghanistan and the conflict in Kashmir is key. The emergence of the MMA as a separate group itself owes much to the regional geopolitical situation in Afghanistan after September 11 and American actions. In October 2001, 26 religious parties and other smaller groups representing a broad spectrum of Sunni and Shiite views, formed the Pak–Afghan Defence Council to protest Pakistan's aid to the US military intervention in Afghanistan.[57] However, it was not able to garner much popular support and was dismantled soon after the Taliban regime was overthrown, part of the Council later re-emerging in the form of the MMA.

Regional geopolitics and US geopolitical interests once again conspired to shift Pakistan's domestic politics. The American intervention in Afghanistan in 2001 was an electoral windfall for the MMA. Asked about the election strategy of the six-party alliance, the deputy general secretary of the JUI described it as "capitalizing on the anti-US emotions in the country following Washington's anti-Muslim role in Afghanistan and Palestine."[58] Without this unifying target, it is not at all clear that the alliance, not known for harmonious relations, could have held together. Indeed, it was the first time in Pakistan's history that the religious parties were able to come together to contest the elections on a single platform. Ever since 1985, when formal democracy was reinstated, the religious parties have taken part in elections independently.

[55] International Crisis Group, *Pakistan: Madrasas*, pp. 3–4.
[56] Quoted in *Dawn*, March 10, 2004.
[57] International Crisis Group, *Authoritarianism*, pp. 13–14.   [58] *Dawn*, August 8, 2002.

Moderate or extremist outcomes

The decision by the Musharraf regime to abandon the Taliban, and its ostensible anti-terrorism alliance with the US, would suggest that global geopolitical compulsions now push the Pakistan military establishment away from policies that tend to promote extremist outcomes. However, regional geopolitical competition with India and continuing ambitions for influence in the new Afghanistan, have not disappeared. Pakistan is caught between two differing geopolitical pressures, and exclusive geopolitical identities that foster religious radicalism are still relevant. The manner in which the government is conducting the "war on terrorism" is instructive. Even with the rise of civilian politicians in 2008, counter-terrorism operations will no doubt be under the military's control, thus leaving intact its dangerous Afghan and Kashmir policies as well.

Dealing with extremists: the military's competing pulls

The military's proximity to the main religious parties is transparent, but its position regarding other domestic groups such as HuM, LeT and JeM is much less easy to decipher. These groups have served a strategic geopolitical function for the Pakistani state (as the chapters on Afghanistan and Kashmir describe), and their loss may not be tolerated by the military.

In the early days of his rule, General Musharraf was fastidious in the way he used the term "terrorism," taking pains to point out that neither the Kashmiri militants nor the Afghan mujahideen could be called terrorists. In the regional context, he reserved the label of terrorism for the methods used by sectarian Sunni and Shia groups within Pakistan, and for Arabs and others from abroad.[59] In the run up to the American attack on Afghanistan in October 2001, Pakistani officials appeared to be straining to keep a balance between past and present policy against "terrorism." During General Musharraf's address to the nation explaining why he had to take the unpopular step of helping the American intervention into neighboring Afghanistan, he conceded that he was picking the lesser of two "troubles" confronting Pakistan.

Since Pakistan joined the US to root out al-Qaeda (and to a less certain degree, Taliban remnants), the Musharraf regime seems to be walking a fine line between cracking down on militants and trying to retain some hold over them for foreign policy purposes in Kashmir and Afghanistan. His crackdown on terrorist groups in March 2002 proved

---

[59] See General Musharraf's remarks in his interview to Bharat Bhushan, executive editor of *The Hindustan Times*, July 6, 2004.

to be a passing phase, with many simply reinventing themselves under different names. This balancing act appears to be increasingly difficult to sustain, as the twin suicide attacks against the president in December 2003 demonstrate. His hand-picked prime minister designate Shaukat Aziz also narrowly escaped a suicide strike in July 2004, as did the interior minister in April 2007.

Musharraf is also under continuing pressure from the US. The response to that American pressure has been evident on a number of occasions. In June 2003, President Musharraf publicly stated that his forces were entering the Federally Administered Tribal Areas (FATA) in a historic break with the past, even suggesting that Osama bin Laden might be crossing the Pakistan–Afghan border in this region.[60] However, he made these statements during a news conference with President Bush in Washington, DC, who was announcing a $3 billion proposed aid package for Pakistan. A year later, the number of al-Qaeda figures arrested in Pakistan had barely gone up, leading US officials to question the extent of Islamabad's willingness to cooperate.[61] The US ambassador to Afghanistan, Zalmay Khalilzad, openly criticized the Pakistanis for providing a "sanctuary" for al-Qaeda and Taliban forces, adding that "We all want Pakistan to deal with the problem." Despite Pakistan's strong reservations about The US troops on its soil, Khalilzad bluntly stated that the American military would move forces into Pakistan if it failed to dislodge the terrorists.[62] For keen observers, it was hard to miss how Pakistan's waxing and waning efforts have been tailored to meet US pressure, as opposed to internal preferences.[63]

Since 2004, Musharraf's offensive has included an apparently increased effort to curb terrorism inside Pakistan, but mostly only those groups which are linked to al-Qaeda and could be characterized as "foreign." In public speeches to commemorate the 57th anniversary of Pakistan's

---

[60] *The Washington Times*, June 25, 2003. Outside forces of any kind were entering FATA for the first time in over a century.

[61] Kronstadt and Vaughn, *Terrorism in South Asia*, p. 11.

[62] www.cbsnews.com, Islamabad, April 21, 2004.

[63] One of the most sensational was the announcement on July 29, 2004 of the capture of Ahmed Khalfan Ghailani, the FBI's 22nd "most wanted" terrorist suspected in the 1998 US embassy bombings in Kenya and Tanzania. According to *The New Republic*, the White House told ISI head Ehsan ul-Haq during a visit to the US in spring 2004 that "it would be best if the arrest or killing of [any] HVT [high value target] were announced on 26, 27 or 28 July," during the Democratic convention to nominate John Kerry as the presidential candidate. Pakistan's interior minister, Faisal Saleh Hayyat, made the announcement of Ghailani's capture on local television at midnight, afternoon local time in New York where John Kerry was preparing to deliver his nomination acceptance speech, leaving open the question as to who the interior minister's real audience was. According to numerous press reports, it turned out that Ghailani had been actually apprehended four days earlier.

independence, Musharraf went to some lengths to focus on "foreign terrorists," stating that it was foreign militants linked to bin Laden who posed the biggest challenge to Pakistan.[64] This would indicate that the military was hesitant to take on some of the most radical Islamist groups spawned in Pakistan by Pakistanis. On this question, the assessment by a well-regarded outside analyst is nothing short of damning. According to Dan Byman, "Indeed, with the possible exception of Iran, Pakistan is probably today's most active sponsor of terrorism."[65] Indeed, the rapid growth of the so-called Pakistani Taliban by 2008 and its flagrant and public campaigns in the NWFP and FATA region challenged the entire basis of US policy of relying on Pakistan to root out terrorists and stem extremism.

Many critics of the government believe that President Musharraf's current fight against terrorism is another tactic to demonstrate the importance of the military having a hold on power.[66] Opinion is split between observers who argue that American pressure has forced (or allowed) Musharraf to seriously attempt to curb militant extremism and rid Pakistan of its ideological and militarized national security framework, and others who suggest that the military is simply changing its façade to bolster the country's public image in a bid to preserve power while waiting for American interest to die down. (The label of terrorism has also become a useful tool in clamping down on opponents of the state, including even peasant agitators demanding greater control over their land tenancy.)[67]

MMA and the war on terrorism

The major religious parties have been caught in the cross hairs of the government's open alliance with the US and their own partnership with the military. The MMA's approach to terrorism has been to challenge the US definition of terrorism to the point of describing America's attack on Afghanistan as "terrorism against humanity."[68] Of all the issues in the MMA's election manifesto, the one that has been the most consistently

---

[64] *The Asian Age*, August 15, 2004.
[65] Byman, *Deadly Connections*, p. 155.
[66] One somewhat cynical view is that without these groups, the necessity of the US to accommodate Pakistan is reduced, leading to a fear of abandonment. In other words, some question whether Pakistan is in effect making the case – "save us from ourselves" – to retain US support.
[67] Rubina Saigol has pointed out how the Pakistani military went so far as to term members of a farmer's movement who challenged the military's control over certain lands "terrorists." "Ownership or Death: A Study of the Tenant Farmer's Movement in Pakistan," paper presented at the Seminar on Non-Traditional Security Formulations: Gender and South Asia, New Delhi, October 30–31, 2004.
[68] Quote by Maulana Fazlur Rehman in *Outlook*, October 22, 2001 during his house arrest in October 2001.

promoted is the anti-imperialist [anti-American] theme.[69] The MMA's position regarding allegations of religious parties' links to terrorism is that it is just a US "pretext for pressurizing the Pakistani leadership."[70]

The government's equivocation when it comes to the religious parties is evident. For example, there were mixed signals from the government regarding alleged links between the JI and al-Qaeda, with interior minister Makhdoom Faisel Saleh Hayat saying in 2003 that "All of the activists and terrorists who have been apprehended in recent months have had links to the Jamaat-i-Islami, whether we have arrested them in Lahore or here [Rawalpindi] or Karachi...They have been harboring them."[71] At the same time, President Musharraf's spokesman General Rashid Quereshi quickly played down the link.

The continued support offered by the MMA to Musharraf, despite his cooperation with the US, demonstrates the political power of the military as well as, perhaps, the MMA's confidence that the military will only take limited action to take to curb radical Islamism. Although the MMA promised to campaign against Musharraf for backtracking on his pledge to give up the post of army chief of staff by the end of 2004 and be accepted in parliament as president after a vote of confidence, it later capitulated on the issue.[72] Likewise, when the idea of moving against foreigner terrorists and the tribal leaders harboring them was raised by the government, the MMA attempted to agitate on the issue but found it difficult to elicit support from other political parties.[73] In any case, Musharraf's registration policy is clearly targeted towards "foreign" elements, and his piecemeal attempts to curb mosque and madrasa non-religious activities are fairly narrowly directed at domestic "sectarian" forces. Since jihadi outfits operating outside Pakistan, which have been linked to groups within the MMA, have not been singled out and are not covered under these policy directives, leaders of the coalition may feel less uncomfortable being associated with the government.

Having gained political power in unprecedented fashion in 2002, there were powerful incentives for the religious parties and the military to

---

[69] The MMA's 2002 election manifesto states the following objective "To get the country and people rid of influence of imperialist forces and their local agents." Available at www.mma.org.pk.

[70] *Pakistan Times*, July 17, 2004.

[71] Gretchen Peters, "Al-Qaeda–Pakistani Ties Deepen," *The Christian Science Monitor*, March 6, 2003. Among high profile al-Qaeda operatives arrested from the homes of JI workers was al-Qaeda operations chief Khalid Sheikh Mohammed in 2003. See "Testimony on Madrasas and US Aid to Pakistan" before the US House of Representatives Subcommittee on National Security and Foreign Affairs by Samina Ahmed, South Asia Project Director, International Crisis Group, May 9, 2007, available as a pdf at www.oversight.house.gov.

[72] *Daily Times*, September 20, 2003. See also *Daily Times*, July 11, 2004.

[73] *The News*, July 8, 2004.

continue working together to retain it. Despite some competing pressures, both the religious groups and the Pakistan military appeared to have found a *modus vivendi* that shored up their power, barring any extraneous shocks. The unexpected crisis triggered by the dismissal by President Musharraf of the independent-minded Supreme Court Justice Iftikhar Chaudhry in the spring of 2007, compounded by the sensational assassination of Benazir Bhutto during her election campaign, have turned out to be twin external shocks that neither could fully weather. The lackluster performance of the MMA and the PML-Q in 2008 and losses at the national and provincial levels are clear setbacks for religious groups and their military partners. On the other hand, the uneasy political compromises between the mainstream parties and the continuing violence provide future opportunities for them both. Meanwhile, the fate of violent extremist groups that function outside established politics will clearly continue to depend on the particular needs of the military and dominant religious parties.

Conclusion

This chapter has shown that there has been a spectrum of identity preferences over Pakistan's history and that the ascendancy of a particular identity is clearly dependent on state sanction or support. As in Afghanistan, we see a three-way tension between religious, geopolitical and secular identities. Again, under conditions of unstable historical secularism, the secular identity remained vulnerable, and its decline is closely connected to the nature of encounters between geopolitics and internal conditions. It is the militarized (and increasingly religion-based) version of state identity that has been the driver of violent extremism at home and abroad for Pakistan. But this religious radicalization has not been accomplished by religious leaders or popular revolution, but made possible in large part by the military.

Left largely to their own devices, as was the case for the first 25 years of Pakistan's history, religious forces in Pakistan were neither sharply political nor narrowly geopolitical. Whether seen in terms of pre-colonial or immediate post-colonial periods, the adoption of religious radicalism as a dominant preference for these groups was not inevitable. From our standpoint, it may also be worth noting that unlike the military, the religious groups do not necessarily need a conflict-ridden environment to exert influence. Although the 1947 partition provides a latent and potentially powerful conflictual identity vis-à-vis India, the geopolitical connotations of such an identity become much more ascendant through the operation of the military. This suggests that the JUI and the JI might also see the military's role differently: as the party closer to "official

Islam," the JI's own geopolitical stand is likely to be closer to the military establishment's. In Pakistan, the addition of geopolitical factors to religious identity has inexorably favoured extremism. Thus, the popular focus on the MMA and other religious groups as the origin of extremism is somewhat misplaced and inadequate. From general trends to specific outcomes, the military's role needs to be recognized.

Pakistan has reached a particularly difficult crossroads in the post-9/11 compromise with the US, with the three competing notions of secular, religious and geopolitical identity in full battle. The military is trying to undo some of the worst excesses of the past but is caught up in too many contradictory policies. The long-term agenda of the politically active religious parties, such as the JI and JUI, are hard to decipher: they are not a monolithic group, and their unity could be undercut by theological, ethnic and regional differences, not to mention political opportunism and some willingness to be co-opted into the political establishment. This sets them apart from other religiously motivated violent extremist groups, particularly the groups of more recent vintage that have formed in reaction to the US war on terrorism. The latter development complicates an unstable environment even further, since the authority of such groups is somewhat in doubt, unlike earlier ones which had links (though often shadowy) to identifiable institutions such as the ISI or religious parties.

One factor in Pakistan's prospects for controlling extremist violence has been the lack of serious participation by mainstream secular parties between 1999 and 2008 in settling the identity struggle. In this context, the geopolitical intrusion of the US has tended to empower illiberal forces, rhetoric aside. For example, after its exhaustive study, the 9/11 Commission reached the conclusion, "we believe that Musharraf's government represents the best hope for stability in Pakistan and Afghanistan."[74] Other observations that the Commission has made regarding the Pakistani army's role are equally surprising. For instance, the Commission mentions the ambivalence that the Pakistan army and intelligence services, "especially below the top ranks," have shown in confronting Islamic extremists, omitting the very common knowledge that it was the ISI chiefs and the military top brass that ushered in and nurtured religious politics and religious militant groups.[75]

Pakistan's democratic interlude (1988–1999) and its unexpected, if partial, resuscitation in 2008 suggests, however, that all things being equal, the popularity of the mainstream "secular" parties in the political

---

[74] *The 9/11 Commission Report, Final Report of the National Commission on Terrorist Attacks upon the United States*, Official Government Edition (Washington, DC: US Government Printing Office, 2004), p. 369.
[75] *The 9/11 Commission Report*, p. 368.

arena is overwhelming in comparison to the religious parties. In the 1997 general elections, only the JUI had any success at all, winning two seats in the 217 member National Assembly, despite the fact that the madrasas were stronger than ever and the Taliban had gained power the year before across the border. Most strikingly, the rise of Islamist radicalism has still not translated into popular support – in 2002 the two mainstream parties captured 61 percent of the vote.[76] Even without Benazir Bhutto, the PPP received a higher number of votes in the 2002 elections than the party that ultimately came to power, the PML-Q. The defeat of the PML-Q and the MMA in the 2008 elections once again reveals this underlying popular impulse. Despite the murkiness of Pakistan's politics, one conclusion may be made with a fair degree of confidence: genuine democratic processes will foster mainstream secular parties and that is the best bet against extremist politics in Pakistan.

[76] In 2002, the PPP won 25.8 percent of the votes, the PML 9.4 percent and the PML-Q 25.7 percent.

5   Conflict and contradiction in Kashmir

The demand by Kashmiri Muslims for greater autonomy burst into a full-fledged insurgency against the Indian government in 1989, and has kept the territory in the grip of violence ever since. The politics and actors involved have, however, hardly been constant. There have been numerous political and ideological formations in the interim, from parties that have held power as part of the Indian state to groups that are largely foreign. There are more facets to the Kashmir conflict than are often acknowledged, with local, national and regional forces affecting Kashmir's political developments.

The most important Kashmiri separatist umbrella organization, the All Parties Hurriyat Conference (APHC), ultimately split in 2004 on the issue of negotiating with the Indian government. The APHC sees itself as the main political representative of the Kashmiri militancy, but there are other armed groups that wield influence, such as the Hizb ul-Mujahideen. The Hurriyat itself defies easy characterization; as the political face of the militancy, its relationship with armed groups is ambiguous.

As in Afghanistan and Pakistan, the way in which competition between the three dominant identity constructions have occurred over time (religious, secular and geopolitical) tells us a great deal about the evolution of the militancy and the balance between moderate and extremist forces. An understanding of the prospects for resolving the conflict based on our findings is more important than ever given some of the powerful changes that have taken place regionally and within India since 2001.

This chapter first considers the efficacy of a number of alternative explanations and then turns to an extended treatment of the dominant religious argument for the evolution of the Kashmir conflict. Next, it lays out the domestic landscape focusing on the character of secularism and secular identity in India, especially in Kashmir. In the subsequent section, it considers the external impact on identity formation and the construction of geopolitical identities in India and Pakistan. Finally, we look at how the interplay between secular, ethno-religious and geopolitical identities tips the balance between more moderate or extremist outcomes.

Attempts to explain extremism

Relative deprivation as an explanation of extremism does not hold up well in the context of the Kashmir conflict. While the Hindu Kashmiri Brahmin minority (known as the Pandits) disproportionately occupied influential positions in the Kashmir Valley as teachers, lawyers and other professionals, it was generally not perceived as occurring at the expense of the majority community.[1] In this regard, the Valley had long been known for its communal harmony rather than hostility. Prior to the insurgency, Kashmir's economic situation was better than other states in India; as were important social indicators like education and health. At four percent, Kashmir still has one of the lowest poverty rates in India, well below the national average. Between 1995 and 2000, during the ongoing militancy, the literacy rate in Kashmir rose from 56 to 65 percent.

In terms of the level of central government support to the states, Kashmir has outstripped all others substantially. The usual practice of the Indian governments funding 20 percent of each state's development needs, with 80 percent raised by the state itself, was reversed in the case of Kashmir from the beginning of the First Five Year Plan in the 1950s onwards until 1990. Since the insurgency, 100 percent of Kashmir's budget has been financed by the Indian government, requiring only 20 percent to be repaid.[2] Some analysts have suggested that the socio-economic improvement that Kashmir has experienced (in spite of the patronage, corruption and ineptitude of the ruling parties in the state) was in a large part responsible for the political mobilization of a new generation of Kashmiris.[3] Greater economic opportunity was not among the major demands of the anti-government movement. The separatists themselves have never made a convincing case

---

[1] Although not an unbiased observer, Jawaharlal Nehru's observations regarding his Pandit community in Kashmir and their close integration into Kashmiri society for "a thousand years or more" contains merit. Jawaharlal Nehru, *The Unity of India: Collected Writings 1937–1940* (London: Lindsay Drummond, 1948), p. 229.

[2] For an overview of Kashmir's economic trends and the heavy government subsidies, see Amy Waldman, "Border Tension a Growth Industry for Kashmir," *The New York Times*, October 18, 2002; Wajahat Habibullah, *The Political Economy of the Kashmir Conflict*, US Institute of Peace Special Report, No. 121 (June 2004), pp. 16–25; Sundeep Waslekar and Ilmas Futehally, *Reshaping the Agenda in Kashmir* (Mumbai: International Centre for Peace Initiatives, 2002), p. 8. and Riaz Punjabi, "Kashmir: The Bruised Identity," in Raju G. C. Thomas (ed.) *Perspectives on Kashmir: The Roots of Conflict in South Asia* (Boulder, CO: Westview Press, 1992), p. 142.

[3] The abolition of landlordism by the National Conference under Sheikh Abdullah in 1950 (uniquely in India) laid a strong foundation for socio-economic transformation. This went a long way in winning loyalty from the lower and middle class Muslims and Hindus. For a discussion of the impact of improvement in a number of different sectors on political mobilization, see Sumit Ganguly, *The Crisis in Kashmir: Portents of War, Hopes of Peace* (New York: Cambridge University Press, 1997), pp. 27–37.

that Kashmir would be better off economically as a separate state rather than as part of India.

The argument that elites manipulated the situation in Kashmir towards conflict for their own purposes is also open to challenge. Kashmiri Muslim elites are not uniform. There is an astonishing diversity even among the disaffected sectors, as later discussion will show. Some key leaders of the armed groups and members of the APHC have repeatedly participated in the state's electoral process whereas others have been jailed for anti-national activities. The militancy drew in both secular and religious leadership. It is difficult to isolate the impact of specific leadership as a causal factor even close to the start of insurgency.

Strictly speaking, the state repression argument suffers from a time lag problem: the imposition of governor's rule in 1990 and army action came in response to the violent outburst in the state in 1989. Kashmir had previously enjoyed continuous religious freedom, and there was no visible suppression of Islam or the Kashmiri identity by the state or central government. Indeed, Article 371 of the Indian Constitution gave Kashmir special privileges from the outset: non-Kashmiris were prohibited from owning immovable property such as land and such policy was viewed as part of promoting cultural autonomy. Hindus could not relocate easily and change the demographics of the state, nor could the state engage in deliberate colonization to change the ethnic balance as it wished (unlike the former Soviet Union, Sri Lanka and elsewhere where there was deliberate change in ethnic composition of target areas, and also in contrast to Chinese suppression of Tibetan Buddhism and key religious figures).

In principle at least, India's flexible federalism also provided a large degree of autonomy. In cases of territorially concentrated minorities, many experts have argued that a federal system holds the best potential for containing ethno-religious conflict. Their critics have argued otherwise: federalism sharpens separatist identities and lays the basis for the future break-up of the country. In Kashmir, separatist tendencies were least when democracy and autonomy were strongest. For example, some Pakistani officials admit to having tried to foment separatism in Kashmir in the 1960s, without success.[4] Even as late as 1983, when the leader of the Jammu and Kashmir Liberation Front (JKLF), Amanullah Khan, attempted to recruit for an armed revolt, he was unsuccessful because of a lack of interest.[5]

---

[4] Jessica Stern notes this point in "Double Edged Sword: The Creation of Pakistan's Jihad Culture," Draft paper, August 29, 2000 (mimeo), p. 2.

[5] Sten Widmalm, "The Rise and Fall of Democracy in Jammu and Kashmir," *Asian Survey*, 37.11 (November 1997), pp. 1007–1008. Widmalm argues that even in the early 1980s, the forces of integration via the democratic process had the clear upper hand in Kashmir.

This brings us to the other element of the state-centric argument – political access, which has a good deal of plausibility when we consider Kashmir's political situation in the 1980s. By first meddling and then resorting to non-democratic methods to gain political advantage in Kashmir, the national Congress Party contributed heavily to Kashmiri alienation. But in the 1980s and previously, when the Congress Party controlled the central government, it engaged in electoral irregularities elsewhere, dismissing other elected state governments and imposing President's Rule under one guise or the other, without generating extremism.[6] Andhra Pradesh, Maharashtra and Tamil Nadu experienced such interference but no violent separatist movement emerged here despite the existence of strong regional identity-based parties and groups in these states. Although central mismanagement and manipulation of politics in Kashmir was an important factor as in other states, we need to explain why it resulted in a violent explosion here and not elsewhere. The dominant "de-institutionalization" of Congress thesis that many analysts put forward is clearly important, but insufficient.[7] We now turn to the remaining standard explanation – religion.

The religious explanation

As a general point, it is useful to reiterate that Assam, one of the three most important secessionist movements India has faced along with Kashmir and Punjab, has a majority Hindu population, casting immediate doubt on a simple religious argument. Conversely, in India's highly diversified state of Kerala, Muslims and Christians comprise 20 percent each of the population and there has been no communal strife and no sign of separatist sentiment. It is easy to make assertions such as that made by respected South Asia expert Ainslie Embree that "religion has been inextricably interwoven with the conflict in Kashmir,"[8] given that the struggle is prima facie between Hindu majority India and its only

---

[6] For an overview of the rise in the Congress' intolerance of opposition in the states, see Prem Shankar Jha, In the Eye of the Cyclone: The Crisis in Indian Democracy (New Delhi: Viking Books, 1993), pp. 48–52.

[7] Well-known proponents of de-institutionalization include Ganguly, The Crisis in Kashmir; Amrita Basu and Atul Kohli, "Community Conflicts and the State in India," The Journal of Asian Studies, 56.2 (May 1997), and Sumantara Bose, The Challenge in Kashmir (New Delhi: Sage Publications, 1997).

[8] Ainslie Embree, "Kashmir: Has Religion A Role in Peacemaking?" paper presented at a meeting at the International Center for Religion and Diplomacy, Washington, DC, December 12, 2000, p. 13. See also his Utopias in Conflict: Religion and Nationalism in Modern India (Berkeley, CA: University of California Press, 1990), p. 8 for the argument that religious identity leads to differing worldviews in India that cannot accommodate each other.

Muslim majority state, located next to Pakistan. However, despite the tendency of many observers to cast the conflict in Kashmir as religiously driven, it is difficult to demonstrate that religion is the primary impetus.

The Jammu and Kashmir region (commonly termed Kashmir) covers an area far beyond the Kashmir Valley where most of the unrest and violence has occurred. "Kashmir" technically consists of Jammu, the Kashmir Valley, Ladakh and the areas under Pakistan's control across the Line of Control (LOC), termed "Azad Kashmir" and the Northern Areas. The LOC coincides in no small part with a linguistic boundary, with Kashmiri the predominant language in the Valley and different Punjabi dialects spoken in Pakistani controlled Kashmir. Two-thirds of Kashmir is in India, and in the 1990s approximately 64 percent of the population was Muslim and 32 percent Hindu. The whole area taken together presents a mixed religious and ethnic picture: apart from Sunni Muslims, the region is also populated by Gujjars, Bakerwals, Sikhs, Sudhans, Hindus and Shia Muslims. The population of Jammu is approximately two-thirds Hindu, one-third Muslim, with a sizeable sprinkling of Sikhs; a little over half of Ladakh is Tibetan Buddhist, with the remainder Muslim; and the Kashmir Valley is nearly 95 percent Sunni Muslim.[9] The Kashmiri Hindu Pandits of the Valley used to form an important minority, but largely fled in 1990, with more than 200,000 living in refugee camps in Jammu or outside the state. In the Northern Areas of Pakistan there is a population mix, with large proportion of Shias and Ismailis, along with Sunni Muslims.

Kashmiriyat and Secular Traditions

With these divergent communities as a backdrop, what has been historically distinctive in Kashmir is the unique syncretic tradition of "Kashmiriyat" or Kashmirihood that evolved from the Kashmir Valley, one that historically fused the culture of the minority Pandits with that of the Muslims.[10] Chapter Two has already discussed the notion of Kashmiriyat, along with Sufism, pointing out their moderating influence on communal and religious sentiment in Kashmir. While both Kashmiriyat and Sufism have suffered setbacks, the latter in particular remains significant for the large majority of Kashmiri Muslims. As one expert notes, "The label 'Muslim' for Kashmir's majority population

---

[9] For a demographic overview of the Kashmir region, see Sumantra Bose, *Kashmir: Roots of Conflict, Paths to Peace* (Cambridge, MA: Harvard University Press, 2003), pp. 10–11; and Leo Rose, "The Politics of Azad Kashmir," in Thomas, *Perspectives on Kashmir*, pp. 248–250.

[10] For an evocative personal narrative on Kashmiriyat from a Kashmiri pandit, see Sudha Koul, *The Tiger Ladies* (New York: Beacon Press, 2002).

slightly obscures the historical interaction between Hinduism and Islam and the Islamic mystics – the Rishi Silsilah – which have given the region a unique character."[11]

In a major poll conducted by the London-based independent market research firm MORI International in April 2002 in Jammu and Kashmir, an overwhelming 92 percent of people opposed the state being divided on the basis of religion or ethnicity, despite 13 years of conflict. There is also wide support (80 percent) for the notion that allowing displaced Pandits to return to their homes in safety will help bring about peace. On the issue of whether Kashmir's unique cultural identity of Kashmiriyat should be preserved in any long-term solution, 76 percent in Srinagar and 81 percent in Jammu agreed that it should be.[12] Similarly, in another poll conducted by A. C. Neilson, the proposal of trifurcating the state in effect by religious majority – into Jammu, Kashmir and Ladakh – was rejected by 87 per cent across the state.[13]

In comparison to some of their co-religionists in Central Asia, Afghanistan and Pakistan, many of the members of the APHC stand out for their lack of a strong affiliation with religious ideology. The APHC's constitution commits it to the following regarding religion: "To make endeavors, in keeping with the Muslim majority character of State, for promoting the build-up of society based on Islamic values, while safe-guarding the rights and interests of non-Muslims."[14] The reference to Islamic values rather than more formal Islamic law or Sharia is telling. During the 1977 elections held in Kashmir (widely seen as the freest and fairest in the state), one factor which stood out was the extremely low level of support for Muslim or Hindu religious parties. The Jamaat-i-Islami (JI), which advocated joining Pakistan, managed to win only one seat. Even in the 1983 state elections, the Hindu nationalist Jana Sangh was wiped out in Jammu and the JI, which had contested 25 seats, sufferred total defeat in the Valley.[15]

The nature of the original militancy itself involved little adherence to politicized Islam. The Jammu and Kashmir Liberation Front (JKLF)

[11] Sten Widmalm, "The Kashmir Conflict," *SIPRI Yearbook 1999* (Oxford: Oxford University Press, 1999), p. 35.
[12] "MORI Publishes Results of Major New Survey," May 31, 2002. Available at www.mori.com. The survey used random sampling to interview 850 respondents from 22 localities of Jammu, 20 in Srinagar and 6 in Leh, as well as three villages around Jammu and four villages around Srinagar. Quotas were set by gender, religion and locality, according to the known population profile of the region.
[13] *The Indian Express*, September 27, 2002.
[14] *The Indian Express*, May 23, 2002.
[15] M. J. Akbar, *Kashmir: Behind the Vale* (New Delhi: Lotus Collection of Roli Books, 2002), pp. 201–203.

which was at the forefront and commanded the widest support initially, was self-consciously secular. Even after nearly 15 years and the rising tide of religious extremism in the region, the JKLF remains committed to secularism as a guiding principle. The most well known separatist leaders themselves rarely make their claims based on religious grounds. A case in point is the Mirwaiz Umar Farooq, head of the Jamia Masjid, the most important mosque in Srinagar, and key leader in the APHC. Indeed, if religion was the singular force, it should logically follow that the vast majority of Kashmiri Muslims would favor joining Pakistan. However, apart from the JI and the Hizb ul-Mujahideen, it is far from clear that uniting with Pakistan is an attractive choice for the Kashmiri Muslims. The dominant choice of many appears to be, loosely, the popular term "azaadi," which could stop well short of independence.[16] But then again on religious grounds, we would have to explain why 145 million Muslims in the rest of India show almost no support for the insurgency that affects four million Kashmiris.

Jean Dreze, a highly respected Indian academic, wrote about the surprising absence of communal sentiment among the Muslims he interviewed during his visit to the Kashmir Valley in 2000. When Dreze enquired whether the ongoing conflict was in part a Hindu–Muslim conflict, "people emphatically said 'no.' Some respondents even had difficulty understanding the question: it simply had not occurred to them to think in those terms."[17] A comprehensive study identifying all communal riots that have taken place in India since 1947 did not find a single outbreak in Jammu and Kashmir.[18] In the Kargil district of Ladakh, which has a 90 percent Shia Muslim population and 5 percent each of Buddhists and Sunni Muslims, there is no open support for the insurgents. (Interestingly, the American attack on Iraq led to the coalescence of groups in Kashmir during 2003 and 2004 around the theme that Muslims and Islam are being targeted by the US, leading to more pointedly religiously motivated demonstrations and protests.)

Over time, religious factors have indeed become more prominent in Kashmir's militancy, but the forces behind this development have less to do with internal religious preferences. The most polarizing religious tendencies have been brought into the conflict by groups who in local parlance are called "jihadi" forces, largely outside of Kashmir. This external penetration occurred partly in conjunction with changing internal perceptions regarding the fate of India's secularism. The upshot

---

[16] Azaadi means different things to different people, from freedom or autonomy to independence. It is hard to find an English equivalent.

[17] Jean Dreze, "Manufacturing Ethnic Conflict," *The Hindu*, March 29, 2000.

[18] B. Rajeshwari, *Communal Riots in India: A Chronology (1947–2003)*, IPCS Research Papers, New Delhi: Institute of Peace and Conflict Studies, February 2004.

was a discernible drift in identity conceptions towards a more radical religious version, though, as the foregoing discussion shows, it has not become deep-seated or dangerously exclusivist among most Kashmiris.

Domestic politics and secularism in India

In contrast to the widely praised election of 1977 in Kashmir, the elections a decade later in 1987 were a critical trigger for Kashmiri militancy. By then, a number of political parties had joined together to create the Muslim United Front (MUF) to contest elections. One of its major goals was to achieve pan-Islamic unity, demonstrating the influence of religious sentiment for the first time.

Many observers cite the rigging and manipulation of the 1987 election by the Congress Party as setting off the revolt by disillusioned Kashmiris.[19] That behaviour by the Congress Party was, in turn, indicative of the party's national decline and the so-called "de-institutionalization" of the Congress from its unrivalled political position at independence. This chain of events at first glance fits in well with the argument that locates the source of militancy in the lack of political access and democratic space that was characteristic of Kashmir during the mid to late-1980s. But, as noted, the ruling Congress Party's misuse of powers such as Article 356 (enabling the President to assume executive powers in a state) to dismiss elected state governments was not confined to Kashmir. The Congress Party's fortunes were in decline in many other parts of India, thanks in large part to the increase of regionally based parties, but something else was clearly at work in the case of Kashmir.

Any explanation that takes into account this difference needs to go beyond just institutional factors. I suggest that the political culture surrounding these institutions is of critical importance; in this case, the key mediating factor was the level of secularism, which by 1989 had reached an all time low in the eyes of many Kashmiri Muslims. This leads us to the book's main concern with how competing identities gained or lost ground.

Symbolism of the Congress–National Conference Alliance

The weakening of the Congress, along with the loss of prestige for the National Conference (the strongest regional party of Kashmir), had

---

[19] The MUF won only four seats in the 1987 elections, but its real strength was not clear given the electoral malfeasance which resulted in the Congress Party and the National Conference taking the rest. For a journalistic account of the increasing alienation of Kashmiri Muslims by a close observer, see Tavleen Singh, *Kashmir: A Tragedy of Errors* (New Delhi: Viking, 1995).

particularly severe repercussions on Kashmir going beyond institutionalism or democratic concerns: for historical reasons, the fate of these two parties was inextricably linked with popular perceptions of the level of secularism. Under Sheikh Abdullah (the so-called "Lion of Kashmir"), the National Conference had set a clear secular tone from the beginning. When Sheikh Abdullah opened his anti-colonial National Conference party to Hindus in the late 1930s, a section split to form the Muslim Conference, which went on to ally with the Muslim League in favor of creating Pakistan. The Sheikh however maintained his strong secular commitment, and managed to remain the most popular Kashmiri leader until his death in 1982. He ruled Kashmir from 1947 to 1953 and again from 1975 until 1982.

Sheikh Abdullah commanded a huge following although pro-Pakistan forces gained ground during the period he was in prison. (He was jailed on numerous occasions totaling nearly a decade, initially under Maharajah Hari Singh.) His original agreement with the Indian government in 1953 had included substantial autonomy for Kashmir, which was then chipped away. His attempts to safeguard Kashmir's position and seeming equivocation on the definition of autonomy led some hardliners to raise suspicions about the Sheikh's commitment to Indian territorial integrity, hemming in the options vis-à-vis Kashmir for his close friend and supporter, Prime Minister Jawaharlal Nehru. Nehru placed huge importance on the Sheikh, seeing him as almost single-handedly managing to steer political activism in Kashmir "out of the narrow waters of communalism into the broad sea of nationalism."[20] Not surprisingly, Abdullah had many detractors on the Pakistani side who believed he was either too independent or too pro-India.[21]

The National Conference began slipping in popularity soon after Sheikh Abdullah's death and his son Farooq Abdullah's succession. The erosion of support for the Conference had reached a critical point when Farooq Abdullah arrived at an agreement with Rajiv Gandhi in 1986 over an election alliance which was viewed as an opportunistic sell-out by most Kashmiris and from which Farooq Abdullah never quite recovered.[22] The election of 1987 which saw the rout of the MUF and

---

[20] Nehru, *The Unity of India*, p. 229.

[21] An excellent analysis of Sheikh Abdullah's strong secularism as well as his changing personal and political relationship to the Indian establishment is given by the historian Ramachandra Guha, "Opening a Window in Kashmir," *World Policy Journal*, 21.3 (Fall 2004).

[22] The manner in which the National Conference (NC) fell out of favor in Kashmir is well known – but a brief synopsis may be given. Until 1983, the Congress did not play an independent political role as a party in Kashmir, and had invariably ceded ground to the NC. The victory of the NC with a two-thirds majority in 1983 was however viewed as a threat by the Congress Party. Thereafter followed a period of opportunism and corrupt practices: in 1984, Farooq Abdullah's government was dismissed by the center, which

the re-instatement of the National Conference, was a turning point. Both Farooq Abdullah and Rajiv Gandhi realized in hindsight that their electoral alliance and coalition government were critical mistakes that partly led to the insurgency.[23] The Rajiv–Farooq agreement had little to do with religion or Hindu–Muslim factors, and everything to do with a central government that had been resisting regional assertions nationwide since 1980 under Indira Gandhi.[24] But the Congress Party's search for power by irregular methods no doubt signaled a broader development for dissatisfied Kashmiri Muslims – that is, the decline of the Nehruvian model, the political embodiment of India's secularism at the national level.

Challenges to Nehru's secular model

Secularism was one pillar of Jawaharlal Nehru's carefully crafted post-independence project for India comprising: democracy, secularism, "socialist" economics and non-alignment. By the early 1980s, the intellectual edifice that Nehru established was coming under pressure, and with it came the "unstable secularism" that characterized South Asia (discussed in Chapter Two).[25] The Bharatiya Janata Party (BJP), created in 1980, became a political instrument of Hindu nationalism, one that became more successful than its predecessors.[26] The BJP was formed following the 1979 expulsion of several leaders from the erstwhile Janata Party, which was an amalgam of anti-Congress groups brought together by common outrage at the imposition of the Emergency by Indira Gandhi. Those expelled included Atal Bihari Vajpayee and L. K. Advani (future prime minister and deputy prime minister). Their expulsion came after

---

actually improved his standing among Kashmiris; but in an about turn, the Congress engineered an electoral alliance with the NC. The credibility problem lay in the manner in which the NC had succumbed to Prime Minister Indira Gandhi's pressure to share a greater portion of political power in Kashmir with the Congress. Although her Kashmir politics followed a pattern in other states including Andhra Pradesh and Karnataka, Indira Gandhi clearly misread political developments in Kashmir.

[23] Akbar, *Kashmir: Behind the Vale*, pp. 212–213.

[24] Wajahat Habibullah, who worked closely with Rajiv Gandhi, offers a different rationale for the electoral alliance, which he too agrees was a mistake in hindsight. According to Habibullah, the alliance was made to stem what was viewed as rising communal tension and the emergence of new religiously oriented parties like the Muslim United Front, which would have provided Pakistan with more of an entrée. The NC–Congress coalition was thus an attempt to bring the two secular parties closer together. In retrospect, he believes the concern was overblown. Wajahat Habibullah, Lecture to the US Institute of Peace, Washington, DC, April 27, 2004.

[25] Khilnani, *The Idea of India*, p. 179 addresses the decline of Nehruvian thought.

[26] For a detailed work on the rise of Hindu nationalism, see Partha S. Ghosh, *BJP and the Evolution of Hindu Nationalism: From Periphery to Center* (New Delhi: Manohar Publishers, 1999).

they refused to sever ties with the Rashtriya Swayamsevak Sangh (RSS), the right-wing cultural bulwark of Hindu nationalism, or Hindutva. (The BJP is often viewed as the political arm of the RSS.) L. K. Advani who stood as the symbolic spearhead for this change appeared to have tapped into latent Hindu communalism to challenge the secular model.

The steep decline of the National Conference's credibility during this period affected its ability to promote the secular ideology as well. As the leading edge of secularism in the Kashmir context, this was seriously damaging in terms of the broader Kashmiri political culture. Likewise, the Congress Party's blatant powerplay in Kashmir over time diminished its previous standing as the champion of India's secularism. The two parties that could have served as the most convincing representatives of political secularism lost their legitimacy in the same period, vacating valuable space for alternative orientations to take hold. This was particularly crippling because on the national scene the Congress Party had become identified closely with the Indian state itself. Thus the de-legitimization of the Congress affected the way Kashmiris viewed the Indian state; the crucial difference between other states and Kashmir was that here it was occurring in tandem with the decline of its most important mainstream regional secular party. Elsewhere, the situation was just the opposite: mainstream regional parties were on the rise. Thus, the perceived level of political secularism, together with the institutional decay of the Congress, brought about the Kashmiri alienation that occurred in the late 1980s.[27] But even so, within this context, Kashmiri opinion was hardly uniform or radical.

Political fragmentation in Kashmir and shifting identities

The opinion of Kashmiri Muslims reflects a broad spectrum ranging from the National Conference and the People's Democratic Party, who operate as part of the Indian mainstream political system, to those espousing the violent overthrow of Indian rule. One dominant feature of the widening political spectrum has been the radicalization of identity constructions, to the point of introducing even religiously driven suicide bombing, a previously unheard-of practice in Kashmir, which has no tradition of martyrdom.

The APHC, itself a conglomerate of some 30 political, social and religious organizations, was formed in 1993 as a political front to further

---

[27] For an unconvincing argument that ties the Kashmir insurgency to Hindu majoritarian communalism, see Ayesha Jalal, *Democracy and Authoritarianism*, p. 179. According to Jalal, "Majoritarian communalism, after all, has been since the early 1980s New Delhi's favorite ideological weapon against movements of regional dissidence." Evidence from Kashmir or other Indian states does not support such a conclusion.

the cause of Kashmiri separatism, and remains dominant. It acts as a central body for the Kashmir militancy and for coordinating approaches to the Indian government and the outside world, especially Pakistan. The Hurriyat's Constitution ostensibly commits the organization to "peaceful struggle" and "negotiated settlement,"[28] but the relationship between members of the APHC and various armed militant groups remains in contention.

The APHC has accommodated a number of viewpoints but, since 2000, there have been fissures. It finally split into two factions in 2004 with the creation of Tehrek-e-Hurriyat-e-Kashmir (Movement for the Freedom of Kashmir). The key difference is between those who are pro-Pakistan and pro-jihad, and others who are more amenable to a dialogue with the Indian government. On paper, their ultimate objective of achieving the "aspirations of the Kashmiri peoples" remain identical. There are no all-Kashmir political groups that successfully bring together the interests of the diverse population.[29]

It is difficult to gauge the extent of popular support for the APHC as it has never contested an election. The APHC has not taken an organizational stand on whether it prefers accession to Pakistan, independence or greater autonomy, and has kept its policy ambiguous in this regard. Some members have indicated their position; the JKLF is for independence, whereas the JI seems to prefer joining Pakistan.

The JKLF, which spearheaded the insurgency, began as an armed extremist group with a secular ideology, but in 1994, its leader Yasin Malik renounced violence as a tool to achieving Kashmiri independence. The Hizb ul-Mujahideen (Hizb) is the largest of the armed militant groups operating in Kashmir, and has been the most effective in the past. Its cadre is generally viewed as comprising mostly indigenous recruits compared to other violent insurgent outfits in Kashmir. The Hizb is often described as the military wing of the JI (Kashmir) although there has been friction in their relationship from time to time. By the time the APHC was established in 1993, the Hizb had reached the status of being the dominant armed group. Once the JKLF gave up violence as a method of struggle, the center of control of the armed movement shifted to the Hizb and, more ominously, to non-indigenous actors.

---

[28] *The Indian Express*, May 29, 2002.
[29] Navnita Chadha Behera, "Kashmir: Redefining the US Role," The Brookings Institution Policy Brief No. 110, (Washington, DC: The Brookings Institution, November 2002), p. 7. Kashmiri Pandits have criticized the Indian government for excluding them from talks related to Kashmir. See for example, *The Hindu*, September 12, 2004.

External intrusions

From 1989 to 2000, the conflict between the Indian government and the militants had by and large reached a political stalemate, although the nature of the movement itself underwent fairly dramatic changes in the early 1990s. Most important of these changes was the influx of foreigners, especially hardened mujahideen from the Afghan war. The JI of Pakistan, through its close backing of the Hizb ul-Mujahideen, and others played a key role in this shift. These new groups included the Pakistan-based Jaish-e-Mohammed (JeM), Lashkar-e-Toiba (LeT) and Harakat-ul-Ansar (renamed Harakat ul-Mujahideen, HuM) – terrorist outfits that introduced more deadly strategies.[30]

The role of the Pakistani military, particularly its intelligence arm, the Inter-Services Intelligence (ISI) and its "Kashmir cell," in promoting and sustaining the Kashmir insurgency is now a fairly familiar story, and need not be repeated in detail here.[31] According to independent experts, Kashmiri insurgent groups had been eclipsed by Pakistan-based Pakistani and other foreign militants by the mid-1990s.[32] The extent of Pakistan's involvement in the Kashmir insurgency however came out convincingly only after the intense scrutiny the country came under from the US in the aftermath of September 11, and public disclosures.[33]

Before that, numerous observers had documented evidence of ongoing Pakistani assistance, but there was no official corroboration by western governments. For example, media reports in early 2001 noted that four out of the five main militant groups active in Kashmir were based in Pakistan, with the deep involvement of the Pakistani military.[34] The most widely recognized organization that openly supports militancy is the United Jihad Council (UJC), a conglomerate of nearly 20 jihadi groups located in

---

[30] The LeT in particular has been identified with suicide attacks. Husain Haqqani, *Pakistan*, p. 299.

[31] For a good account of the growing foreign involvement, see Jonah Blank, "Kashmir: Fundamentalism Takes Root," *Foreign Affairs*, 78.6 (November/December 1999). See also Saifuddin Soz, "Kashmiriyat versus Militancy," *Economic Times*, February 2, 1995. For a cataloguing of militant groups involved in the Kashmir conflict by the Institute for Defence Studies and Analyses in New Delhi, see K. Santhanam, Sreedhar, Sudhir Saxena and Manish, *Jihadis in Jammu and Kashmir: A Portrait Gallery* (New Delhi: Sage Publications, 2003). Another excellent related work is Rashid, *Taliban*.

[32] See for example, Jessica Stern, "Pakistan's Jihad Culture," *Foreign Affairs*, 79.6 (November/December 2000); and Blank, "Kashmir."

[33] See for example, David Sanger and Michael Wines, "Bush Joins Putin in Urging Pakistan to Use Restraint," *New York Times*, May 26, 2002.

[34] For a discussion of the details pertaining to the Pakistani military's involvement in cross-border terrorism based on on-the-ground reporting, see Ghulam Hasnain, "Inside Jihad," *Time Asia*, February 5, 2000.

Pakistan and headed by Syed Salahuddin of the Hizb ul-Mujahideen. The LeT, JeM and HuM are among those reported to be members of the UJC.[35] Western corroboration regarding Pakistan's activities took away any "plausible deniability" that the government might have hidden behind in the past. Post-9/11, there were even allegations of new Taliban and al-Qaeda training camps and relocation of existing training camps into Pakistani-controlled Kashmir.[36]

Apart from the military dimension, Pakistan's strategic policy is also linked to its identity construction which this book argues has shaped the direction of Kashmiri insurgency. The ensuing discussion shows how clashing geopolitical identities, on both sides of the border, help fill important gaps in the explanations considered at the beginning of the chapter.

Geopolitical identities

India's worldview

The Indian elite's geopolitical identity constructions have been shaped by a combination of factors: the need to cohere a highly diverse populace and a particular view of India's place in the world. The state has promoted India's identity as cosmopolitan and secular. The constitutions of every other state in South Asia except India have ended up incorporating religious identity into national identity in some form or other. Contrary to this trend, the Indian government has historically sidestepped the issue of religion in its definition of nationalism and, in the case of Jammu and Kashmir, it has avoided it even more studiously. This stands in some contrast to how the British laid the ground for observers to view Kashmir as a *communal* rather than a territorial dispute. The British version of the Kashmir conflict following the 1947 outbreak skipped over the legal issue of aggression by Pakistan on India's territory and focused instead on religious affinity for a resolution (and the US then more or less adopted this as its own policy).[37]

India's pro-Arab foreign policy in the Middle East, and Kashmir's historically low level of politicized Islam, have worked to keep the Kashmir conflict from catching the imagination of the Islamic world.

---

[35] International Crisis Group, "Kashmir: The View from Srinagar," ICG Asia Report No. 41, Islamabad/Brussels, November 21, 2002, p. 10.

[36] See for example, K. Alan Kronstadt, "Pakistan's Domestic Political Developments: Issues for Congress," Congressional Research Service Report for Congress, January 5, 2004. After 9/11, US officials indicated that there might have been infiltration by al-Qaeda into the "disputed Kashmir region." *New York Times*, June 13, 2002.

[37] Francine Frankel, "Kashmir: Onset of India's Suspicion of the United States," mimeo.

Indeed, Kashmir did not figure significantly in either neighboring Afghanistan or Bangladesh. Even when Afghan mujahideen began filtering into Kashmir, Afghanistan's involvement was not direct; it was second-hand via Pakistan. Apart from the brief Taliban period, Indo-Afghan ties have been excellent, in contrast to the strained relations between Afghanistan and Pakistan since 1947. Until the introduction of foreign fighters, Kashmir by and large stood isolated from the core influential Islamic countries such as Saudi Arabia and Iran.

So far, India has been viewed as a sympathetic state by Arabs and Iranians, a result of policies that Indian leaders of all persuasions have followed.[38] Even under the BJP-led regime of Atal Vajpayee, relations with Arab states were protected, despite the controversial cultivation of ties between India and Israel. For example, in January 2002, Salim ben Amer, an envoy of Libyan leader Muammar Qaddhafi, who met Prime Minister Vajpayee in New Delhi and later President Musharraf in Islamabad, concluded afterwards that "Nobody can set a time frame for resolution of the Kashmir problem which has been lingering on for over 50 years."[39] India's interests in the Middle East are also tempered by the presence of nearly 3.5 million Indians working there who could become vulnerable to unpopular regional politics.[40] Finally, domestic politics is a factor: although Muslim clerics took a lead in organizing large-scale protests against the Iraq war, Iraq is not seen as a "Muslim" issue in India but more as an example of America's aggressive unilateralism, with opposition from different quarters.

The release of three Indian hostages working for a Kuwaiti transport company in Iraq without harm after nearly six weeks of captivity in 2004 was viewed by many as vindicating India's close and extensive ties with the Islamic countries of the Middle East. It was also seen as reflecting India's ability to set itself apart from the US-led agenda in the Middle East in general, and Iraq in particular, despite India's increasing ties with the US on regional counter-terrorism. As a country with the second largest Muslim population in the world, Indian policymakers seem to be keeping this factor in mind when crafting global policies against radical Islamist groups. (It may be noted that India has the largest number of Shiites after Iran.) During the Indian hostage crisis, leaders of India's Shia community strongly condemned the abduction as an act of "psychological terror."[41] Shia community leaders in India used their contacts with Shia clerics in

---

[38] For a more extended treatment, see Ollapally, *US–India Relations*, pp. 4–6.
[39] Javed Naqvi, "Losing Kashmir Will Break Up India: Advani," *Dawn*, January 25, 2002.
[40] Siddharth Srivastava, "Now Indians Cry Foul Over Iraq," *Asia Times Online*, May 8, 2004.
[41] *The Telegraph*, July 23, 2004.

Iran and asked them to use their moral authority for the release of the Indian workers.

The Organization of Islamic Conference (OIC) has at times criticized India's human rights record in Kashmir and at other times simply called on India and Pakistan to settle the dispute through negotiations, prompting the United Jihad Council in Muzaffarabad at different points to call on the OIC "to move beyond symbolic gestures and routine resolutions," on Kashmir.[42] In 1994, Pakistan succeeded in getting the OIC to establish a Kashmir Contact Group, and the APHC has observer status within the OIC.[43] Ten years later, however, at the June 2004 foreign ministers' meeting in Istanbul, some members of the OIC were apparently quietly trying to convince Pakistan to soften its customary anti-India resolutions about Kashmir, with the representatives of Algeria, Saudi Arabia and Sudan among others arguing that the OIC should not complicate ongoing peace talks between India and Pakistan by taking an aggressive stand on Kashmir.[44] Indeed, Saudi Arabia went to surprising lengths not to appear to be narrowly supporting Indian Muslims, even after the communal carnage in Gujarat in March 2002 in which nearly 2,000 Muslims were massacred. During a visit to its traditional ally Pakistan in October 2003, the Saudi foreign minister Prince Saud al-Faisal refused to be drawn into an attack on India over Gujarat. In the presence of his Pakistani counterpart Prince Faisal said, "They [Indian Muslims] are people with substance. They are people with courage to stand for their interests by themselves and not to wait for the help of others. I would hate to think of the Muslims in India as a minority, coming from a country that has less Muslims than India. So these Muslims are not tattered in the wind."[45]

Kashmir and the Indo-Pakistan geopolitical identity struggle

Pakistan's view of Kashmir has been dominated by a religiously informed geopolitical identity – one that stands in sharp contrast to India's, and is distinguished even from Kashmiri Muslim perceptions. The identity that serves as the "cement" for a fractured Pakistani polity may be viewed as highly geopolitical in character, with India as the logical "other." Both the Indian and Pakistani leaderships agree on one point however: opposition to full independence for Kashmir. An independent Kashmir is viewed as affecting the geopolitical interests and identity of both states negatively.

---

[42] *Daily Times*, June 26, 2004.
[43] *Milli Gazette*, 3.5, March 1–15, 2002.
[44] C. Raja Mohan, "The Armitage Mission," *The Hindu*, July 5, 2004.
[45] Pranay Sharma, "Saudi Snub to Pakistan on Gujarat," *The Telegraph*, October 21, 2003.

It is generally believed that the Hizb was launched with the aid of Pakistan in 1990; Pakistan's main objective in doing so was to counter the JKLF which was calling for independence and had a secular platform. The JI of Kashmir already had a wide following, allowing the Hizb to draw a large number of its militants from the JI itself and, across the border, the JI of Pakistan was an important partner for the military, enjoying good ties with civilian leaders from the Pakistan Muslim League (PML). The Hizb ul-Mujahideen advocated Kashmir's merger with Pakistan and the Islamicization of Kashmir. Much as in Afghanistan, the creation of a more "Islamist" group beholden to the Pakistan military was far more useful for foreign policy purposes vis-à-vis India than the JKLF that Pakistan could not control. Nonetheless, with its substantial Kashmiri cadres and local connections, even the Hizb's orientations have at times diverged from the objectives of its patrons. For example, several senior Valley-based Hizb commanders were dismissed by the Pakistan-based leadership in 2002 when they showed signs of softening their armed strategy.[46]

Indian dilemmas   For India, Kashmir's location on its periphery has been an important consideration in its geopolitical calculations (as with Punjab and the Northeast). Its strategic position, bordering China on the north and northeast (Tibet), Afghanistan on the northwest and Pakistan in the west has guaranteed the attention of India's security managers, even under the best of circumstances. The introduction of polarizing religious identities as a geopolitical instrument by Pakistan via a "proxy war" makes it particularly difficult for the Indian state to disentangle geopolitical threats and vulnerabilities from religious identity, much as it might wish to. Kashmir has come physically and metaphorically to represent India's "secular" state model; partly for this very reason, the Pakistan state has been wedded to challenging India in Kashmir. Kashmir also provided the Pakistani military a "low cost" strategy of bleeding its much larger neighbor and hence keeping alive the notion of political parity. It is not surprising that the Kashmir conflict became redirected and redefined well beyond an uprising against India's central government.

The Indian government adopted a two-pronged strategy in Kashmir which it persisted with until 2002 with little success: to use the Indian army in massive numbers to defeat the insurgency militarily; and, politically, to rely on the Abdullah family and the National Conference in Jammu and

---

[46] Abdul Majid Dar, former chief of the Hizb, who opposed tactics like suicide attacks used by other groups, was killed under mysterious circumstances in March 2003. For a description of the falling out between local and Pakistan-based Hizb leaders, see *Daily Times*, March 24, 2003.

Kashmir as alternative leadership for Muslim and non-Muslim Kashmiris. The government appeared caught off-guard and unprepared for the vehemence of the insurgency, and its initial reaction was the imposition of governor's rule under Malhotra Jagmohan, whose heavy-handed counter-insurgency measures earned him few friends among the population. In addition to the Indian army and Border Security Forces (BSF), "special forces" were set up over time using so-called "surrendered militants" who were more familiar with the territory. The government has been criticized by international and local human rights organizations for the repressive measures its military and paramilitary forces have engaged in to bring the insurgency under control. Since the mid-1990s, human rights organizations have also taken militant organizations to task for their brutality. In a clear break with the past, however, by 2000 Indian government leaders at the highest level had begun overtures to the separatists which culminated in direct talks with the separatist APHC in 2003.

The government's new strategy cannot be understood without taking into account both the internal and external environment. Since independence, Indian elites have assumed a much larger global role for India than its actual material capabilities might suggest. More than ten years after economic liberalization in 1991, and with growth rates reaching impressive levels of 7–8 percent, India was clearly beginning to realize long-held aspirations of being recognized as a major power. For key sections of the Indian leadership, particularly the nationalist BJP that was at the helm of the National Democratic Alliance (NDA) coalition, the nuclear tests of May 1998 underlined this status in politico-military terms. In order for India to play this emerging global role fully, however, the Kashmir "millstone" needed to be cast off. At the same time, the post-9/11 environment forced sections of the separatists to be more forthcoming on negotiations. The changing geopolitical realities of the region no doubt influenced the Hurriyat, particularly the greater scrutiny that Pakistan came under for its support for jihadi groups, and the lower tolerance of the US for terrorist violence.

India's flexible discourse   The Indian state's overtures to the Kashmiri separatists was orchestrated in such a way that it protected its strategic and identity needs. The discourse on negotiation was ambiguous and flexible enough to accommodate the concerns of the militants, without undermining the state's sovereignty and security interests. The term "azadi" came to be interpreted in numerous ways, from full independence to autonomy. Well-known Indian jurist Ram Jethmalani of the non-governmental Kashmir Committee, which was set up with the tacit blessing of the government to probe the militants' interest in negotiations, has described how "azadi" was an especially useful concept in initial interactions with Kashmiri militants highly suspicious of his Committee.[47] Likewise, the introduction of "insaniyat" or a "humanitarian" framework by Prime Minister Vajpayee during his visit to Srinagar for unconditional talks (the first Prime Minister to address a public meeting in the city in 15 years since Rajiv Gandhi) may be viewed as an attempt to break the logjam of official language. ("Unconditional" itself was left undefined.) This framework avoided previous statist language wrapped around the Indian Constitution, or the militant's most uncompromising understanding of azadi. The central government, along with the newly elected People's Democratic Party at the state level (which had finally toppled the National Conference in 2002), also tried to project an image of normality in Kashmir as a counter to the dominant conflict-ridden image, and chose to hold a series of all-India meetings, such as the Inter-State Council, in the state.[48]

The introduction of a bus route across the Line of Control between Srinagar and Muzaffarabad in 2005 was a symptom of India and Pakistan trying to find a way of preserving their geopolitical identities. Pakistan had been opposed to Kashmiris on both sides traveling on passports with visas (as India preferred) with the objection that it would amount to a recognition of the Line of Control as the international border. Instead, it wanted them to go across the LOC on the basis of documents issued by local authorities, which India resisted.[49] Kashmiris on both sides had been pressing for a direct bus service, and both India and Pakistan had indicated their willingness, but it took three years of diplomatic wrangling to create a unique form of travel documentation that would neither challenge nor erode the sovereignty of the two countries. Their unique capacity to innovate demonstrates once more the critical interpretive power of the state.

Pakistan's predicament   From Pakistan's perspective, there has been a continuing dilemma, not just about India but about Kashmiri Muslims and their tendency towards a secularized identity. Even in the part of Kashmir that it administers, the Pakistani state's own identity needs have pressed the Kashmiris towards a more "official" Islam in the legal, educational and social arenas. As Leo Rose puts it, "The general tendency in Azad Kashmir had been to assume that all of its citizens were good Muslims and the government did not have to go about forcing the people to be what they already are. But the collapse of the 'Two Nation' theory in the context of the Bangladesh rebellion and the Indo-Pakistan

---

[47] Discussion with Ram Jethmalani, Center for Strategic and International Studies, Washington, DC, November 8, 2002.

[48] The symbolism was noted by many commentators. See for example, Priya Sahgal, "Hard Selling a Hotspot," *India Today*, September 15, 2003, pp.10–11.

[49] *The Hindu*, October 26, 2004.

War of 1971, led to some changes on this subject, in Azad Kashmir as in Pakistan."[50]

Pakistan's predicament is best illustrated by its relationship with the National Conference from the beginning. Prior to British withdrawal, the heterogeneous Kashmir was ruled by the Hindu Dogra Maharaja Hari Singh, who at partition was given the choice of joining either India or Pakistan. As late as October 1947 (two months after partition), the Maharaja had still not decided. The political leadership in Delhi began to see Sheikh Abdullah, the head of the regional party Kashmir National Conference, and a fierce opponent of Hari Singh, as the preferred partner.[51] The Hindu-dominated Indian leadership had little problem in identifying with Sheikh Abdullah against the Maharaja – the state's interest lay with him irrespective of religion. Abdullah's interest also leaned towards India; his letters of 1947–1948 indicate that he believed that Kashmir's "distinctiveness" could be best preserved within a plural India.[52] During a much-vaunted visit to Pakistan in May 1964, commentary by the pro-establishment newspaper *Dawn* was revealing: "especially his [Abdullah's] references to India's so-called secularism, have caused a certain amount of disappointment among the public in general and the intelligentsia in particular." The newspaper also found fault with Abdullah for having "taken up the role of an apostle of peace and friendship between Pakistan and India, rather than that of the leader of Kashmir, whose prime objective should be to seek their freedom from Indian bondage."[53]

This underlying Pakistani apprehension has remained despite the militancy. Various Pakistani observers have even commented on this situation. For example, a former Pakistani policymaker notes that within two years of the insurgency, "the ISI concluded that it could not leave the insurgency to the Kashmiris only."[54] Pakistani military officers apparently considered indigenous Kashmiri commanders based in Kashmir less reliable than foreign jihadis and Pakistan fighters. As another Pakistani observer concluded, "In a replay of Afghanistan – the ISI playing favorites and exerting control over the Afghan resistance – the Kashmir resistance found itself hijacked by Pakistan-based elements, a nationalist movement thus transformed into an enterprise looking suspiciously as if sponsored by

---

[50] He goes on describe the changes introduced. See Rose, "The Politics of Azad Kashmir," pp. 248–249.
[51] Widmalm, "The Kashmir Conflict," p. 35.
[52] This is the opinion of Wajahat Habibullah after conducting research on the Sheikh's correspondence. Wajahat Habibullah, Lecture to the US Institute of Peace, Washington, DC, April 27, 2004.
[53] Quoted in Guha, "Opening a Window in Kashmir," p.90.
[54] Haqqani, *Pakistan*, p. 287.

Islamabad."[55] By the early 1990s, important Pakistani commentators were noting the "transformation" of the movement with its "symbolism changing from the secularism of Amanullah Khan's JKLF to the Islamic slogan of the newer, younger militants," and the increasing "Islamic component" versus the JKLF which "traditionally espoused a secular line seeking an independent Kashmir."[56]

Pakistan's proxy war   Foreign militants have since been reshaping Kashmir's drive for greater independence into an Islamist proxy war for Pakistan. One of the shared characteristics of foreign-based groups, as distinct from more indigenous Kashmiri outfits, is their pan-Islamist agenda. Nearly all accounts place the responsibility for the expulsion of native Hindu Pandits from the Kashmir Valley and their targeting by insurgents with radical Islamist groups backed by the ISI.[57] The targeted killings of Sikh and Hindu civilians in Kashmir over time has been generally attributed by the Indian police and army to foreign-based terrorist organizations. Organizations seen as indigenous Kashmiri have rarely claimed responsibility.

Ten years after the insurgency began, the Lashkar-e-Toiba and Harakat ul-Ansar were being singled out as culprits along with, to a much lesser extent, the Hizb ul-Mujahideen.[58] Tellingly, in the MORI poll of April 2002, two-thirds of people in Jammu and Kashmir were of the view that Pakistan's involvement in the region over the preceding ten years had been negative. Only 15 percent believed that it had been good for the region.[59] All this suggests that the violent subculture that the Pakistan military propagated appears to have taken only limited root among Kashmiris themselves.

Since 2001, Pakistan has seen its geopolitical interests diverge regionally and globally. The so-called "core issue" of Kashmir has driven Pakistan foreign policy towards India for decades, with the jihadi groups being the government's, especially the military's, instrument for this policy. Although Pakistan has come under international pressure over al-Qaeda

---

[55] Ayaz Amir, "The Grass and the Elephants: Why Kashmiris are Wary of the Indo-Pak Peace Process," *The Asian Age*, October 11, 2004.

[56] Quoted in A. G. Noorani, "Contours of the Militancy," *Frontline*, 17.20, September 30–October 13, 2000, p. 9.

[57] Haqqani, *Pakistan*, p. 386. The ISI reportedly shifted its support away from Hizb ul-Mujahideen after it refused to go along with some of the ISI's more radical plans such as targeting non-Muslim Kashmiris.

[58] See US Department of State, *Annual Report on International Religious Freedom for 1999: India*, Bureau for Democracy, Human Rights and Labor, Washington DC, September 9, 1999.

[59] "MORI Publishes Results of Major New Survey," May 31, 2002. Available at www.mori.com.

and the Taliban, regional dynamics has led Pakistan to try and retain influence over jihadi groups for its Kashmir policy.

In this connection, as we saw in Chapter Four, Musharraf has been walking a fine line between so-called foreign and domestic extremist groups to reconcile these opposing pressures. As the Indian government opened up a dialogue with sections of the militant movement in 2000, Pakistan was faced with the prospect of being overtaken by events. Pakistan's patronage of separatist groups has continued and has impacted the way that the Indian government's negotiations with the Kashmiri separatists have fared. The differing tendencies in the militancy, which has left it vulnerable to outside influence, have affected the twists and turns of the negotiations and are examined in the next section.

Dialogue with New Delhi

Within five years of its formation, signs of divergence within the APHC became evident when the leader of JI Kashmir, Ghulam Mohammad Bhat, indicated his party's intention to sever all links with armed groups, in particular, the Hizb ul-Mujahideen. The Jamaat chief cited the Hurriyat's constitution (which had not then been publicly released) as committed to working for the spread of Islam through peaceful means.[60] Although links were not in fact severed, two years later in July 2000, in a move that signalled a possible shift in the strategy of the Kashmiri insurgents for the first time, the Hizb ul-Mujahideen itself declared a three-month ceasefire and hinted at possible talks with the government. The Indian government had been suggesting the possibility of talking with Kashmiri militants earlier in the year when home minister L. K. Advani announced that he was working "to create a climate in which if any section of the Kashmiri people wishes to discuss issues with the Government of India, discussions can take place."[61]

The Vajpayee government responded to the Hizb by suspending all offensive military action for the first time since the insurgency had broken out. But the militants' ceasefire proved short-lived, partly due to differing expectations about the Indian government's flexibility regarding pre-conditions for the talks, the Hizb ul-Mujahideen's stand on Pakistan's status in the talks and, ultimately, pressure from its Pakistan-based leadership. However, in November 2000, Prime Minister Vajpayee did announce

---

[60] Praveen Swami, "A Break with the Past," *Frontline*, 15.5, December 5–18, 1998. As early as the mid-1990s, some Indian analysts were urging the government to negotiate with the militants given the increasing militarization of positions in the Valley. See for example, Prem Shankar Jha, "Kashmir: A Strategy for Peace," *Indian Express*, July 23, 1994.

[61] Praveen Swami, "Strategic Shift?" *Frontline*, 14.11, May 27–June 9, 2000.

unilaterally that security forces would suspend combat operations against militants in Jammu and Kashmir during the Islamic holy month of Ramadan. The government then extended the ceasefire for six months until May 2001, despite provocations such as an attack on New Delhi's historic Red Fort on December 23, 2000 for which the Pakistan-based LeT claimed responsibility.[62] Although the dialogue with the armed Hizb failed to make any headway, the government used it as a further opening to make overtures to the Hurriyat.

Since 2000 there have been several attempts to keep the dialogue on track. Talks between the Kashmir Committee (established in August 2002 and comprising respected and distinguished non-governmental leaders) comprising and Hurriyat members were the first real sign that dialogue still remained an option. The Committee clearly had the backing of Prime Minister Vajpayee and Home Minister Advani who, since his elevation to deputy prime minister, had been known to have dropped his objection to a dialogue with separatist groups. Likewise, the chairman of the APHC, Abdul Gani Bhatt and Shabir Shah, one of the most prominent separatist figures outside the APHC, were favorably disposed to the Committee. The Kashmir Committee's biggest success was that it went some distance in fostering goodwill with the APHC membership. Jethmalani's descriptions of his initial meeting with leaders in the Valley revealed the importance of establishing personal rapport and credibility and the willingness to take risks to prove it.[63]

The Hizb ul-Mujahideen chief Syed Salahuddin, however, based in Pakistan, had strong criticism for the Kashmir Committee and asked the Hurriyat not to "beg" for talks with New Delhi. In response, the Hurriyat chairman told reporters in Srinagar that "We are in politics … politics consists of reconciliation, balancing and interpreting various opinions … We will consider the opinion of Syed Salahuddin but it is not imperative that we go by his opinion. We have our own independent stand in this regard."[64] The joint statement released by the Kashmir Committee and the APHC said, "The APHC and Kashmir Committee unanimously agreed that all concerned parties must rise above their traditional positions, abandon all

---

[62] cnn.com, "Timeline: Conflict Over Kashmir," www.cnn.com, May 24, 2002.

[63] According to Ram Jethmalani, chairman of the Kashmir Committee, during his first visit to the Valley to ascertain prevailing viewpoints, no group responded specifically to his request for a meeting. He then checked into a hotel in Srinagar and made it known that he was open to meeting anyone who wished to talk to him. He then described how, one by one, he was able to meet a variety of individuals with whom he ended up having discussions for several hours. Discussion with Ram Jethmalani, Center for Strategic and International Studies, Washington, DC, November 8, 2002.

[64] *The Times of India*, October 12, 2002.

past extreme stands, and show the necessary flexibility and realism to reach an acceptable, honorable and durable solution."[65]

The decision by Deputy Prime Minister Advani to engage in direct talks with the Hurriyat produced an unprecedented meeting between the center and a five-member Hurriyat delegation in January 2003. Advani's personal engagement in the dialogue instantly elevated the process and, given his hawkish reputation and close association with Hindutva groups, imbued it with the weight that the dialogue had thus far lacked.[66] Two rounds of talks were held, with a third slated to discuss so-called "substantive issues" that were left unspecified.[67]

The third meeting never occurred as a result of the stunning reversal of fortune suffered by the ruling NDA coalition in May 2004. This left the APHC moderates, who had been participants in the dialogue in a politically uncomfortable position, with little to show as accomplishments as the "substantive issues" had yet to be discussed, but open to continuing denunciation from the hardliners. The rift between the moderate and hardline factions had by then become irreparable, with Syed Shah Geelani suggesting an alternative party, Tehrek-e-Hurriyat-e-Kashmir. Geelani declared that the party would gain inspiration from Islam, rather than secularism, socialism or communism, and argued that his Hurriyat faction was the "real one."[68]

With the assumption of power by a new Congress-led coalition government in New Delhi in May 2004, the dialogue process slowed down considerably. The United Progressive Alliance (UPA) government under Prime Minister Manmohan Singh initially stated that talks with the Hurriyat would be held only within the Indian Constitution, a position that immediately alienated the group. The level at which the talks would take place was also an issue given that the Hurriyat's first two interactions were with the deputy prime minister, whereas the new government indicated its team would be led by the home minister.

The moderate wing of the Hurriyat was also hard pressed to make any moves towards dialogue in the face of sustained threats and assassination attempts, especially against Mirwaiz Umar Farooq, the caretaker chairman. The level of intimidation had reached nearly intolerable proportions by the time Geelani suggested a new party. The Mirwaiz's uncle had been assassinated; the Mirwaiz's own home had been attacked; and the historical Islamia School set up in 1898 by the Mirwaiz's great granduncle, attended

---

[65] *The Times of India*, September 9, 2002.
[66] Iftikhar Gilani, "Ceasefire, Detenues' Release Key Issues in APHC Talks," *Kashmir Times*, January 22, 2004.
[67] See outlookindia.com, February 25, 2004 and March 27, 2004.
[68] See *The Hindu*, September 16, 2003 and August 8, 2004.

by generations of the elite of the Valley, was razed to the ground, all within a matter of weeks.[69] Unable to persuade the hardliners to join forces with them, the moderate faction became reluctant to expose themselves to further danger in a dialogue that was unlikely to produce quick results. At this point, the Indian government tried to inject some fresh life into the process with the announcement in September 2004 that no conditions would be attached to talks with the separatist group.[70]

Interference from Pakistan

From 2000 onwards, the Indian government's modified strategy of engaging directly with the Kashmiri separatists was hamstrung by Pakistan's interference in the background. The collapse of the ceasefire between the government and Hizb in August 2000 may be partly blamed on Pakistan's opposition and the JI in Pakistan's attack on the ceasefire as a ploy to divide the movement. The question of why the Hizb offered the ceasefire in the first place begs an answer. It has been suggested that it had fallen out of favor with Pakistan's ISI, which now favoured groups such as the new JeM, LeT and HuM, because they were viewed as being more malleable and closer in ideology.[71] It was also likely that the agenda of the Hizb and the newer militant groups were not entirely aligned, given the latter groups' much broader pan-Islamic agenda.

The Pakistan factor was openly raised in the government–APHC talks when the APHC initially stressed the need to hold tripartitie talks between the governments of India, Pakistan and the APHC, as well as have a Hurriyat delegation visit Pakistan for consultations. Not surprisingly, India resisted such pressure, but it is instructive that the government went on to invite Pakistani chief Musharraf to enter into bilateral peace talks. But the Agra summit between Prime Minister Vajpayee and President Musharraf in July 2001 did little to move the two sides closer on the Kashmir issue, and by the end of December 2001, India and Pakistan were heading towards a possible military showdown after the terrorist attack on the Indian parliament, allegedly by the Lashkar-e-Toiba operating from Pakistan. Between December 2001 and January 2004, relations between the neighbors hung in the balance, with some relief only in late 2002 when India pulled back its

---

[69] *The Asian Age*, July 6, 2004 and July 15, 2004.
[70] *Dawn*, September 26, 2004.
[71] Suba Chandran, "Recent Developments in Kashmir – I: Hizbul Ceasefire – Why?" Article No. 401, Institute for Peace and Conflict Studies, August 7, 2000.

troops from the international border after a ten-month stand-off, and fully breaking the stalemate at the South Asian Association for Regional Cooperation (SAARC), meeting in Islamabad in January 2004.

The long-awaited elections in Kashmir took place in October 2002, during this so-called composite crisis between the two countries. Earlier that year on January 26, India's Republic Day, Prime Minister Vajpayee had declared that "There would be free and fair elections in Jammu and Kashmir this time," conceding in effect that the previous election was not. Pakistan staunchly opposed the participation of militants in these elections, either as individuals or as part of the Hurriyat. The Hurriyat Conference had its own reservations about giving legitimacy to the elections but Pakistan's opposition sealed the matter. The assassination of prominent APHC leader Abdul Ghani Lone, whose People's Conference had hinted at contesting or supporting outside candidates in the election, no doubt dissuaded any further participants.[72] The moderates thus found themselves in an increasingly precarious position, while Pakistan's position emboldened the hardliners.

Tilting the balance: moderate and extremist outcomes

The promise of democratic secularism

In Kashmir, religious and geopolitical identities since the late 1980s have both worked to produce greater polarization and increased levels of militarization. An outcome that would maintain Kashmir's traditional inclusive identity and move away from violent hostility is very much dependent on a change of attitude in Pakistan. The tilt towards religious extremism in Kashmir is all too closely linked to Pakistan's geopolitical identity needs. The extent to which Pakistan can play an intrusive role will be partly dependent on India's continued protection of open, secular politics, and the free play of democracy in Kashmir, reinvigorated by the elections in 2002.

Kashmir's (by all accounts free) state elections in October 2002, and India's national elections of May 2004 bringing to power a coalition led by

---

[72] In an emotionally charged statement, Lone's son Sajad accused the ISI and Syed Ali Shah Geelani of involvement in his father's assassination. See Lawrence Lifschultz, "A Voice From Kashmir," *Frontline* 19.16 (August 3–16, 2002). See also *The New York Times,* May 22, 2002; *Dawn,* May 22, 2002; R. Vinayak and L. Iyer, "Ballot vs. Bullet," *India Today International,* June 3, 2002; *The Hindu,* September 3, 2002. According to a report in the Frontline, "the Pakistan-based United Jihad Council has been handing out threats to centrists as well in the secessionist formation [APHC], because of what was seen as a lack of a serious anti-election campaign." Praveen Swami, "The Collapse of an Initiative," *Frontline,* 19.15 (July 20–August 2, 2002).

the historically more secular Congress Party, were two key developments which supported more open and non-violent structures. The new Kashmiri leadership had campaigned on the promise of unconditional talks with the separatists and offering a "healing touch."[73] The peace process with Pakistan restarted by the BJP in January 2004 was also taken forward by the UPA coalition. One notable step by Manmohan Singh's government has been the promotion of greater transparency in Kashmir, most spectacularly the visit of a delegation of 16 Pakistani journalists in October 2004 (the first time in 56 years) to Jammu and Kashmir.[74]

The Indian state's political secularism had become increasingly strained, particularly since the 1980s and then reaching its lowest point during the Gujarat riots of 2002. During the BJP period, the National Centre for Educational Research and Training (NCERT), the institution that draws up model textbooks for teaching history in schools, came under attack for allegedly trying to rewrite history to serve the ideology of the Hindu right wing. This would have seriously departed from the post-independence national agenda of teaching history in a way that would promote the principle of a composite Indian identity, a widely shared national imperative.[75] Since the BJP's defeat, one of the priorities of the new government has been to restore the more secular agenda in the critical sector of education. In this new round of textbook revision, greater attention seems to have been paid to the unstable nature of secularism in India and the need to introduce a strong "modernist" perspective, but in a more nuanced manner.[76] A key institution that has consistently upheld "political secularism" is the Indian Supreme Court.[77]

The ousting of the BJP and the rise of the Congress, left-wing and other secular parties has put the Hindutva groups on the defensive and in distinct disarray. In the post-election "chintan baithak" (brainstorming session), these groups tried to explain their defeat as resulting from a lack of "ideological orientation" signaling a return to a hardline agenda.[78] But this

---

[73] Mehbooba Mufti, vice president of the People's Democratic Party and daughter of the new chief minister was at the forefront of this new approach. *The Hindu*, September 2002.

[74] For reports of the visit, see *The Times of India*, October 17 and 20, 2004.

[75] For a discussion of the varying ideological strands in India's educational sector, see Meenakshi Gopinath, "Restoring the Canvas of Coexistence: A Role for Education in India," in Aall and Ollapally (eds.), *Perspectives*.

[76] Personal discussions with S. Settar, member of the Review Committee set up by the Human Resources Development Ministry to examine the NCERT textbooks. Bangalore, India, July 2005.

[77] For strong argument in favor of the role of the Court, see Editorial by one of India's leading news journals, *India Today*, July 21, 2003, p. 6; and Brenda Cossman and Ratna Kapur, *Secularism's Last Sigh? Hindutva and the (Mis)Rule of Law* (Delhi: Oxford University Press, 1999), pp. 76–77.

[78] Neena Vyas, "Advani in a Dilemma," *The Hindu*, October 25, 2004.

shift has proven unsuccessful: for example, BJP firebrand Uma Bharati's lackluster performance in stimulating popular support, the BJP's inability to unseat the Congress in state elections in the key state of Maharashtra despite widespread dissatisfaction with the incumbent, and the resistance of the BJP's coalition partners in the National Democratic Alliance (NDA) to strident Hindutva, all point to the limits of single-issue politics in India.[79]

Besides, although there have been challenges to secularism, no alternative has emerged to replace it, nor is it very likely. For example, the BJP's election platform included a call for the creation of a uniform civil code (overturning the existing system of personal laws being governed by religious injunctions if an individual prefers it), but once in power, this was not pursued. The call for a uniform civil code was an attempt to use secular language for a non-secular agenda, highlighting the hold that secularism has on Indian discourse and the fact that arguments and counterarguments tend to occur within that secular context. The comments by BJP President Advani describing Mohammed Ali Jinnah as "secular" on a visit to Pakistan in June 2005 is a case in point. While in power, the top BJP leadership itself felt compelled to underline India's secularism.[80]

Beyond the state, careful research suggests that, on the narrower issue of inter-communal peace, the prognosis for India is good. Ashutosh Varshney's research team found that only 5 percent of India (the same eight cities over time) is riot prone, and it is largely an urban phenomenon.[81] Soon after coming to power, the UPA government indicated that it would introduce a "model law" to tackle communal violence in a comprehensive manner after discussion with the country's security personnel and civil groups.[82] These trends in India clearly contribute to producing a better environment for the moderates on all sides in the Kashmir conflict. But even under the best of circumstances within India, Pakistan's ability to play a spoiler role in moderating Kashmiri politics is enormous.

[79] This constraint has not been entirely lost on even Hindutva leaders. See *The Asian Age*, July 19, 2004.

[80] For example, prior to elections in 2002, L. K. Advani asserted in Parliament that India could never be converted into a Hindu state or rashtra. He went on to add that the people would neither condone communal violence nor tolerate pseudo-secularism (in a barbed reference to Nehruvian secularists). See www.rediff.com, November 18, 2002. This brought about a strong reaction from the head of the Shiv Sena who suggested that Advani, so far viewed as "a strong votary of the Hindutva," needed to explain why he was behaving like Prime Minister Vajpyaee who is "all the time performing a circus act to keep his secular image intact." *The Hindu*, November 22, 2002.

[81] According to him, eight cities in India have accounted for almost all the communal conflict in the twentieth century: Ahmedbad, Aligarh, Hydrabad, Meerut, Baroda, Calcutta, Delhi and Bombay. Ashutosh Varshney, *Ethnic Conflict and Civic Life: Hindus and Muslims in India* (New Haven: Yale University Press, 2002), pp. 7–9.

[82] *The Hindu*, November 4, 2004.

Pakistan's persisting policy

Although Islam may be losing its political appeal for Pakistan's foreign policy, thanks to major changes in the geo-strategic environment and American pressure, there is little evidence of a fundamental shift by Pakistan vis-à-vis Kashmir. The United Jihad Council operating out of Pakistan unanimously backed Geelani in his battle with moderates in the APHC. He was favored because he was viewed by many Pakistanis as the only political leader in Kashmir still favoring jihad.[83] During critical negotiations between the moderate wing of the APHC and the Indian government, the United Jihad Council's statements decrying those taking part in the dialogue as "traitors" served to vitiate the environment for political action by the moderates, and raised the risks for them.[84] Moreover, it was shortly after his meeting with the Pakistani foreign secretary in New Delhi that Geelani broke rank with the moderates in the APHC for good and created a new party, which many perceived as having Pakistan's strong blessing.[85]

While it is difficult to pinpoint where external patronage of and internal receptivity to extremism meet, local militants appear to have different incentives for engaging in violence than do foreign fighters. This is well illustrated by the divergences found between cases of government–militant stand-offs in Kashmir. There are several examples, but the siege of the Hazratbal and Charar-e-Sharief shrines in 1993 and 1995 respectively are telling.[86] Both takeovers and accompanying sieges occurred during the 1990s, when the Indian government and militants were unrelentingly pitted against each other – but the Hazratbal stand-off ended peacefully, whereas the Charar-e-Sharief situation exploded in violence. A critical difference between the two sieges was that the militants in the Hazratbal shrine were clearly local, whereas those in and around Charar-e-Sharief were foreigners. In the first case, the government was able to utilize the assistance of well-known local leaders, who commanded the respect of Kashmiris of almost all stripes, as mediators. On the other hand, at Charar-e-Sharief, the foreign militants were not viewed as amenable to appeals from local leaders. Another factor that in all

[83] Amir Rana, "Jihadis Call for Gillani to Form New Party," *Daily Times*, August 25, 2003.
[84] The United Jihad Council's denunciations are detailed in "Action against India to Continue: Jihad Council," *Dawn*, April 19, 2004.
[85] Seema Mustafa, "J&K Rebels Will Meet Kasuri This Week," *The Asian Age*, August 31, 2004.
[86] Wajahat Habibullah, "Siege: Hazratbal, Kashmir 1993," *India Review*, 1.3. Habibullah, the Divisional Commissioner of Kashmir, was the top Indian administrative authority for the area and the chief interlocutor, but his account has not been seriously challenged.

likelihood influenced the local–foreign militant distinction was their view of Sufism and, by extension, the sanctity of shrines.

In the past, as we have repeatedly seen, US geopolitical interests contributed heavily to developing religious extremist conceptions in South Asia. In the case of Kashmir, pre-9/11, American appeals to Pakistan against the use of jihadi groups for foreign policy purposes was muted, a situation that has changed at least in rhetoric. The nuclearization of South Asia has also produced a shift. A senior member of the South Asian bureau at the State Department put the American position starkly: "When two countries have nuclear weapons, the US position is to avert any violence that could lead to escalation, i.e., changing the status quo. That will be the overriding US position on Kashmir now and in the foreseeable future."[87]

Despite the mixed regional geopolitical environment, the simultaneous Indo-Pakistan talks and the internal Kashmir dialogue process may take away the edge from the most aggressive forms of geopolitical identity construction. The idea of a "softer" Line of Control or possible "adjustments" to sovereignty have been floated in recent times by not only public intellectuals but sources close to government.[88] The innovative way of dealing with travel documents for Kashmiris to travel across the Line of Control, for example, revealed that, with the right degree of political will and imagination, geopolitical and other identity interests could indeed be reconciled towards moderate outcomes.

Conclusion

The destiny of Kashmiris lies well beyond the various internal groups that make up the political landscape in Kashmir. This chapter has not attempted to examine possible solutions to the conflict, but we may conclude that the cultivation of religiously polarized and militarized identity constructions by the external groups that we find in Kashmir, will be a huge obstacle.

To cite religion as the driving force for militancy, however, would be largely misplaced; and relying on religion for solutions is only likely to deepen divisions in such a diverse environment. Even where we might most expect the religious identity argument to be used, such as in the statements

---

[87] Background comments by a senior State Department official at a discussion forum on "US–South Asia Relations: A Discussion with Qazi Hussain Ahmed, Jamaat-I-Islami, Pakistan" at The Brookings Institution, July 12, 2000.

[88] See for example, "India Prepared to Make LOC 'Softer,'" *The Times of India*, September 3, 2004; and Lt. Gen. Vinay Shankar (Retd.), "Can We 'Adjust' Soverignty?" *The Asian Age*, October 1, 2004.

of the Mirwaiz Umar Farooq, it does not figure prominently.[89] The role of external actors, in contrast, has tended to distort the contours of the Kashmiri conflict, most often pushing it towards greater violence and religious extremism. Chapter Four showed how the Pakistani military never gave up its policy hold on two conflicts in the neighborhood – Afghanistan and Kashmir – no matter who was in power. The effects of this are borne out in the evolving nature of the militancy, in which Pakistan's geopolitical identity clashes with India have made Kashmir one of the most intractable conflicts.

[89] The Mirwaiz has consistently argued against any further communal or ethnic partition of the state, and that the state's "immense diversity" must be kept intact. See for example, Luv Puri, "No Partition of J&K: Mirwaiz," *The Hindu*, November 21, 2004.

6 Sri Lanka's violent spiral

The long-running conflict in Sri Lanka appeared to have finally run its course in 2002 when an unprecedented ceasefire agreement was signed by the newly elected government of Prime Minister Ranil Wikramsinghe and the separatist Liberation Tigers of Tamil Eelam (LTTE). By 2008 however, after a series of political upheavals among the dominant Sinhalese, a devastating tsunami that killed 35,000 people, new factional fighting among the Tamil militants, and renewed clashes between the LTTE and the military, peace on the island has crumbled under the force of another violent spiral. Like the rest of South Asia, there was little in the island's history to predict the conflict that has dominated Sri Lanka's political landscape for more than 25 years and claimed nearly 65,000 lives. The rise of rigid and polarized ethno-religious identities that have fed violent confrontations has edged out more moderate and accommodating voices on all sides.

How did Sri Lanka's strong secular ethos at independence in 1947 crumble and distort one of the most promising democratic experiments in the developing world? As in the cases of Afghanistan, Pakistan and Kashmir, this chapter traces the rise of extremism in Sri Lanka by looking at a three-way identity struggle between secular, ethno-religious and geo-political identity conceptions. The chapter argues that as the influence of these three elements has waxed and waned in Sri Lanka, it has created conditions that foster extremism and violence. The emergence of the LTTE, from a people known more for their culture and professional achievement than warfare, is an anomaly. While the militancy of the LTTE is well-known, extremists within the ranks of the Sinhalese political class and religious clergy have increasingly carved out greater political space and need to be considered as well. The ultra-nationalist, leftist Janata Vimukti Peramuna (JVP) and the activist Buddhist monk organization Eksath Bhikkhu Peramuna, in particular, stand out for their unremitting intransigence towards Tamils.

The LTTE, commonly referred to as the Tigers, dominates groups articulating Tamil grievances and commands the greatest popular support.

In the past, however, there has been a spectrum of opinion in the Tamil community. This included the early moderate parliamentary parties culminating in the Tamil United Liberation Front (TULF), as well as several other militant groups that emerged in the 1970s and 1980s such as the Eelam People's Revolutionary Liberation Front (EPRLF), Tamil Eelam Liberation Organization (TELO), Eelam Revolutionary Organization of Students (EROS) and People's Liberation Organization of Tamil Eelam (PLOTE). Although their stated objective of an independent Tamil homeland was the same, there were divergences on strategy and a willingness to compromise on that ultimate goal. These differences came out most openly between the LTTE and the EPRLF in the political flux during the Indian intervention of 1987–1989.

This chapter begins by questioning the purely ethno-religious explanation for the rise of violent extremism in Sri Lanka, as well as a number of other conventional approaches. It then looks at the decline of political secularism domestically and the way in which geopolitical identity preoccupations at the Sri Lankan state level have exacerbated dormant ethno-religious prejudices. We will see how the LTTE came to eclipse the decades-old traditional groups, which left little room for new and alternative political formations such as the TULF and EPRLF to gain political traction. For all the key actors in the Sri Lankan conflict, neighboring India's actual and perceived role has been crucial. We cannot fully understand the evolution of extremist politics in Sri Lanka without an appreciation of the link between domestic politics in Sri Lanka and perceptions of India's regional geopolitics. As in other countries, the balance towards violent militancy has been tipped by a combination of domestic and external forces, but here the geopolitical aspects are less explicit and more ambivalent. The combined effects, however, are no less deadly.

Attempts to explain extremism

The ethno-religious factor

On the face of it, the Sri Lankan situation appears squarely to meet popular notions of ethno-religious conflict.[1] According to census data, Sri Lanka's population of 16 million comprises 74 percent Sinhalese, 18 percent Tamil (including 5.6 percent so-called Indian Tamils brought in by the British as plantation labor in the nineteenth century) and 7 percent

---

[1] For an argument that Sinhalese–Tamil communalism has deep historical roots, see Lakshmanan Sabaratnam, *Ethnic Attachments in Sri Lanka: Social Change and Cultural Continuity* (New York: Palgrave, 2001), pp. 9–36.

Tamil-speaking Muslims. The overwhelming majority of Sinhalese are Buddhist and most Tamils are Hindus. From the Tamil minority's perspective, divisive majoritarian politics and government repression have added up to a deliberate effort of disempowerment. They point to the systematic marginalization of Tamils from opportunities in education and employment since the 1970s, and of being targeted by the police and the military. In contrast, many Sinhalese view Tamils with suspicion, out to destroy the unity of the country by establishing a Tamil homeland in the north and eastern parts. The violent insurgency, the government's heavy-handed military tactics and the high degree of insecurity felt by ordinary citizens have radicalized sentiment and pitted the two communities against each other. Within the span of Sri Lanka's distant or even more recent history, however, this is far from characteristic.

Historically, Tamil identity has always been well developed and strong, but it existed in its own right, not in opposition to the majority per se or as a breakaway notion. Many Tamils were at the forefront of the movement to create a "Ceylon national-consciousness" during the agitation for independence.[2] As part of the anti-colonial movement, the Ceylon National Congress (CNC) had been established by both Sinhalese and Tamils in 1919. The CNC's first president was Ponnambalam Arunachalam, a prominent Tamil politician. In 1925, his successor, H. J. C. Pereira, a leading Sinhalese, declared that "The salvation of Ceylon depends not on the growth of communalism or racialism, but on the growth of the true national spirit which the Congress would always foster."[3] Early Buddhist and Sinhalese revivalist movements, because they concentrated their attack on foreign rule, were not generally viewed as threatening by Tamils. The Buddhist revival at the turn of the century focused on challenging Christian dominance and British expansion.

The absence of any alliance between the "Indian Tamils" and indigenous or Sri Lankan Tamils points to another weakness of ethno-religious ties. Indian Tamils are largely concentrated in the tea-growing areas of central Sri Lanka and share the same language and religion but have not made common cause. Tamil Muslims, too, have for the most part avoided direct confrontation on the government's policies. In 1948, when the Indian Tamils were summarily deprived of citizenship rights, the only significant action taken was by independent Tamil leader C. Suntheralingam who

---

[2] Chelvadurai Manogaran, *Ethnic Conflict and Reconciliation in Sri Lanka* (Honolulu: University of Hawaii Press, 1987), p. 30.
[3] Quoted in K. N. O. Dharmadasa, *Language, Religion, and Ethnic Assertiveness: The Growth of Sinhalese Nationalism in Sri Lanka* (Ann Arbor: The University of Michigan Press, 1992), p. 226.

resigned from the central cabinet in protest.[4] Such a blatantly unfair measure failed to set off a communal crisis. As one observer put it, "if race were all that mattered, the Ceylon and Indian Tamils would make a common cause against the Sinhalese."[5] Such a united front has never materialized, even during the current conflict.

The dominant stand of Tamils prior to independence in 1948 and into the 1970s was to work within the politico-economic set-up of Sri Lanka. This made good sense as they held a huge stake in the success of the new country: Tamil representation in the professions and state bureaucracy was high and, as a minority, they had not been visibly marginalized. Much like India, one of the distinguishing features of the anti-colonial and post-colonial political leadership in Sri Lanka was its relatively broad ethno-religious base and shared ideological tolerance. Indeed, the splits *within* the majority community were often no less rancorous than divisions between the majority and minority communities.

While it is true that the political parties were for the most part arrayed along ethnic and religious lines, that did not translate into separatist demands. This identification simply reflected the realities of a multi-ethnic society and not necessarily sharp social antagonisms. In the 1952 general elections, for example, both leading Tamil parties presented moderate platforms: the Tamil Congress (TC) led by G. G. Ponnambalam allied with the dominant Sinhalese United National Party (UNP) to work within a unitary system, while S. J. V. Chelvanayakam's Federal Party, a break-away from the Congress, fought for the federal option of a linguistic Tamil state in the northern and eastern provinces. The collaborators won the day, with the UNP and Tamil Congress gaining 40 percent of the northern votes to the Federal Party's 27 percent; in the east, the UNP won 40 percent and the Federal Party managed only 4 percent.[6] Political conflict that did flare up following British withdrawal was mostly secular, urban and non-communal and gave no real sign of what was to follow.[7]

There is little to suggest that the Sri Lankan identity of the Tamils at the national level was somehow diluted. (The situation may be compared to ethnic relations in Afghanistan where ethnic identities were also well developed without separatist sentiment.) If Sinhala–Tamil identities had been hostile in Sri Lanka, we would have expected the demand for a

---

[4] W. Howard Wriggins, *Ceylon: Dilemmas of a New Nation* (Princeton, NJ: Princeton University Press, 1960), p. 145.

[5] Quoted in Manogaran, *Ethnic Conflict*, p. 28.

[6] Wriggins, *Ceylon*, p. 146.

[7] A good deal of it was due to labor disputes. John Richardson, *Paradise Poisoned: Learning About Conflict, Terrorism and Development from Sri Lanka's Civil Wars* (Kandy, Sri Lanka: International Centre for Ethnic Studies, 2005), p. 130.

separate Tamil homeland at the point of independence, when state structures were in flux.

Political access and elite manipulation

There are many commentators who blame the conflict on the drawbacks of the Westminster-style democratic machinery that Sri Lanka inherited at independence.[8] The argument is that the one person, one vote system would inevitably lead to majoritarian politics at the expense of minorities. In Sri Lanka, the "ethnic bidding" for votes that has taken root indicates the danger in such a set-up. But does the institutional structure offer a sufficient explanation? For example, why did the same political structure in Malaysia not lead to conflict?[9]

Given Sri Lanka's strong democratic tradition and extremely favorable development indicators, we might have expected the democratic process to be sufficiently robust. The early political elites from all communities showed enough faith in the country's institutions, even though they failed to reach an agreement over special provisions to protect minority interests. The dominant Sinhalese political vision was for a democratic, secular state that would be dominated by the majority but sensitive to minority concerns. The potential for this consensus to go awry was not lost on the Tamils, even though the requirements for "political secularism" seemed to be in place.

Democracy in Sri Lanka had more going for it than its electoral apparatus, including a strong, independent judiciary, a dynamic civil society and a growing non-governmental sector. In fairly short order, the country also attained widespread economic development that set it apart from the vast majority of other developing countries, including all its neighbors. It has been repeatedly cited in development literature as a "success story." As a group, the Tamils were not historically shut out of the political arena nor denied access to political organizations. All these indices of a credible, rather than nominal, democracy placed Sri Lanka in an advantageous position to counteract the vulnerability of the election process to majoritarian bias.

---

[8] One of the best-known scholars suggesting that the traditional Westminster model would not work in majoritarian multi-ethnic societies is Arend Liphart. See his *Democracies: Patterns of Majoritarian and Consensus Government in Twenty One Countries* (New Haven, CT: Yale University Press, 1984).

[9] On the Malaysian experience, see H. P. Koon, "The New Economic Policy and the Community in Peninsular Malaysia," in *The Developing Economies* 35.3, 1997; and F. H. Abdullah, "Affirmative Action Policy in Malaysia: To Restructure Society, to Eradicate Poverty," in *Ethnic Studies Report*, 15.2, July 1997.

Its abject inability to do this suggests that we need to go beyond the institutional political processes. The way in which political engagement degenerated over time to the point of outright violence is only partially explained by shortcomings of the election system.

Relative deprivation and state repression

We can identify the beginning of a radical shift that seriously undercut these stabilizing advantages with deliberate steps taken by the Sri Lankan state in the early 1970s to enhance the economic status of the Sinhalese majority – a reverse affirmative action program. One of the most detailed studies done on economic inequalities and the ethnic conflict in Sri Lanka concludes that "up until the early 1980s, the difference between ethnic groups with respect to real income remained insignificant, albeit with fairly marked urban–rural disparities in the case of all ethnic groups."[10] Interestingly, this challenges the popular notion among Sinhalese nationalists that as a group the Tamils were much better off than the majority community.

In 1970, the government intervened in the university admission process so that, in effect, Tamil students had to obtain higher marks than Sinhalese students for admission. This came as a huge blow to the Tamil youth who were strongly focused on gaining an education and entering professions due to the lack of economic alternatives in their stronghold of Jaffna in the north, a terrain that was singularly inhospitable for most traditional farming, and distant from the commercial centers of the country. Tamil students were particularly hard hit in medicine and engineering where they had been performing well for decades. For example, the percentage of Tamil students gaining university admission in the sciences fell dramatically from 35.3 percent in 1970 to 14.2 percent by 1975.[11] This chipping away of the economic rights of the Tamils was clearly a factor in the outbreak of Tamil militancy for the first time in 1977.

But are economic arguments sufficient? There was nothing to indicate that Sri Lanka would not continue to perform well in economic and development terms, with an expanding economy that could have absorbed preferential economics. At independence, Sri Lanka had substantial foreign exchange reserves and a balance of payments surplus. Its macroeconomic planning was particularly well developed in comparison to others. The government carried out one of the few peaceful successful land reform

---

[10] G. H. Peiris, "Economic Inequalities and Ethnic Conflict in Sri Lanka," *International Relations in a Globalizing World*, 1.2 (July–December 2005), p. 315.

[11] C. R. De Silva, "Sinhala–Tamil Relations and Education in Sri Lanka: The University Admissions Issue – the First Phase, 1971–1977," in Robert B. Goldman and A. J. Wilson (eds.) *From Independence to Statehood* (London: Pinter Publishers, 1984), p. 131.

and wealth redistribution programs in the developing world, and provided free primary school education and health care. Sri Lanka also performed noticeably well on the Physical Quality of Life Index (PQLI), in a small category of countries with low per capita incomes which still provided for the physical wellbeing of their population. In 1990 when the new Human Development Index (HDI) was introduced, it showed Sri Lanka still outdoing most other developing states, despite seven years of civil war.[12] Remarkably, the combination of the two major political parties' different economic orientations (the UNP's market-friendly outlook versus the Sri Lankan Freedom Party's interventionist agenda) ended up producing a well-regarded outcome across the board. For example, in 1984, adult literacy stood at more than 85 percent, and life expectancy at 69 years, rivaling even developed countries; on the economic side, plantations, farming, industry, trade and commerce were doing remarkably well.[13]

The real challenge to ethnic harmony was that "affirmative action" for the Sinhalese was symptomatic of a wider and more dramatic meddling by the Sinhala-dominated state, systematically dismantling critical and long-standing structures of "political secularism." Along with the changes in the educational sphere was a pronounced move to promote a Sinhala state identity, a shift that signaled a precipitous decline of the country's past secular identity. With the state taking the lead in what amounted to a frontal assault on Sri Lankan pluralist principles, the political secularism that had helped to keep the country together was no longer available. The state changed the rules of the political game and arguably paved the way for militaristic solutions all round: state repression and Tamil insurgency being in full force by 1983.

As in most other South Asian cases, the state's role in perpetuating or creating certain identity conceptions over others has to be understood by considering both domestic and external factors or, as this book suggests, its geopolitical identity needs. In the Sri Lankan case, the geopolitical aspect has been more latent than explicit but its imprint is nonetheless unmistakable.

Adding geopolitics to the equation

The polarizing chauvinism that came to characterize state policies was intimately tied up with a Sinhala viewpoint best described as a "majority

[12] Richardson, *Paradise Poisoned*, pp. 51–52 and 61–66.
[13] This is the conclusion reached by Paul Sieghart in a detailed report on a mission to Sri Lanka in January 1984 on behalf of the International Commission of Jurists and its British Section, JUSTICE. See *Sri Lanka: A Mounting Tragedy of Errors* (London: International Commission of Jurists and JUSTICE, March 1984), p. 6.

with a minority complex."[14] This complex had to do with the existence of 60 million Tamils in the Indian state of Tamil Nadu and exaggerated fears of Indian dominance. Sinhala ethno-religious nationalism and its geopolitical content is currently expressed, for example, in the increasingly extreme positions taken by a section of the Buddhist monks and the JVP. Their stand amounts to equating Tamil separatist demands with alleged Indian regional hegemonic ambitions, together with the view that the neighboring Tamils are hankering after a Tamil homeland within Sri Lanka.[15] Yet there is no serious Sinhala observer of the conflict who does not see a role of some sort for India in its resolution.[16] This mixed reality has spurred the Sri Lankan state to act in seemingly contradictory ways – from overtures to extra-regional actors in an anti-Indian bid to countenance direct intervention by India.

It may well be that even without the Indian shadow, the Sri Lankan state would have engaged in repressive policies against the Tamils. Identity politics have become brutally violent under many different circumstances elsewhere in the world. However, we would be wrong to ignore how India came to play a part in the Sri Lankan state's identity construction. Indeed, the state's simultaneous overreaction and defensiveness, the continuing hold of a destructive "majority–minority" complex and its ambivalent foreign policy orientations are inexplicable without considering the India factor. Conversely, the Indian state had its own set of contradictions. To an extent, the Tamil insurgency served potent domestic political interests, but India's own anti-state movements (especially in Punjab during the 1980s), and its philosophical commitment to secular pluralism served as a brake. At the same time, India's increasingly clear role as the regional manager ensured that it had to play some role; it could not be seen to be sitting on the sidelines. This has put India in an awkward position: from condoning sanctuaries for Tamil militants in South India to proscribing the LTTE; from resisting outside intervention in Sri Lanka to allowing Norwegian mediators to take the lead in the peace process since 2002.

These geopolitical workings need to be added into the equation in order to comprehend the contours of extremism of various shades in Sri Lanka. But we first turn to the domestic sphere and the decline of political secularism, which, as argued above, had a decisive impact in spurring the militancy.

[14] This is a common assertion by analysts. See for example, S. J. Tambiah, *Ethnic Fratricide and the Dismantling of Democracy* (Chicago: University of Chicago Press, 1991), pp. 92–93.

[15] For a background of the JVP, see Shelton Kodikara, "The Continuing Crisis in Sri Lanka: the JVP, the Indian Troops and Tamil Politics," *Asia Survey*, 29.7.

[16] See, for example, Jehan Perera, "Exploring the Solution to the Communal Problem," in Committee for Rational Development (ed.) *Sri Lanka: The Ethnic Conflict* (New Delhi: Navrang Publishers, 1984), p. 105.

Domestic structures and political secularism

Waxing and waning of secularism

The political class in Sri Lanka at independence was one of the most cohesive and secular-minded, and strong "ethnic" parties had yet to emerge. With the exception of a few isolated voices on both sides, the idea that the Sinhalese and Tamils were bound to collide was not much considered. The multi-ethnic elite seemed to have a working consensus on the direction of national policy, and the withdrawal of the British was accomplished peacefully. Some have credited this to a "co-fraternity" among the elites.[17] English-speaking and steeped in the liberal tradition, neither the Sinhalese nor the Tamils in the Ceylon National Congress were overly concerned about the possibility of ethnic fracturing in the new state. The constitutional period did point to potential fissures, though, with many Tamils unsuccessfully arguing for safeguards against the "territorial electorates" (over communal representation), which would inevitably lead to a large majority of seats for the Sinhalese. Ultimately, the 1946 Soulbury Constitution simply stated that the state should not favor one community or religion over another. That these same elites could become seriously infected with exclusionary identity politics seemed not to be taken very seriously.

There were good reasons for the absence of open ethno-religious acrimony. Similar to minorities in other South Asian states, the Tamils had a long history of co-existence and even political partnership with the Sinhalese. For example, one of the best known South Indian Tamil rulers, Elara, who came to power in Sri Lanka in 145 BC, was well-known for his justice and impartial administration. Despite revisionist Sinhalese attempts to show themselves unequivocally as the earliest settlers of the island, other historians argue that Tamils arrived as invaders and migrants no later. These historians, including the highly respected K. M. De Silva, suggest that although the dates of these settlements cannot be definitively established, both communities have been there for more than two thousand years and that the country from very early in its recorded history has been a "multi-ethnic society."[18]

The anti-colonial movement, although not as prolonged or intense as in India, further fused the communities. At the political and social elite level, there were strong class ties across communities, forged in part through

---

[17] See for example, Neil DeVotta, "Ethnolinguistic Nationalism and Ethnic Conflict in Sri Lanka," in Michael E. Brown and Sumit Ganguly (eds.) *Fighting Words: Language Policy and Ethnic Relations in Asia* (Cambridge, MA: MIT Press, 2003), p. 107.

[18] See K. M. De Silva, *A History of Sri Lanka* (London: C. Hurst & Co., 1981), p. 13, and Manogaran, *Ethnic Conflict*, p. 21.

common educational institutions and a fairly cosmopolitan and open cultural ethos in the capital city, Colombo. Although the Tamil population was concentrated in the northern peninsula of Jaffna, there were significant numbers in the south who were integrated into the mainstream political and economic structures, from government bureaucracies to commercial banks. The conclusion by noted scholar Tambiah that "Sinhalese–Tamil tensions and conflicts in the form known to us today are of relatively recent manufacture," is widely supported.[19]

Sri Lankan Tamils thus had a clear stake in the country and, just as importantly from the perspective of this book, no aspirations for a pan-Tamil, India-oriented independent state. Given the existence of the Indian state Tamil Nadu just 22 miles across the shallow Palk Straits from Jaffna, the conspicuous lack of political links between Tamils on both sides is surprising. This is not to suggest that ties were not strong but they were confined to the cultural sphere. Citing the physical separation as increasingly a social separation, anthropologists studying Sri Lanka refer to the emergence of a distinct Sri Lankan Tamil identity. Hindu religion was also a common bond but not an exclusive one given the considerable number of Christians within the Sri Lankan Tamil society.[20] It may be noted that among the Tamil militants and their most ardent supporters, there is little to distinguish Hindu and Christian compatriots, whereas similarities between Sinhalese and Tamil Christians are few, once again pointing to the weakness of a purely religious explanation for the current conflict.

Despite the relative complacency of the early liberal leadership, there were two competing tendencies of proto-communalism and proto-secularism. The proto-communal tendency first reared its head in the form of language politics: the demand by sections of the majority to privilege Sinhalese at the national level. This language agitation started at the grassroots but, within a decade of independence, Sinhala political elites seized the issue for their own purposes. Given the control of state machinery by these same leaders, gradual but increasing state intervention into such communal controversies dealt a decisive blow to political secularism. The first "official" site of communal sentiment was located in the politics of language but it was inextricably linked to the broader Sinhala national identity encompassing religion, ethnicity and the "majority's minority complex."[21]

---

[19] Tambiah, *Ethnic Fratricide*, p. 7.
[20] One of the most important Tamil political figures was S. J. V. Chelvanayakam, a Christian who led the Tamil Federal Party.
[21] The UNP's break with its tradition of inter-communal cooperation and descent into language chauvinism was one of the most ominous developments. On the UNP's shift, see Wriggins, *Ceylon*, p. 145.

State sponsorship of communal policies

That the Sri Lankan state would end up repudiating its politically secular roots so drastically was unexpected. Even S. W. R. D. Bandaranayake of the Sri Lanka Freedom Party (SLFP), most closely identified with changing the secular discourse of the country at the state level as Prime Minister in 1956, had begun by clearly calling for both Sinhalese and Tamil to replace English as the official language.[22] In 1944, J. R. Jayawardene from the UNP (future prime minister and president who too went on to erode the secular basis of the constitution) had sponsored a bill in the legislative body to make both Sinhalese and Tamil official languages. In 1949, the country's first Prime Minister, D. S. Senanayake, had declared that "our essential task is to create a nation, and that our people speak not one language, but two or perhaps three."[23] The Swabasha (native language) Movement itself had begun as a way of uplifting the Sinhala and Tamil masses that were unable to take advantage of educational and economic opportunities that went to the English literate classes. Even those who might have been most inclined to seek a preference for Sinhalese initially included Tamil in their appeals.[24]

The drive towards chauvinistic "ethnic bidding" originated thanks to a potent emergence of Buddhist activism and personal political divisions within the Sinhalese political class. It then became entrenched when the state machinery was deployed in its service.[25] The role of the bhikkus or Buddhist monks was critical in the decline of secular political discourse, but only once had they gained state patronage. Bhikkus enjoyed an elevated standing in cultural terms prior to independence and into the 1960s but were politically marginal. One well-known expert points out that "there had been no succinct exposition of Buddhist grievances and relatively simple prescriptions for its rejuvenation. There was a strong tradition of monks remaining aloof from organized political activities. Until the 1956 election, and for many centuries, there had been no organized armature of Buddhist monks and laymen."[26] The bikkhus functioned mostly under the Eksath Bhikkhu Peramuna (EBI – United Buddhist Front), although there

---

[22] For a comprehensive political biography of Bandaranayake which mirrors Sri Lanka's tension between cosmopolitan reforms and Sinhala chauvinism, see James Manor, *The Expedient Utopian: Bandaranaika and Ceylon* (Cambridge University Press, 1989).

[23] Quoted in Jehan Perera, "Exploring the Solution," p. 100.

[24] A comprehensive account of language politics is found in Neil DeVotta, "Ethnolinguistic Nationalism," p. 118.

[25] The SLFP was created by Bandaranayake when he faced unexpected competition inside the ruling United National Party (UNP) as a cabinet minister, rather than any strong ideological differences.

[26] Wriggins, *Ceylon*, pp.343–344.

were numerous sangha sabhas (bhikku associations) that were supportive and could be activated. Other important and powerful groups also worked together with the bhikkhus: for example, the Young Men's Buddhist Association, the Theosophical Society, the Ayurveda Sangamaya (Congress of Indigenous Medical Practitioners), the Bhasa Peramuna (Language Front) and the Lanka Jatika Guru Sangamaya (Sinhalese Teachers' Association).[27] In their increasingly strident appeals, the monks and their supporters managed to bring the incendiary issues of language, ethnicity and religion into the political arena all at once.[28]

There is little evidence that mainstream Sinhalese politicians had considered the bhikkus as serious political actors, and the monks were most often simply tolerated. The political tactics of S. W. R. D. Bandaranayake, which catered to narrow Buddhist sentiment, was the most visible break with the past. As the elections approached in 1956, Bandaranayake presented himself as the Buddhist candidate claiming that he had the active support of 12,000 bhikkus (65 percent of all bhikkus in Sri Lanka). As it turned out, this was hugely overblown, with numbers closer to 3,000.[29] However, with the SLFP's sponsorship of the Sinhala Only positon, the politicization of ethno-religious belief came under the remit of the state, a development that spelled the beginning of the end of the political secularism that political leaders had largely adhered to, and an elevated and inflated position for ultra-nationalist ideologues.

Once the 1956 Official Languages Act enshrining Sinhala was passed, Bandaranayake belatedly tried to placate the Tamils. The Bandaranayake–Chelvanayakam Pact of 1957, which many see as a historic "missed opportunity" to settle the ethnic issue by establishing an autonomous Tamil linguistic state within a united Sri Lanka, was hijacked by activist Buddhist monks of the EBP and supporters who denounced it as "surrendering" to the Tamils. The critical turning point was the sudden backing they received from the opposition UNP and its leader J. R. Jayawardene.

Unholy alliances

Over time, both the SLFP and UNP have flip-flopped on the question of accommodating or repudiating Tamil demands and on how far to go to get a peace process off the ground. Meanwhile, hardline Buddhist organizations have gained in stature and, by 2005, had positioned themselves as

---

[27] Neil DeVotta, "Ethnolinguistic Nationalism," pp. 120–121; and Jeyaratnam A. Wilson, "Politics and Political Development since 1948," in K. M. de Silva ed. *Sri Lanka: A Survey* (London: C. Hurst & Co., 1977), p. 301.

[28] The 1956 elections coincided with a year-long celebration of 2500 years of Buddhism.

[29] Wriggins, *Ceylon*, p. 347.

coalition partners with extremist Sinhalese groups such as the JVP. Two major issues have been at the forefront for them: the level of accommodation with the Tamil minority; and any external involvement in the ethnic conflict and peace process. The SLFP has been the most willing to openly link up with these groups, most recently exemplified in how it brought down the UNP government in 2004 citing foreign influence and national security concerns connected with the Norwegian-facilitated peace process. As a noted scholar asserted, "increasingly in the 1970s and now in the 1980s, we have a formulaic Buddhism which says that to be a Sinhalese is to be automatically a Buddhist and Aryan, and to be Buddhist is to be able to make a total claim – territorially and politically – over Sri Lanka."[30]

The period from 1956 to 1977 saw the deepening of Sinhalese nationalist politics with tragic consequences for Sinhalese–Tamil relations. From language policies to educational quotas, state-instituted measures favored the majority community. The most pointed reminder of this was the change in the 1972 Constitution, making Sinhalese and Buddhism the official language and religion respectively. The country's name was changed from Ceylon to Sri Lanka, recalling ancient Sinhalese mythology. Minority protections were eroded or eliminated and federalism was explicitly prohibited. The state ushered in educational policies which gave the Sinalese majority a weighted advantage and unfair quotas in admission to universities. For example, the implementation of the so-called backward district quotas reduced the number of Tamils admitted to university science programs by one third in a single year.[31] In addition, the deliberate "colonization" by the government of traditional Tamil areas in the north and particularly in the east, by giving the Sinhalese incentives to migrate, began changing the demographics.

The election of Jayawardene in 1977 and the defeat of the more populist SLFP government seemed to hold promise. The SLFP had lost so much support that the leadership of the Opposition went to A. Amrithalingam, head of the largest Tamil parliamentary party. Even the shift from a Westminster-type parliamentary system to a Gaullist presidential format, engineered by Jayawardene through the UNP's five-sixths majority, was initially welcomed by many civil society groups.[32] They believed that the new system, which encouraged candidates to look beyond their party or ethnic group in the absence of an absolute majority for a second preference backing from other groups, was better equipped to deal with minority

[30] Tambiah, *Ethnic Fratricide*, p. 58.   [31] Richardson, *Paradise Poisoned*, p. 297.
[32] Gananath Obeysekera, "Political Violence and the Future of Democracy in Sri Lanka," Committee for Rational Development (ed.) *Sri Lanka: The Ethnic Conflict* (New Delhi: Navrang Publishers, 1984), p. 83.

grievances. However, within Jayawardene's cabinet itself were members publicly identified with virulently racist perspectives.[33] Against initial hopes, the communalization of politics at the state level reached its apogee during Jayawardene's term with the outbreak of unprecedented ethnic violence in July 1983. The state's complicity or at best callous indifference during anti-Tamil riots in which some 3,000 Tamils were massacred, with thousands fleeing into refugee camps and to India, has been well documented.[34] For most Tamils, this brought them to a point of no return.

Fracturing and consolidation of Tamil politics

The radicalization of Tamil politics occurred gradually but once it took shape in the form of the LTTE, power remained concentrated. This evolution can be traced directly to the precipitous decline of political secularism, beginning with the Sinhala Only bill of 1956. The growing identification of the state with perceived majority grievances invariably undercut the atmosphere of co-existence that had been dominant. Minority confidence in the state as a neutral arbiter was no longer secure, replaced by feelings of intense vulnerability despite the formal democratic machinery. The eclipse of moderate Tamil parties did not occur overnight; their credibility was eroded over time as success in negotiating with the government on Tamil rights became more and more elusive. Tamil support for an armed solution came reluctantly and cannot be separated from egregious violations perpetrated by the state. Under such pressure, despite the mixed picture of Tamil politics and range of opinion historically, the ascendancy of the LTTE has drowned out other shades of opinion.

Traditional Tamil politics had converged around the moderate, liberal Tamil Congress, the party that had been in partnership with the UNP during the independence movement. The first calls for a separate Tamil homeland (Eelam) had come in the 1960s but went largely unheeded. While the champion of Tamil Eelam was a highly respected community leader, he was clearly ahead of his time and was never able to gain widespread popular support.[35] Most Tamils threw their support behind politicians who saw their future inextricably tied into the mainstream

---

[33] Cyril Mathew, Minister of Industries, addressed parliament and published inflammatory material challenging the patriotism of Tamil officials and military officers, and even referred to "South Indians" running important parts of Colombo.

[34] For graphic descriptions of these fateful days, see Dayan Jayatilleka, "The Ethnic Conflict and the Crisis in the South," in Committee for Rational Development (ed.) *Sri Lanka: The Ethnic Conflict* (New Delhi: Navrang Publishers, 1984), pp. 87–89; Tambiah, *Ethnic Fratricide*, pp. 15–33; and Sieghart, *Sri Lanka*, pp. 19–22.

[35] The idea of Eelam was introduced in 1959 by C. Suntheralingamu, MP from Vavuniya, who formed the Unity Front of Eelam Tamils and called for an independence struggle.

Sri Lankan polity. Thus what the proponents of Tamil Eelam were not able to accomplish for themselves, the Sri Lankan state did for them.

While there was no appreciable agitation for a separate state until 1983, the need for some form of regional autonomy to safeguard Tamil rights was recognized in response to the Sinhala Only movement. Indeed, regional autonomy agreements stopping well short of independence were reached early on in 1957 and 1965 under the SLFP and UNP regimes. Support by these two different parties showed that such formulae were not seen by Sinhalese leaders across party affiliations as threatening the integrity or interests of the country. The first was negotiated between the SLFP's Bandaranayake and S. J. V. Chelvanayakam, leader of the Tamil Federal Party, and the second by UNP Prime Minister Dudley Senanayake, again with Chelvanayakam. These agreements never saw the light of day as one by one Sinhalese leaders caved into chauvinistic sentiments and Tamil leaders, in turn, made tougher demands as time passed.

Various proposals on devolution, power sharing, federalism and autonomy have come and gone since 1956, but the lack of political will on the part of Sinhalese politicians and disagreement over specific details have consistently got the better of Tamil and Sinhalese dealmakers, even when it appeared that a peace settlement was finally around the corner, most spectacularly in 2002–2004. Hardline Sinhalese have seized on characterizing autonomy or federal solutions as a first step to secession, fanning the fears of the majority. But most often, the cost of autonomy arrangements are psychological, not material. There is little evidence that conceding autonomy leads inexorably to independence.[36] Rather, it would seem that it is the increasingly intransigent Sinhalese position on autonomy that has turned the Tamils towards the goal of independence and a willingness to use extremist methods to achieve it.

The hardening of Tamil identity and formation of militant groups

The displacement of moderate Tamil parties that sought to continue the state's original plural democracy and make their appeals through the parliament began occurring in earnest by the late 1970s. Several groups, including the longstanding Tamil Congress, converged under the banner of the Tamil United Liberation Front (TULF) to contest the 1977 elections on a separatist platform. In reality however, they held out a strong hope for a regional solution rather than one of independence. The traditional voice of Tamil opposition continued to rely on

---

[36] Perera, "Exploring the Solution," provides good evidence from global experience to make this point. See pp. 101–104 and 110–114.

non-violent civil disobedience tactics along the lines of the pre-independence Gandhian movement.

However, the TULF's preferred parliamentary route hit a dead end when the Sixth Amendment was passed in 1983 disallowing a separatist platform in the political arena. This effectively stripped Tamil "moderates" of any viable alternative to the gathering militant opinion in the community. Subsequently, younger groups espousing an armed approach who had been on the periphery took center stage. The rise of more extremist Tamil groups had two effects: the survival of moderate politics on the Tamil side became shaky; and on the part of the Sri Lankan government, hardliners pushing a military line against "terrorism" and those driven by fears from the unexpected emergence of successful armed Tamil groups coalesced to unleash an iron-fisted state policy.[37]

The most important of the new Tamil groups were the LTTE, led by V. Prabhakaran, and the Eelam People's Revolutionary Liberation Front (EPRLF). Within ten years, and after the intervention by India in 1987, the LTTE became the clear front runner, but only after painful and violent splits among these Tamil groups on strategy and ideology. The stated agenda of all these groups (and the TULF) contained nearly indistinguishable objectives on Tamil Eelam, and there was even a significant effort to put forward a united front when dealing with the Sri Lankan government and, at times, with India. Behind the common front, however, the level of flexibility on the demand for separate statehood and the willingness to espouse armed rather than political strategies differed.

After the Indian intervention, in particular, these differences could not be contained. The LTTE assured its supremacy in part by targeted assassinations of its opponents, including the top TULF leader, A. Amrithalingam, in July 1989.[38] No viable alternative to the LTTE has existed since then and it continues to receive large-scale support from the Tamil population. It is this political reality that has accorded the Tigers the political space to deal with international organizations, the Indian government and, most recently, the Norwegian interlocutors despite its proscription as a "terrorist" entity by the US, India, the UK and the European Union. Notwithstanding the LTTE's history of

---

[37] The Sri Lankan army's phenomenal growth is an indication of the government's military route: its size increased from a mere 10,309 in 1978 to 39,098 in 1988 to 122,505 in 2005. See Shantha Kottegoda, "Sri Lanka's Conflict in the North and East and Challenges to the Army, *International Relations in a Globalizing World*, 1.2 (July–December 2005), p. 208.

[38] Although the LTTE rarely takes responsibility for eliminating its opponents, most independent observers of the conflict see the culpability of the Tigers in a rash of killings over time.

ruthlessness, the ceasefire agreement of 2002 suggested war weariness on all sides. The notional acceptance by the Tigers of autonomy within a united Sri Lanka in 2002 also showed important flexibility that harked back to the early politics of the country.

Accounts differ, but by the mid-1980s there were between 20 and 30 Tamil groups of varying shades of opinion.[39] Each of the non-LTTE groups has exerted limited influence intermittently, with the EPRLF in particular gaining sudden prominence during the Indian intervention between 1987 and 1990. This period provides a glimpse into the direct interaction between domestic ethno-politics and geopolitical identities, taken up next. The Sri Lankan government, the Indian central government and Tamil Nadu politicians, as well as key Tamil militant and political groups were all actors in this complex of competing strands of identity politics at the external regional level.

Geopolitical identities

Ethnic affiliation and strategic purposes

As in other cases, we can see how the peculiarities of identity at the strategic level elevated the ethnic conflict in Sri Lanka beyond domestic politics. The Sinhalese sentiment driving the ethnic conflict operated at two levels: anti-Tamil and anti-India. At different points in time, this combination served the strategic and political purpose of Sinhala elites, although the dictates of realpolitik did not allow the ruling party at any given time to let relations with India to get completely out of hand. Still, as the geopolitical identity of the Sri Lankan state took on increasingly strident Sinhala Buddhist tones from the 1970s onwards, it vitiated both the internal and regional atmosphere. The tendency has been for Sinhala nationalists to exaggerate the "Indian threat" despite the reality that Tamil nationalism and militancy were in fact tolerable only up to a point for India, as we see in the post-1987 period. In the longer run, India's geopolitical identity needs had to be consonant with its own secular pluralism – opposed in principle to narrow Sinhala nationalism and Tamil separatism. Indeed, the changes that having been occurring in Indo-Sri Lankan relations from the early 1980s onwards demonstrate that geopolitical identities are not necessarily static and that external forces can have a salutary or at least benign impact on domestic structures, unlike what we have seen in previous chapters.

---

[39] K. N. O. Dharmadasa, *Language, Religion, and Ethnic Assertiveness*, pp. 73–77.

Sri Lankan insecurity complex

The Sinhalese "majority's minority complex" that contributed heavily to the deterioration of ethnic harmony, is intimately connected to its perception of India. Sri Lanka's ancient history and mythology have produced a discourse that lends itself to projecting an antagonistic relationship between Tamils and Sinhalese on the one hand, and Sri Lanka and India on the other.[40] The onset of ethnic hostilities presented an opening to Sinhala chauvinists to resuscitate the more self-serving accounts. Revisionist versions of Sri Lanka's past emphasized battles that were won against South Indian princes, the perceived political treachery of the Tamils and the usurping of Sinhala power. They repudiated or glossed over the strong Tamil–Sinhala partnership in ancient politics and the episodes of Sinhalese rulers seeking assistance from various South Indian rulers in their own power games.[41] But although such revisionism existed, this proto-communal tendency lay dormant for the most part (as in the rest of South Asia). Sinhala nationalists also failed to take into account the extended and nearly unbroken history of peace and non-intervention by its powerful neighbor, focusing instead on the demographic threat posed by India, over which the latter naturally had little control.

In this discourse, the role of Buddhist monks has been significant, especially in further inflaming the nationalist ideology set forth in the Mahavamsa chronicle by monks in the fifth century AD. The Mahavamsa ideology articulated a symbiotic relationship between the Buddhist sangha and Sinhalese rulers, as well as their special stewardship or protection of Buddhism. This ideology formed the basis for the notion of a Sinhala-Buddhist kingdom defended against intrusions and invasions by South Indian kingdoms. It provided the "founding myth" conflating Buddhism, Sinhala people and the territorial unit of the island. It overlooks the fact that until the Chola period, South India itself had a strong Buddhist heritage in certain areas which were Sri Lanka's key partners in Buddhist learning. Moreover, the assimilation aspects are flatly not recognized although, throughout the early history, there was a significant influx of South Indian migrants who intermingled with the Sinhalese. Leading anthropologist Tambiah explains how such misconceptions and misinterpretations have fueled the majority–minority complex: "[it is] partly a

---

[40] For one account of the historical exploits of Sri Lankan kings over India, see Kottegoda, "Sri Lanka's Conflict," pp. 205–206.

[41] There is much literature on the distortions of Sri Lanka's history. See for example, Tambiah, *Ethnic Fratricide*, pp. 81–94; Vincent Coelho, *Across the Palk Straits: India–Sri Lanka Relations* (New Delhi: Palit & Palit, 1976), pp. 153–155; and De Silva, *A History of Sri Lanka*, pp. 3–16.

product of Sri Lanka's miniscule size, both territorially and demographically, and the nature of exchanges with India, especially South India, that have been interpreted in certain (tendentious) ways and inscribed in the traditional chronicles and translated as the true past."[42]

Apart from the activist Buddhist monks, the most virulent anti-India group has been the JVP. The group's odd mixture of left-wing politics and Sinhala chauvinism is distinguished by its anti-India sentiment. The JVP's left ideology of "anti-imperialism" is focused almost entirely on what it sees as Indian expansionism and hegemony, though it does not tolerate outside involvement from anywhere. The distorted development of labor politics in Sri Lanka historically played into the contemporary politics of the JVP as well. Important sections of the radical left leadership had by the late 1920s moved away from representing a united workers' front; for instance, A. E. Goonesinghe went on to narrowly champion Sinhalese working class interests.[43] The JVP is at once ultra-nationalist and anti-statist with its combination of anti-Indian, anti-Tamil and radical leftism.

The perceived Indian threat thus has been one latent historical preoccupation, without proportionate cause. The case of "Indian Tamils" and the extrapolation of their strength is a good example. This group has been among the weakest and most impoverished in Sri Lankan society, offering little resistance from the time when their citizenship rights were denied at independence. Historically, the Indian government had a "hands off" policy regarding their interests. Far from zealously taking up their cause, the Indian government dragged its feet until the Sirimavo–Shastri agreement was literally thrust upon it in 1964, in which India belatedly agreed to repatriate 525,000 of a total of an estimated 975,000 Indian Tamils. Yet, the sentiments expressed by Sinhala political elites over time have been all out of proportion, whipping up images of the "Indian menace." In the late 1920s, contemporary journals were warning that "The day will come when Ceylon will be swamped by the Indian hordes, unless something is done to put an effective check."[44] During the discussion on constitutional reforms at independence, Sinhalese political leaders preferred to reject any recommendation (such as those by the Donoughmore Commission) which granted the Indian Tamils a large degree of self-rule if it also meant granting the franchise.[45] It is the Indian government's conspicuous lack

---

[42] Tambiah, *Ethnic Fratricide*, pp. 92–93.

[43] K. N. O. Dharmadasa citing E. F. C. Ludowyk in *Language, Religion, and Ethnic Assertiveness*, p. 229.

[44] Quoted in K. N. O. Dharmadasa, *Language, Religion, and Ethnic Assertiveness*, p. 229.

[45] A phobia expressed was that the Tamil estate workers would "submerge" the Sinhala villager in the hill country where the plantations are located. Coelho, *Across the Palk Straits*, p. 155.

of action on behalf of disenfranchised Indian Tamils that has been noteworthy rather than any interference.

India's strategic dilemma

The post-1983 environment in Sri Lanka that shut out even the moderate and traditionally strong forces of the TULF, led to a re-grouping of Tamil opposition of all shades into neighboring India, giving some credence to Sinhalese nationalist fears. But Sri Lankan Tamil activism in India was a break with past history, and although Tamil alienation and ultimate radicalization found a receptive audience in India, India's particular geopolitical identity needs meant that it would not be a simple relationship. The unraveling of ethnic relations in Sri Lanka had a number of repercussions for India: Tamil interests in Sri Lanka aligning with ethnic and domestic political interests in Tamil Nadu; at the center, the ruling Congress Party's declining fortunes in Tamil Nadu and its search for regional party alliances; and the need for balancing India's geopolitical interests as the pre-eminent regional power against unconditional support for separatist forces in the neighborhood. To make matters more complicated, India's own commitment to secular pluralism and territorial sovereignty was being violently challenged in Punjab at the same time.

India's response to the ethnic conflict next door has been described by some analysts as an exercise in "hegemony," with an Indian version of the Monroe Doctrine. The hegemonic argument is simplistic and misplaced. For example, Alan Bullion contends that "India had to manage the ethnic conflict in Sri Lanka itself, in order to both maintain its hegemonic role and keep external powers out of its 'backyard.'"[46] The objective of keeping hostile external powers at bay is insufficient evidence of hegemony, although Bullion seems to simply conflate the two. Conversely, he gives too little credence to the compulsions of cross-strait ethnic affiliation and the way in which it shaped *Sinhalese geopolitical identities* which, if not contained, was bound to put it on a collision course with India. In this context, it should have been clear to any Sinhalese political leader that Sri Lankan ethnic relations could not remain insulated given the importance of Tamil Nadu in India's democratic system. That this did not serve as a visible brake on the Sri Lankan government suggests the actual limits of India's influence.[47]

[46] Alan J. Bullion in *India, Sri Lanka and the Tamil Crisis 1976–1994: An International Perspective* (London: Pinter, 1995), p. 51.
[47] Barbara Crossette calls India "the regional meddler," a loaded term at best, but it reveals a certain amount of confusion on the part of outside observers. See Barbara Crossette, "Sri Lanka: In the Shadow of the Indian Elephant," *World Policy Journal*, 19.1 (Spring 2002), p. 25.

India clearly saw the intrusion of outside powers into the region (particularly acute during the Cold War years) as a threat to its interests. The underlying and even obsessive drive in Indian security and foreign policy has been to achieve strategic autonomy. But India's "strategic culture" militated against developing aggressive strategic doctrines that could guide policy; its hallmark was ambivalence and even an ideological aversion to realpolitik.[48] There has been an underlying vision of India as the inheritor of the British Raj, enjoying unchallenged supremacy in the Indian Ocean region, but its articulation has been by a small minority and on the margins. India's behavior with regard to Sri Lanka bears out the ambivalent and equivocal nature of its policy rather than a hegemonic pursuit of power.

During the 1977–1979 interregnum under the Janata government, New Delhi remained more or less neutral and noncommittal, despite rising Tamil grievances against the Sri Lankan government. When the Congress Party returned to power, Indira Gandhi's overbearing approach shifted from the Janata government's more self-conscious "good neighbor" policy, but her attitude was colored by Cold War anxieties. The early 1980s was a period of uncertainty for India, with renewed US–Soviet rivalry in nearby Afghanistan and the re-arming of Pakistan by the US as a frontline state. In stark contrast to India, Sri Lanka joined Pakistan in condemning the Soviet intervention in Afghanistan. Two controversies surfaced specifically between Sri Lanka and India: the port of Trincomalee and the Voice of America station. Given its strained relationship with the US, India was worried about Trincomalee being turned into another Diego Garcia base by the US so close to its borders; it was also concerned about the proposed expansion of Voice of America facilities north of Colombo, slated to be the largest of its size outside the US, with greater monitoring and eavesdropping capacities.

Balancing versus bandwagoning by Sri Lanka

As the Sri Lankan government launched an increasingly military response to the insurgency after 1983 and Tamil guerrillas found sanctuaries in Tamil Nadu, Jayawardene sought training for his military from sources perceived as anti-India. Sri Lanka's turning to Pakistan, China and, reportedly, Israel during this period put India on notice. According to leading analyst, S. D. Muni, Indian policymakers interpreted these moves

---

[48] See the author's "India's Strategic Doctrine and Practice: The Impact of Nuclear Testing," in Raju G. C. Thomas and Amit Gupta (eds.) *India's Nuclear Security* (Boulder, CO: Lynne Rienner Publishers, 2000).

as a strategy to "isolate India in the region by facilitating the strategic presence of the forces inimical to India's perceived security interests"[49] Even before then, Sri Lanka had shown a willingness to adopt a foreign policy that risked alienating India, as opposed to the arguably safer "bandwagoning" that realist theory might predict.[50] A successful balancing behavior for Sri Lanka was in fact inherently difficult, given its location and the absence of compelling alliance partners to keep India in check (unlike even Nepal situated between rivals India and China).

Sri Lanka's behavior suggests that a purely strategic explanation is insufficient. To understand why bandwagoning has not been the predominant choice, we have to bring in geopolitical identity factors – specifically, the implicit identification of Sri Lankan Tamils with Indian Tamils and, by extension, the Indian state. Given this linkage, any open embrace of India would be dissonant from a strategic cultural perspective, not to mention the potential negative fallout for state leadership at the domestic political level from Sinhala nationalists.

Indeed, Colombo has been widely assailed – on the one hand by Sinhala nationalists when there has been any whiff of interference from New Dellhi and, on the other hand, by a section of the more cautious analysts who have warned against provoking India, pointing to Sri Lanka's dangerous isolation and vulnerability.[51] The Committee for Rational Development (CRD), created by highly respected public figures from both communities in the aftermath of the riots in 1983, questioned the Sri Lankan government's policies (emotionally satisfying to many Sinhalese) which appeared to put it on a "collision course" with India, noting that the Tamil "political underground" operating from Tamil Nadu could only be controlled by the Indian and Tamil Nadu governments. After pointing out the futility of dealing with internal opponents purely through confrontation, the CRD maintained that "There may be forces within the government which are urging it to pursue a similar [confrontationist] strategy in the international arena. Given our size and bargaining power, such a strategy would be suicidal. Non-alignment and the strengthening of relations with India must remain the 'front line' of our foreign policy."[52] This set of conflicting pressures for Sri Lanka, along with India's own geopolitical ambivalence,

---

[49] S. D. Muni, *Pangs of Proximity* (New Dehli: Sage Publications,1993), p. 52

[50] Earlier, the Sri Lankan government had taken other provocative stands against India such as allowing Pakistani aircraft to overfly its territory during the 1971 Bangladesh war when India prohibited it, thus providing an alternate route to the Pakistan military.

[51] Jayatilleka, "The Ethnic Conflict," p. 237.

[52] Committee for Rational Development, "Selected Documents of the Committee for Rational Development, July 1983–March 1984," in Committee for Rational Development (ed.) *Sri Lanka: The Ethnic Conflict* (New Delhi: Navrang Publishers, 1984), p. 63.

became most evident during the intervention of the Indian Peacekeeping Force (IPKF) in 1987.

Prelude to intervention

Rajiv Gandhi, who succeeded his mother as Prime Minister in 1984 after her assassination by Sikh bodyguards (thus falling victim to the separatist politics of Punjab), negotiated the Indo-Sri Lanka Accord paving the way for India's direct intervention. This did not however represent a break in India's strategic ideology. The international environment had changed to India's benefit, signaled by the 1984 Memorandum of Understanding between India and the US for greater cooperation in the economic, technological and defense spheres. This was interpreted as an endorsement of sorts for a more assertive role in ensuring regional stability, thus easing India's geopolitical options.[53]

India had not become directly involved in negotiating with Sri Lanka until the ethnic rioting of 1983. At the same time, it was an open secret that India backed various Tamil militant groups operating in Tamil Nadu, largely thanks to pressure from Tamil Nadu Chief Minister M. G. Ramachandran, who became a leading spokesman for Tamil groups, especially the LTTE. The orientation of New Delhi and Tamil Nadu politicians however was not always congruent: the latter were motivated by ethnic bonds and gaining local political mileage; the ruling Congress Party wanted to shore up its sagging support in this key state, as well as ensure that India would be the regional power broker. The Congress had been dislodged from Tamil Nadu since 1967 as a result of bitter caste politics and Tamil nationalism and could hardly afford to be seen as insensitive to Tamil grievances.

The leading edge of Tamil nationalism in Tamil Nadu during the 1960s was the Dravida Munetra Kazhagam (DMK) party, but it broke apart with the creation of the All India Anna DMK, only to splinter again. Intense competition between these parties have led them to espouse the cause and outbid each other for the sponsorship of the Sri Lankan Tamils, and lead to greater "internationalization" of the conflict.[54] While ethnic affiliation afforded fairly easy entry into Tamil Nadu politics for leading Sri Lankan Tamil political and cultural leaders, it is difficult to find material support

---

[53] S. D. Muni, "India and the Post Cold War World: Opportunities and Challenges," *Asian Survey*, 31.9 (September 1991), p. 866; and Wilson, *The Break-Up of Sri Lanka*, pp. 199–200. The only discordant note came from China, which was perceived to be close to Sri Lanka then.

[54] See for example, Shelton U. Kodikara, *Foreign Policy of Sri Lanka: A Third World Perspective* (Delhi: Chanakya Publications, 1982), pp. 40–41.

until after the 1983 ethnic carnage, and even DMK support was not unlimited. An editorial in the leading daily in Tamil Nadu, *The Hindu*, in 1977 proclaimed that "The TULF leaders should forget, once and for all, the idea of a separate state, and work peacefully with the Sinhalese, and it is for the Government to act swiftly to create the necessary climate of confidence, so that the Tamils no longer feel they are a neglected lot and mere second class citizens."[55]

Rajiv Gandhi's own preference seemed to be for negotiations by the Tamil groups rather than armed insurgency. Given India's sensibilities, it is not surprising that, in 1985, Rajiv Gandhi made a public statement that Sri Lankan Tamils should not expect a separate state but something similar to what India has.[56]

Sinhalese commentators criticized India's perceived "double-track" strategy of arming Tamil groups as a pressure tactic, while conducting negotiations. According to knowledgeable sources, however, India also wanted to prevent Tamil militant groups from finding support from hostile powers or becoming powerful enough to divide the island.[57] Well-known Indian experts have noted India's interest in limiting the level of Tamil militancy and concern about the LTTE's growing autonomy.[58] The impact of a divided Sri Lanka was not a welcome prospect for India, even though Tamil Nadu's ethnic restiveness was no longer an issue. This was clearly not lost on LTTE leader V. Prabhakaran who, in a series of exclusive interviews granted to noted Indian journalist Anita Pratap well before the 1987 IPKF episode, predicted that "Eventually, I will have to battle India ... Even more than Sri Lanka, India will not allow us to create Tamil Eelam because of its own 55 million Tamils in Tamil Nadu."[59]

Between 1983 and the IPKF intervention in 1987, India's main role was as a facilitator to get the Tamil militants and Sri Lankan government to the negotiating table. Immediately after the 1983 riots, the Indian government appointed G. Parthasarathy, a seasoned diplomat, as its envoy for the talks. (Contrary to assumptions in Colombo given Parthasarathy's Tamil

---

[55] Quoted in Kodikara, *Foreign Policy of Sri Lanka*, p. 42. There is no consensus on precisely when the Indian government began covertly assisting Tamil militants; the first public revelation was by investigative reporting in *India Today* in late March 1984.

[56] Wilson, *The Break-Up of Sri Lanka*, p. 183. Wilson was a close Tamil associate of Jayawaradene and served briefly as an intermediary in the conflict.

[57] Ketheshwaran Loganathan, *Sri Lanka: Lost Opportunities* (Colombo: Centre for Policy Research and Analysis, University of Colombo, December 1996), p. 91. Loganathan was a key figure in EPRLF.

[58] The South Asia Analysis Group, based in Chennai, provides ample evidence of this continued thinking on the part of influential Indians.

[59] Quoted in Anita Pratap, *Island of Blood: Frontline Reports from Sri Lanka, Afghanistan and Other South Asian Flashpoints* (New York: Penguin Books, 2001), p. 68.

Brahmin background, those who interacted with him point out that he actually stressed the need for moderation and reconciliation to the Tamil groups.)[60] The highlight of India's efforts was the Thimpu talks begun in 1985, in which it managed to get all the relevant Tamil groups involved. But in January 1987, the Sri Lankan government launched "Operation Liberation," precipitating a crisis that eventually brought India directly and militarily into the fray.

The Indian intervention

The experience of the Indian Peacekeeping Force led to major changes in the nature of the Sri Lankan conflict and it contributed to some re-writing of Indo-Sri Lankan relations that had seemed unlikely. Peter Gourevitch's explanation is highly relevant here: geopolitical thrusts had far more impact than at the purely international level, reaching well into the domestic sphere.

The Indian intervention came at the invitation of Sri Lankan President J. R. Jayawardene, but it may well have been a face-saving gesture by a man whom many dubbed the "fox" for his legendary cunningness. The immediate cause of India's stepped-up involvement was a looming humanitarian crisis precipitated by the Sri Lankan government's massive military offensive against the LTTE guerrillas in May 1987, which included an unprecedented and all-out embargo in the north, even of food and medicine. Civilians were reeling under what some Sinhalese were labeling a final assault, and calls for aiding the beleaguered Tamils were gaining loud momentum in Tamil Nadu. In an uncharacteristic show of resolve, the Indian government defied the Sri Lankan government's blockade of the north and air dropped tons of food and medicine into Jaffna during early June. Although it violated Sri Lankan sovereignty, it was presented as a form of "humanitarian intervention," a term that had yet to gain currency in the international context. In a reversal of longstanding Sri Lankan policy, Jayawardene requested Indian "peacekeeping" assistance, leading to an immediate agreement with Rajiv Gandhi's government, the arrival of Indian forces into Sri Lanka and an abandoning of the military offensive. Under Indian pressure, it was agreed that negotiations would re-open to bring the civil war to an end.

The Indo-Sri Lanka Accord of July 1987 was a milestone in Sri Lanka's domestic and international politics. The Accord was to serve as the basis for a negotiated settlement, with India as the guarantor. It committed both parties to supporting a multi-ethnic, multi-religious plural society while

[60] Personal interviews, Colombo, Sri Lanka, December 1996.

preserving the territorial integrity of Sri Lanka. Meanwhile, India agreed to ensure that its territory was not used for activities against the Sri Lankan government, even permitting naval cooperation in this regard. Militants were expected to give up their arms, with Indian troops based as peace-keepers in the north and east. In return, India was reportedly able to extract a commitment vital to its geopolitical interests, contained in an "exchange of letters" between the leaders. Sri Lanka purportedly agreed that the port of Trincomalee or any other port in Sri Lanka would not be made available for military use in a way that was prejudicial to Indian interests.[61]

The implementation of the agreement, however, proved to be a debacle for India as its involvement turned from being a peacekeeping buffer between the government and the LTTE, to fighting the very Tamils who had originally viewed India as their patron.[62] The LTTE quickly came to view India as having betrayed their "Eelam" demand and resisted India's heavy-handed military presence because of the requirement to disarm before negotiations. Fifty thousand troops and over 1,000 casualties later, the IPKF withdrew. From the perspective of peacemaking, the episode was a critical lost opportunity. Since then, Indian involvement has receded but not disappeared. Throughout the various twists and turns during the intervention, India's preference for political pluralism has been consistent.

Hardline versus moderate outcomes

The balance between moderate and hardline elements had shifted drastic-ally by 1983, with Sinhalese opinion leading the way. The ultra-nationalist Sinhala forces such as the JVP were facing off with moderate and liberal compatriots. In Tamil Nadu, politicians favored the radical LTTE, thanks in large part to the LTTE's organizational and popular strength. The rise of the LTTE was also due to its serious fundraising capacity (especially from the Tamil diaspora) and its access to the international arms market.[63]

Developments at the politico-institutional level in Sri Lanka were also shutting out traditional avenues for moderate opinion among Tamils and Sinhalese. The use of draconian legislation and emergency meas-ures, along with changes in the political structure, inched the state

---

[61] Although these letters have not been made public, its plausibility is affirmed by most experts.

[62] There was even some speculation that the "wily" Jayawaradene drew the less experienced Rajiv Gandhi into this "trap" of getting India to fight the Sri Lankan government's battle.

[63] The LTTE's ability to sustain itself independent of Indian support has been repeatedly demonstrated. The politico-economic backing of the Tamil diaspora which was forced to flee the island in different waves since 1983 is well known. See for example, Richardson, *Paradise Poisoned*, pp. 412–413.

towards a more authoritarian stance, the abuse of power and rampant human rights violations. The political space to challenge government policies or mount alternative prescriptions narrowed during the 1980s, making it difficult for non-governmental, public interest and progressive civil society groups to exist, let alone flourish.[64] This was a huge blow to the development of critical civil society groups (a growing sector in the country) in both the Sinhalese and Tamil communities. The public education sector was also increasingly used as a site for cultivating polarizing identities, led by state actors.[65]

On the Tamil side, the large number of militant groups and the stiff inter-group competition for support pushed them towards more extremist positions, making it politically (and physically) inadvisable to advocate positions which could be interpreted as a compromise. It was all too easy to slap the label of "traitor" onto those who were willing to risk entering into negotiations with the Sri Lankan government, which in the past had repeatedly exposed its biases. India's support in the form of safe havens and training camps in Tamil Nadu provided an implicit bargaining advantage for the LTTE vis-à-vis the Sri Lankan government. The IPKF intervention brought about a severe reaction and was seen as a "betrayal" of the Sinhalese people by opposition parties led by the SLFP's Sirimavo Bandaranayake in alliance with the JVP. Despite this outcry about India's intervention, India's support for Tamil militancy as a whip against Sri Lanka, and Sri Lanka's "loss of sovereignty," what is ironic is that the IPKF interlude revealed a marked preference by India for more "moderate" Tamil forces and the settlement of the ethnic conflict through the traditional political system.

The IPKF episode and breakdown of relations with the LTTE

Had the Indo-Sri Lanka Accord been implemented in its entirety, it would have resulted in a devolved political structure for Sri Lanka, an objective that had continually eluded the country since the aborted Bandaranayake–Chelvanayakam Pact of 1957. (Indeed, the Accord closely resembled this pact, which ironically Jayawardene had been instrumental in scuttling 30 years earlier. The B-C Pact is often said by Tamils to be only agreement negotiated in "good faith" by Sinhalese politicians.) The Indo-Sri Lankan Accord also provided for the recognition of Tamil as an official language, along with Sinhala, to address a longstanding Tamil demand. In November 1987, the Sri Lankan parliament passed the 13th Amendment by a

---

[64] For an independent assessment of how far Sri Lanka's democratic norms had slipped, see Sieghart, *Sri Lanka*, pp. 22–92.

[65] This theme is explored in Aall and Ollapally (eds.) *Perspectives*.

two-thirds majority and made Tamil another official language, with English to be a so-called link language, and laid out the procedures for the devolution of power under Provincial Councils. This landmark legislation would have been highly unlikely without Indian involvement, pointing to the deep and potentially moderating influence of India on Sri Lanka's domestic structures and politics.

As the guarantor of the Accord, India had hoped to persuade the well-known parliamentary party TULF to participate in the North-East Provincial Council elections mandated under the agreement and thereby confer legitimacy on this process.[66] India's expectations were high despite reservations from the LTTE; after all, Jaffna Tamils had welcomed Indian troops with garlands. The TULF, however, opted to stay out of the elections, partly to avoid displeasing the LTTE which had begun to view the IPKF as an "occupying force" rather than "liberators." India then turned to the Tigers' rival EPRLF, clearly a more pliable partner and hence no doubt attractive. The EPRLF also shared the Indian government's preference for following the electoral path at that point and was willing to give up arms. The group's ideology could be described as leftist but its platform envisioned a secular and democratic coalition of forces, something eminently suited to India's own political conceptions.

One of the casualties of the IPKF experiment was the Indian government's support for the Tigers. When an LTTE female suicide bomber was implicated in the assassination of Rajiv Gandhi in Tamil Nadu during his campaign for re-election in 1991, the Tigers fell from grace along with their backers in Tamil Nadu. The Tamil Nadu state administration cracked down hard and destroyed much of the LTTE infrastructure. Worst of all for the LTTE, Rajiv Gandhi's assassination turned Indian opinion hostile. The chief ideologue of the LTTE, Anton Balasingham, conceded by 2001 that, in retrospect, the assassination of Rajiv Gandhi had been "a historical blunder."[67] In an interview to the Indian NDTV in June 2006, Balasingham appealed to the Indian public to forget the past.

The negotiation path

Since 1991, the LTTE has found it difficult to regain its support base in India but under their enigmatic leader, V. Prabhakaran, it has proven extremely resilient. The Tigers have also shown themselves to be surprisingly capable of acting in the political sphere through intermittent

---

[66] For one close-up perspective on the Accord and its implementation from an EPRLF viewpoint, see Loganathan, *Sri Lanka*, pp. 126–162.

[67] Pratap, *Island of Blood*, pp. 125–126.

negotiations with both SLFP and UNP-led governments, starting in earnest in 1994, although the first much-publicized ceasefire broke down within a matter of four months in April 1995. The increased political and geopolitical isolation of the Tigers from India on the other hand, most likely made the Sri Lankan state more receptive to India. Abandoning direct involvement, India left open the door in order to nudge the militants towards talks while lobbying the government for a settlement based on substantial autonomy.

From the mid-1990s onwards, the idea of negotiations had become an integral part of the bitter conflict, a development which owed much to India's previous efforts. India's stand cannot be understood without seeing its particular set of geopolitical identity needs vis-à-vis the Sri Lankan government and the militants, pushing the protagonists towards less extremism and a non-military path. By 2002, the breakthroughs achieved by the Norwegian-brokered negotiations between the LTTE and the newly elected UNP government of Prime Minister Ranil Wikramasinghe suggested that the militant group had evolved into a viable political actor. The Tigers' new thinking was dramatically illustrated with their unilateral declaration of a ceasefire in December 2001, laying the path towards a peace agreement.

The Ceasefire Agreement reached in February 2002 represented historic compromises on both sides and some astute finessing all around. The willingness to re-assess separate statehood on the one hand and federal options on the other, "without prejudice to pre-existing positions" for instance, allowed the LTTE and the government to begin negotiations without outright concessions. Wikaramasinghe had come to power trouncing the Sinhala nationalist parties on a "peace" platform. The process also had universal and open support from key outside actors: India, the US, the UK, Japan, the European Community and even donor agencies. According to one prominent Sri Lankan commentator, "In terms of its long-term impact on the conflict and peace processes in Sri Lanka, the CFA of February 2002 is second only to the Indo-Sri Lanka agreement ... Both of these documents, although they have not led to the cessation of Sri Lanka's ethnic war, in a very fundamental way redefined major dimensions of the conflict and pointed towards possible trajectories of settlement."[68]

While the Norwegians took the lead, India was content to play a background role for several reasons: there was no longer the same pressure from Tamil Nadu politics; the peace process was going in a direction India preferred; and, unlike earlier periods, India was confident of the tacit and

---

[68] Jayadeva Uyangoda, "Three Years After the Ceasefire Agreement: Where Have We Gone?" *Daily Mirror*, March 17, 2005.

even explicit acceptance by outside powers of India's stabilizing role.[69] Besides, India's economic liberalization progress was having a particularly positive impact on Indo-Sri Lanka relations, highlighted by the signing of the Indo-Sri Lankan Free Trade Agreement in March 2000. (The Indo-Sri Lankan FTA has been held up by India as a model for its relations with its neighbors.) Thus, for the first time in decades, geopolitical and domestic forces were simultaneously moving in a benign direction, reining in extremist, militarist and non-secular elements.

The role of spoilers

Even under such favorable circumstances, the treat of the "spoilers" had not been eliminated. In this instance, it was a combination of state and non-state actors that posed the biggest challenge. With Wikaramasinghe's victory, a unique but awkward situation of having an SLFP President alongside a UNP Prime Minister emerged. This could have finally provided the basis for a united mainstream Sinhala front to back the peace process; instead the co-habitation resembled a blood feud, wrecking the prospects for collaboration. President Kumaratunge (daughter of S. W. R. D. and Srimavo Bandaranayake), bolstered by the JVP and nationalist support, ultimately brought down the government using her executive powers in February 2004. Since then, the more liberal, pro-peace forces have steadily lost ground, first in the parliamentary election of April 2004 when the SLFP alliance returned to power and then again in November 2005 when SLFP presidential candidate Mahinda Rajapakse (seen as a hardliner) narrowly beat Wikaramasinghe.[70]

The 2004 and 2005 elections and the SLFP's choice of alliance partners gave the JVP and Jathika Hela Urugayu (JHU, a party of Buddhist monks which openly advocates a state based on Sinhala–Buddhist supremacy) a huge opening to influence the national agenda. The JVP managed to get 39 seats in parliament (far exceeding its earlier ten seats largely due to a no-contest electoral arrangement with the SLFP) allowing it to play a critical "kingmaker" role. Kumaratunge's justification for bringing down the UNP government for being "soft" on the Tigers during negotiations and conceding too much sovereignty to international actors,

---

[69] Personal interviews with high level policymakers in the Ministry of External Affairs, New Delhi, India, November 1–2, 2004. The Tamil Nadu government in August 2006 went so far as to deny permission for the holding of an international conference by the well-known World Tamil Congress in the state, claiming it feared that LTTE cadre and sympathizers of other banned groups might enter the state during the conference. *The Hindu*, August 11, 2006.

[70] New presidential elections were necessary since Kumaratunga's term expired.

jeopardizing "national security," played directly into the hands of the JVP and JHU. The brand of ethno-nationalism of the JVP and JHU that brooks little accommodation with the Tamil minority and opposes outside involvement, whether from Norway or India, continues to be an enormous impediment (whether working inside or outside the government).[71]

The high profile consecutive elections of 2004 and 2005 allowed the Sinhala nationalists to keep up a withering attack against the peace process and international involvement.[72] Ranil Wikaramasinghe, the Sinhalese leader most closely identified with the peace negotiations (six rounds had been held), found himself on the defensive and facing an extremely tight presidential race. Moreover, his natural support base among the Tamils failed to materialize when they stayed away from the polls in large numbers. Although the LTTE had not called for a formal boycott, their various pronouncements were not lost on anyone. In demonstrating its own "strength," however, the LTTE weakened the liberal forces in the UNP, bringing about what could be the worst outcome yet.[73] In his first policy statement to the Parliament, President-elect Rajapakse demanded a new ceasefire agreement with the LTTE and indicated a U-turn on the concept of federalism that his party had previously agreed to. The country has once again slid into violence, much like the many frustrated attempts at peace-making, only worse because this time a settlement had seemed so close.

Conclusion

This chapter has shown how over time the dormant proto-communal tendency in Sri Lanka came to produce extremist politics in both the Sinhala and Tamil communities. The LTTE's meteoric rise was particularly anomalous given that the Tamil movement had for long never accepted an "ideology of violence."[74] The rise of Sinhala nationalism and the decline of political secularism clearly stoked Tamil militancy. The peculiar version

---

[71] Some Sinhalese commentators questioned Norway's role by arguing that it shifted from being a facilitator to a mediator, and that it tilts towards the LTTE. See, for example, Shanth Hennayake, "Realities of Sri Lanka Today," paper presented at a panel on Sri Lanka: Broadening the Discourse on Peace and Security, Sigur Center for Asian Studies, George Washington University, Washington, DC, April 9, 2004.

[72] For coverage of the lead-up to the election and its aftermath, see BBC at www.bbc.co.uk, November 14–21, 2006; and Reuters at http://in.today.reuters.com.

[73] The LTTE had been accusing the UNP government of encouraging and aiding rebels within the LTTE, most notably Colonel Karuna in the eastern province, as a way of weakening the Tigers even as negotiations were on. This is probably one reason that the LTTE had little remorse in contributing to the defeat of the UNP.

[74] On this point, see Radhika Coomaraswamy, " 'Through the Looking Glass Darkly:' The Politics of Ethnicity," in Committee for Rational Development (ed.) Sri Lanka: The Ethnic Conflict (New Delhi: Navrang Publishers, 1984), p. 194.

of the Sinhalese majority's historical "minority complex" vis-à-vis Tamils in India created a geopolitical identity that went beyond a purely strategic interest, sharpening chauvinism against Sri Lankan Tamils. The Sri Lankan state's use of threat inflation regarding India, especially strong during periods of eroding legitimacy and declining democracy, also ensured that Indo-Sri Lankan relations would not be friction free.

India has periodically given Sri Lanka good reason to feel insecure, especially since backing Tamil militants after 1983, but long periods of non-intervention are even more noteworthy. Indeed, even during its most intense period of involvement during the IPKF episode, India's own geopolitical identity needs ensured that a settlement via democratic methods most amenable to the secular "moderates" was its preferred outcome rather than an ethnically splintered island that New Delhi could dominate. The 2002–2004 interlude in which the UNP–LTTE ceasefire agreement held saw the beginning of a re-emergence of "political secularism" at the same time that geopolitical forces were benign, and even beneficial. It suggested that geopolitical identity conceptions need not be static, nor condemn states in South Asia to unrelenting competition, often feeding extremism in the process. The Sri Lankan case suggests that the important factor is how South Asia's delicate balance between secular, ethno-religious and geopolitical identities ultimately gets tilted, with the state as a mediating factor.

7   Bangladesh: divided politics and geopolitics

Bangladesh's short history since independence in 1971 has produced several surprises. Economically, it has defied those who dismissed its prospects from the beginning and has even been an innovator in small-scale economic development. Politically, it has moved haltingly towards a democratic framework that has been durable, if turbulent. Bangladesh's society, too, has been notable for its pluralist ethos and religious co-existence. For the most part, it has also managed to remain relatively insulated from major geopolitical upheavals that have shaken the region and beyond.

Since the elections of 2001, however, politics in Bangladesh has become unexpectedly divisive, exposing sharp polarizations on secular, religious and geopolitical identities. A critical question is whether the increasing violence in the political sphere is a reflection of these fundamental issues or, more simply, competition among parties for political spoils. The rise of Islamist extremism in the country and its implications beyond its borders suggests that we cannot ignore this question, despite the country's promising origins. In addition, as a Muslim majority country, Bangladesh has stood in some contrast to Pakistan and Afghanistan, providing us with a counter-example to developments in the region. For the purposes of this book, the focus here is on how the various identity strands in Bangladesh have interacted over time, with the country first escaping the worst forms of polarization, only to be confronted with them later. Unlike the other chapters, it is the *potential* for sustained violent extremism that is of concern. In this sense, Bangladesh is a "test case," with the jury still out.

At the strategic level, Bangladesh's attitude to India has swung from attraction to aversion. This inconsistent policy orientation in large part mirrors its increasingly conflicted geopolitical identity in the South Asian region. India's security preoccupations in its northeast borderlands, abutting Bangladesh (and China), have not made bilateral relations any easier. Assam, with the largest linguistic community in India's northeast, provides a good example of how India's sovereignty and identity concerns clash with Bangladesh's changing strategic and identity interests.

This chapter will begin by laying out Bangladesh's largely secular political foundation and how its particular socio-cultural ethos supported such an orientation. Next, we will consider the erosion of this political culture and the lead up to the current climate. In the unfolding struggle between various notions of secular, religious and geopolitical identities, we will give special attention to how the Indo-Bangladesh relationship has played its part. As we have seen in previous chapters, the role of the state in fashioning an internally and externally polarizing identity conception in this regard is significant. Finally, the chapter looks at the mounting evidence of a possible transformation of Bangladesh's politics and geopolitics and what mitigating factors may avoid a fatal tilt towards an extremism that threatens the country and the region.

Common bonds and fragmented identity

The ethnic composition of Bangladesh makes it the most unified state in South Asia. It is almost entirely Bengali in ethno-linguistic terms, barring a 500,000-strong tribal population out of a total of 145 million. It has a sizeable Hindu minority at 12 percent, a tiny Christian and Buddhist following in tribal areas, with the remainder of the population being Muslim. Historically, the Bengali language has played a highly significant role, first as a medium of national prominence during India's anti-colonial struggle, and then as the leading edge of the Bangladeshi independence movement against Pakistan. More than 1,000 miles of Indian territory separated the eastern and western wings of Pakistan at the time of its creation, but the distance turned out to be much more than physical.

Except for their religion, Muslims in east and west Pakistan had little in common, whereas religion was the only factor separating Hindu and Muslim Bengalis.[1] In the words of Maulana Abdul Kalam Azad, the most well-known Muslim Congress leader of the Indian independence movement, "It is one of the greatest frauds on the people to suggest that religious affinity can unite areas which are geographically, economically, linguistically and culturally different"[2] Indeed, during the Lahore Conference of the Muslim League in 1940 during which the Pakistan Resolution was first officially adopted, it called for "independent states" in the northwest and

---

[1] The dismal fate of 300,000 Urdu-speaking non-Bengali Muslims (termed Biharis) in the country after 1971 points to the critical importance of language. On the traditionally broad identity notions, see, for example, Robert Jackson, *South Asian Crisis* (London: Chatto & Windus, 1975), pp. 14–15; Verghese, *An End to Confrontation*, pp. 20, 146–147; and Rounaq Jahan, *Pakistan: Failure in National Integration* (Dhaka: University Press, 1972).

[2] Maulana Abdul Kalam Azad, *India Wins Freedom: An Autobiographical Narrative* (Bombay, 1959), p. 227.

east (current day Pakistan and Bangladesh). The basis for this lay in the well-recognized cultural and geographical differences of the two areas. It was only in 1946 that the Resolution was amended in favor of one Muslim state.[3]

The Awami League, which went on to lead the movement for Bangladeshi independence, had broken from the Bengal Muslim League and formed the Awami Muslim League (AML) in 1949. Within the AML were dissidents whose ideology was not very different from that of the Muslim League, but a large section of the party was secular, opposing even the term Muslim in its title. (The word "Muslim" was dropped in 1955 to emphasize the party's secular character.)

At the time of partition, there was concern in Pakistan's government that India would be able to exercise undue influence in East Pakistan, particularly because of the large Hindu minority. Government leaders at the center launched anti-Hindu programs to counter India's potential influence but found little support among Bengali Muslims.[4] Unified political opposition to Pakistani rule made the socio-cultural ethos binding the two communities over centuries even stronger. Bengalis of all stripes saw discrimination at the hands of Pakistani authorities in every arena – economic, political and military. The percentage of East Pakistanis in the critical Pakistan armed forces is a case in point: in 1963, estimates put it at a mere 3.9 percent.[5] The perceived contempt of the Pakistani elite for their Bengali compatriots and their blatant unwillingness to share power more equally set the stage for revolt against Pakistan in 1971.[6] Secular Bengali nationalism under the Awami League provided the major impetus for autonomy and, later, independent statehood, shattering the two-nation theory in the process.[7] India's critical patronage of the Bangladeshi movement, culminating in war with Pakistan, only underscored the complexity of identity in the new state.

This well-developed Bengali identity came under increasing strain, however, in 1975, with the military coup that overthrew the Awami League government of Sheikh Mujib Rahman. Since then, the major struggle has

---

[3] Bhuiyan, *Emergence of Bangladesh*, pp. 16–17.

[4] Charles Peter O'Donnell, *Bangladesh: Biography of a Muslim Nation* (Boulder: Westview Press, 1984), p. 27.

[5] Bhuiyan, *Emergence of Bangladesh*, p. 79.

[6] For example, during the rule of Ayub Khan under martial law decrees from 1958 to 1962, the ruling group did not include a single Bengali. Talukder Maniruzzaman, *The Bangladesh Revolution and Its Aftermath* (Dhaka: Bangladesh Books International Ltd, 1980), p. 9. See also Mizanur Rahman Shelley, *Emergence of a New Nation in a Multi-Polar World: Bangladesh* (Dhaka: Academic Press and Publishers Ltd., 2000), p. 131.

[7] Bhuiyan, *Emergence of Bangladesh*, provides a good account of the consolidation of the AL's hold on the masses. (It should be noted that Bengali nationalism did marginalize the non-Bengali minorities, especially the tribal population in the Chittagong Hill Tracts.)

been between a more secular Bengali socio-cultural identity and a religious identity based on Islam for Bangladesh. Since the incoporation of the Jamaat-e-Islami (JeI), the leading Islamic party in the country, into the Bangladesh National Party (BNP) government in 2001, this debate has intensified (please note that I will be using JeI in this chapter rather than JI, as it is more commonly associated with Bangladesh). Scattered communal incidents in the aftermath of the elections, as well as the shocking and unprecedented political violence from 2004 onwards blamed on Islamist extremists, suggests that the politics of identity have reached a critical stage in Bangladesh. Latent in this debate is the question of relations with India, another potent element of its geopolitical identity.

Moderating tendencies

Bangladesh was faced with seemingly insurmountable challenges at independence: devastating floods and cyclones, a galloping population growth, extremely low industrial capacity and abysmal literacy rates. Its economic relations with the western wing had resembled a "colonial structure," with cheap raw material going from the "periphery" into value-added goods at the center, leaving the new state in a perilous situation.[8] Still, the Awami League, under independence leader Mujib Rahman, had been swept into power on a wave of popularity after leading the liberation movement, and a democratic structure was set up. The preamble to the first Constitution enshrined the four principles of nationalism, democracy, secularism and socialism, and strongly reflected the Indian model. In the first parliamentary elections held in 1973, the Awami League won handily, with nearly 75 percent of the votes. (All religious political parties were disbanded after independence.) The government's form of secularism attempted to maintain an equidistance from all religions rather than completely separating from them; for example, on the government-controlled television and radio, excerpts from the holy books of Islam, Hinduism, Buddhism and Christianity were read. Thus, at the highest level of the state, "political secularism" was being dramatically propagated, with apparent popular support.

There was little vocal opposition to such an approach, except from the small JeI. The Jamaat was weak in Bangladesh, having established its roots there only since the early 1950s, when members from the parent body in the western wing arrived to form a party in the east.[9] In the first free and

---

[8] Robin Blackburn (ed.) *Explosion in a Subcontinent* (New York, Penguin Books, 1975); See also Jackson, *South Asian Crisis*, pp. 19–21.

[9] One of the most detailed studies of the JeI in Bangladesh is by Razia Akhtar Banu, "Jamaat-i-Islami in Bangladesh: Challenges and Prospects," in Jussain Mutalib and Tajul Islam Hashmi (eds.) *Islam, Muslims and the Modern State* (London: Macmillan Press, 1994), pp. 85–86.

fair national election ever held in Pakistan (in 1970), the Islamic parties had fared badly: they won less than 7 percent of the vote in the East, in contrast to the Awami League's 76 percent. The Awami League had won all but two seats in East Pakistan (giving it a majority and the privilege of forming the next Pakistan government, something which the western wing was not prepared to accept, thus sparking the immediate crisis towards civil war).[10] The JeI's activism spawned its own student group Islamic Chattra Sangha (ICS) which emerged against the growing ranks of radical left-wing student groups agitating on the language issue and on a platform of secularism, non-communalism and anti-imperialism.[11]

The Jamaat had conspicuously bucked the Bengali nationalist trend from the beginning, opting to align firmly with Pakistan's central authorities. The JeI's support (as informants and fighters) despite the violence unleashed by the Pakistan armed forces against Bengali civilians, especially the intelligentsia and minorities, led to the group's infamy as "collaborators of Pakistan's army" versus the "patriots and freedom fighters."[12] Mujib Rahman's government banned the JeI and stripped its top leadership of citizenship, and a number of them moved to Pakistan. The Jamaat's adoption of religious affiliation over Bengali nationalism in the face of Pakistan's brutal suppression of their compatriots had not only sealed the Jamaat's fate but also discredited any official or political role for religion in the new state.

Indeed, close analysts were dismissive of the prospects of any major political inroads by the Jamaat even 20 years after Bangladesh's independence. Most importantly, the predominant view was that the three-decade-old struggle with the power elite of Pakistan had solidified a political culture that was incompatible with the "fundamentalist" religious ideology of Jamaat.[13] According to one expert, "In the secularized politics of Bangladesh, religion would not have the degree of salience it had in former United Pakistan."[14] Support for secularism had grown the more the Pakistani rulers were seen to exploit Islam to try to save a united Pakistan.

The marginal role for religion in politics was natural in the Bengal polity given the dominant form of Islam. The arrival of Islam in East Bengal between the thirteenth and fifteenth centuries had been peaceful, with conversions by and large of desperately poor landless peasants trying to

[10] Jackson, *South Asian Crisis*, p. 24.
[11] Maniruzzaman, *The Bangladesh Revolution*, p. 57.
[12] These are commonly used terms in Bangladesh in this connection.
[13] Razia Akhtar Banu, *Islam in Bangladesh* (Leiden: E. J. Brill, 1992), pp.163–169.
[14] Maniruzzaman, *The Bangladesh Revolution*, p.241. Along with U. A. B. Banu, Maniruzzman offers some of the most detailed research on religion and politics in Bangladesh.

escape the Hindu caste system. Bengali identity itself had taken strong shape since the ninth century and thus could not be easily displaced. The form of Islam that emerged combined elements of Hinduism and local popular culture with Sufism. This amalgamation, along with the Bengali language, served to set apart the eastern and western wings of Pakistan from the start, making for an extremely uneasy national identity based on statist notions of "official Islam."[15]

Civil society groups

In its more recent history, Bangladesh's social fabric has been deeply influenced by the rise of an unusually vibrant civil society. Voluntary action had been the historical norm largely because of the frequent natural disasters that devastated the country, but the mass mobilization and popular resistance during the civil war, and a catastrophic cyclone in its aftermath, were critical for the development of new non-governmental organizations (NGOs).[16] The huge international relief effort that followed became a mainstay of Bangladesh's development and, by 1982, the country had become the "aid capital of the world."[17] Bangladesh was absorbed quickly into the global aid industry, making subsequent access to funds easier, and the NGO effort eventually became widespread. Estimates suggest that 20 to 35 percent of the population received some NGO help, usually credit provision, health or education services.[18] Despite large-scale support from foreign donors, the voluntary sector is dominated by indigenous NGOs developed and run by Bangladeshis, in contrast to most other poor countries that are aid dependent.[19] With the exception of a few large indigenous NGOs like the Bangladesh Rural Advancement Committee (BRAC), the Grameen Bank and Proshika, most NGOs are local, very small and voluntary.

---

[15] For a general discussion, see Asim Roy, *Islamic Syncretistic Tradition in Bengal* (Princeton University Press, 1983).

[16] David Lewis, "On the Difficulty of Studying 'Civil Society': Reflections on NGOs, State and Democracy in Bangladesh," *Contributions to Indian Sociology*, 38.3 (2004) (New Delhi/Thousand Oaks/London: Sage Publications, 2004), p. 306.

[17] Shelley Feldman, "NGOs and Civil Society (Un)stated contradictions," *Annals of American Academy of Political and Social Science* 554 (November 1997), p. 53.

[18] David Lewis, "NGOs, Donors, and the State in Bangladesh," *Annals of American Academy of Political and Social Science* 554 (November 1997), p. 34.

[19] There are some who suggest that Bangladesh suffered an identity crisis due to its overwhelming reliance on foreign aid and the international development community. Imtiaz Ahmed, "Governance and the International Development Community: Making Sense of the Bangladesh Experience," *Contemporary South Asia* 8.3 (November 1999) p. 295.

The non-formal primary education arena is one arena in Bangladesh in which NGOs have clearly made an impact; for example, they have been critical in raising the literacy rate in the country from 35 percent in 1991 to 64 percent in 2000. The major beneficiaries have been women, given the large number of NGOs that target this group. Indeed, according to World Bank economists, the "gender gap" in education is the narrowest of all the South Asian states.[20] During the 1990 transition to a democratic government, many NGOs backed the opposition to the military government. Over time, some NGOs have added good governance and election monitoring to their agendas. The result has been a seemingly permanent strengthening of civil society. BRAC, formed during the independence movement, is now comparable in size and influence to Bangladesh government departments or local corporations.[21] The dominant impulse of these civil society groups has been non-religious and open, if not actually secular.[22]

Thus Bangladesh inherited a favorable tradition and has had a more recent past that has captured the South Asian ethos. In the early 1990s, one analyst wrote about the JeI: "The Jamaat ideological stream in Bangladesh's political system will continue to be narrow, but it will remain deep and perennial."[23] Similarly, another noted scholar suggested that, "capacity for expanded community is Bangladesh's hidden strength. And although contemporary forces have tried to subvert that tradition, it lingers on and offers the peoples of Bangladesh a possible way out of their state-building dilemma."[24]

Polarizing tendencies and the role of the state

The injection of religion into the political arena was not the result of a popular upsurge – it was state-led under military rule. The violent overthrow of Mujib Rahman in 1975 marked the beginning of a new trend in this direction. There had been growing disaffection with the post-independence Awami League government – not with its defining principles, but with its overpersonalization, patronage, ineptitude and perceived corruption. The military coup by General Zia ur-Rahman, however, left little

---

[20] Shantayanam Devarajan, "Making Services Work for the Poor in South Asia," paper presented at the Sigur Center for Asian Studies, George Washington University, Washington, DC, February 10, 2005.

[21] Lewis, "NGOs, Donors, and the State in Bangladesh," pp. 36–37.

[22] Riaz, God Willing, p. 9.

[23] Banu, "Jamaat-i-Islami in Bangladesh," p. 96.

[24] See Lawrence Ziring, Bangladesh: From Mujib to Ershad, An Interpretive Study (Karachi: Oxford University Press, 1992), p. 218.

room for popular mobilization and state consolidation on these issues; the new leadership turned to religion as a legitimizing tool.

General Zia's introduction, in 1977, of constitutional amendments on Islam pointed to the first formal break with the state's founding principles. While he initially publicly subscribed to democracy, nationalism and even socialism in accordance with the original constitution, he pointedly dropped secularism as a basic feature. Even so, there was little indication that it was being jettisoned wholesale. "Absolute trust and faith in the Almighty Allah as the basis of all actions" was termed a Fundamental Principle of State Policy but "no discrimination against any citizen on grounds of religion, race, caste and sex or place of birth" was also given as a Fundamental Right.[25] Zia (as others before and after him) did not change the national flag because it has no Islamic symbolism or the national anthem because it was written by a Hindu (Rabindranath Tagore) despite such demands by the Muslim League and other Islamic parties.

At the same time, Zia took other measures that signaled longer-term objectives. The head of Jamaat, Ghulam Azam, was allowed to return to Bangladesh in 1978 and apply for citizenship. (Neither the military governments of Zia ur-Rahman nor his successor H. M. Ershad gave Azam citizenship, revealing how deep the JeI stigma was; but Zia did restore the citizenship of most other JeI leaders.) And the ban against the Jamaat was officially lifted in 1979.

Education sector

The education sector has not been immune from growing Islamicization.[26] Zia's government directly intervened in the educational sector, setting up a new committee on curricula and syllabi that sought to dramatically control the content of textbooks and sanction what may be called "official" Islam. The Ministry of Education implemented a compulsory class on Islamiyat in all grades until the eighth and then as an elective class in the ninth and tenth grades. (In a sign of the country's tolerant traditions, students from minority communities were given the option of taking similar courses on their religions.) Once the curriculum content was changed in this manner, it became "political suicide" for any regime to suggest a reversal or even modification.[27]

[25] See Marcus Franda, *Bangladesh: The First Decade* (New Delhi: South Asian Publishers, 1982), pp. 50–57 and 223; Ziring, *Bangladesh*, pp. 87–90.
[26] This topic is taken up in detail in Aall and Ollapally (eds.) *Perspectives*. This section relies heavily on the contribution by Imtiaz Ahmed.
[27] Ahmed, "The Role of Education," in Aall and Ollapally.

Madrasa education (longstanding in Bangladesh as in other Muslim societies) saw not only dramatic growth after independence but also a change in direction. There are two main types of madrasa education in Bangladesh: Alia and Qawmi madrasas. Alia madrasas are overseen by the Bangladesh Madrasa Education Board (BMED), an autonomous body but mostly funded by the government. They offer traditional religious studies and general subjects such as mathematics, social science, general science, Bengali and English. The modern curriculum contents were added into these madrasas by the government following independence. (During the liberation war, many of the madrasa graduates were discovered to be antagonistic to the idea of an independent state from Pakistan because the appeal was on language, not religion.)

In contrast to the Alia system, Qawmi madrasas are private and function outside state regulation. They generally only teach religious knowledge and tend to depend on local and diaspora charities and funding, Muslim foundations based in the Middle East and commercial ventures. The training received is inadequate for the job market but their numbers have risen: in 1971, there were an estimated 1,350 madrasas with 300,000 students in Bangladesh; by 2004, the number of Alia madrassas had climbed to 25,200, with three million students. The number of Qawmi madrasas stood at 8,000, speculated to cater to nearly a million students. At the same time, the number of mainstream government schools fell from 78,595 in 1996 to 65,610 in 1999. Even the Alia madrasas have come under criticism from Bangladeshi scholars for conveying a legalistic and formal understanding of Islam that denigrates the spiritualism and mysticism of Bangladesh's Sufi traditions. Indeed, they note that while Alia madrasas teach non-Muslim Bengali writers like Rabindranath Tagore and Promath Choudhury, the great Sufi masters like Rumi and Hafez are left out, thereby promoting "official Islam" over more popular versions.

Deepening Islamicization

In 1978, General Zia created the Bangladesh Nationalist Party (BNP), ostensibly a political party but firmly within the control of the military and bureaucratic elite. Zia's assassination in 1981, and General Ershad's successful military coup a year later, only deepened the country's drift away from its secular foundations. The Ershad regime (1982–1990) incorporated Islam more dramatically into the political sphere, winning the eighth constitutional amendment in June 1988 that declared Islam as the state religion. This amendment had come on the heels of a worsening political crisis with civilian parties beginning in 1983, which came to a head in late 1987 over continuing military rule.

General Ershad's Islamization program played havoc with the country's identity.[28]

Ershad had managed to stay in power in large part by successfully dividing the civilian opposition but, even as late as 1987, he had not gained the full support of Islamic political organizations. The JeI, for instance, participated in protests and strikes along with the Awami League and BNP opposition alliances, agitating for democratic rule which finally came to pass in 1990. The unbroken civilian rule since then: by Khaleda Zia's BNP 1991–1996, Sheikh Hasina's Awami League 1996–2001, and Khaleda Zia's BNP 2001–2006 has also been accompanied by acrimonious political competition that threatens Bangladesh's political future. In this competition, the state (most notably under the BNP) has become an active participant in the production and perpetuation of symbols and discourses that have accelerated the Islamization process, especially since 2001.[29] This has implications well beyond the domestic sphere, not only in how relations with its neighbors proceed, but also the manner in which Bangladesh engages with the unfolding global scenario on Islamist extremism and terrorism.

Bangladesh is often described as having been partitioned twice: in 1947 and 1971. Unlike Pakistan where the trauma of the 1947 partition is dominant, for Bangladesh, it is still 1971. The partition of 1947 did not resolve East Bengal's identity dilemma; 1971 seemed, on the face of it, to do so. But the politics of division begun by the military governments, taken to new heights by BNP, has brought it to the fore again: at the political and geopolitical levels.

External environment and geopolitical identity

The observation by one astute student of sub-continental politics early on remains more pertinent than ever: "Nothing is more important to Bangladesh than its relationship with India. While this is widely realized in Bangladesh, it is less well realized in India."[30] Bangladesh is almost entirely surrounded by India on its 1,200 miles (4,096 kilometers) of land boundary, except for a small section that is adjacent to Myanmar and the Bay of Bengal to its south. India's overwhelming military superiority and economic clout, as well as its geo-strategic encirclement of Bangladesh and its status as the upper riparian state, arguably creates one of the rare instances in realist theory that calls for "bandwagoning" rather than balancing behavior. Coupled with the uncomfortable reality for Dhaka that no other major power has a sufficiently deep and enduring interest in the

---

[28] For a good discussion of Ershad's policies, see Ziring, *Bangladesh*, pp. 169–183.
[29] Riaz, *Unfolding State*, pp. 232–234.   [30] Franda, *Bangladesh*, p. 75.

country to serve as a balance to India, it looks even more compelling.[31] Yet, since 1975, Bangladeshi identity constructions have been geared towards distancing Bangladesh from India and, in the process, creating conditions for a more contentious geopolitical environment. Domestic power struggles in Bangladesh politics have led to antagonism with India being a proxy for "nationalist identity" credentials.

India's geographical position is not entirely without drawbacks: Bangladesh happens to lie between India's strategically located northeastern states of Assam, Arunachal Pradesh, Tripura, Meghalaya, Mizoram, Manipur, Nagaland and the rest of northern India. The main lines of communication between these states and other areas of India run along the northernmost tip of Bangladesh through the Siliguri Corridor, a thin stretch of Indian territory which separates Bangladesh from China's southern Tibetan area of Nathu La.[32] For India, its northeast borderlands which have been convulsed by insurgencies in Nagaland and Assam, and a restive population in Manipur, remain vulnerable to Bangladesh and even Chinese manipulation.[33] This region (surrounded by Bangladesh, Nepal, Myanmar, China and Bhutan and geographically isolated from the rest of the country) has been second in strategic importance only to Kashmir, and has been a persistent thorn in Indo-Bangladesh relations.

Bangladesh's uncertain geopolitical identity

Bengali alienation from Pakistan had predisposed it to good relations with India. The movement to make Bengali one of the state languages of Pakistan had begun as early as 1948, with Sheikh Mujib Rahman serving as an important student leader. Urdu was understood by less than one percent of the Bengalis. The anti-Pakistan sentiment grew over time among a wide Bengali political spectrum, with only factions of the Muslim League and Islamist parties in favor of a strong central government. These latter groups also believed in a hostile posture towards India, much like their western compatriots; among them the JeI was the most organized.[34] India's critical role in the 1971 war against Pakistan

---

[31] During the 1971 war, as the USS Enterprise headed towards the Bay of Bengal in a show of support for Pakistan, Mrs. Gandhi apparently assured her nervous cabinet that no other country was willing to sacrifice blood or treasure on behalf of Bangladesh and that India had nothing to worry about.

[32] Shelley, *Emergence of a New Nation*, p. 51.

[33] See, for example, Kanti P. Bajpai, *Roots of Terrorism* (New Delhi: Penguin Books, 2002), pp. 62–104.

[34] Maniruzzaman, *The Bangladesh Revolution*, pp. 29–30.

and the warm ties between the Indians and Mujib's regime thus went against the ideology of the Jamaat.[35]

Close relations with India also did not sit well with important sections of Bangladesh's military forces.[36] While India's diplomatic and military backing for the Mukti Bahini guerrilla movement won many friends, there were some military leaders who resented what they came to view as India getting too much credit for the victory or "robbing them of the glory of liberating the country." Accordingly, this created "almost rabid anti-Indianism in the Bangladesh armed forces."[37] India's clear lines of authority, with the military being subordinate to the civilian political elite, could also not have been missed. Moreover, Bangladesh's officer cadre had been trained by the Pakistan military establishment, which no doubt left a lingering imprint. Beyond this, the military's insecurity lay in the common perception that it was the non-professional, guerrilla groups drawn from the populace that made independence possible, not the conventional military. Prior to the assault of the Pakistani military in March 1971, East Pakistan's armed forces showed little interest in the political ferment.[38] In its political incarnation, the Bangladeshi military has been the coolest to closer relations with India, while the mainstream political leadership remains divided.

Yet, all Indo-Pakistan wars had been fought on the western front, despite the reality of East Pakistan's vulnerability. Indeed, the 1965 war, in which East Pakistan was left virtually unprotected, called into question

[35] On India's role in the 1971 war, opinions ranged from India's reluctant but forceful entry to India fomenting the movement in order to destabilize Pakistan. On balance, it would seem that the unprecedented movement of ten million refugees into adjoining Indian states (at the rate of 60,000 per day by May 1971) was unsustainable and provided a proximate cause for Indian intervention. Richard Sisson and Leo E. Rose, *War and Secessions: Pakistan, India and the Creation of Bangladesh* (Berkeley: University of California Press, 1992), p. 152; and Shelley, *Emergence of a New Nation*, pp. 133–134. The refugees included a fair number of Muslims but they were overwhelmingly from the Hindu minority, whom the Pakistan army, in league with local non-Bengali elements and the JeI, was targeting with particular ferocity. See Bhuiyan, *Emergence of Bangladesh*, pp. 207–214. Observers have noted India's highly effective relief work with the refugees, for example, avoiding communal incidents despite the tremendous population pressure over a very short span of time. See Franda, *Bangladesh*, pp. 113–115.

[36] Jackson, *South Asian Crisis*, p. 149,

[37] Maniruzzaman, *The Bangladesh Revolution*, p. 238. The consensus among independent analysts is that India's intervention on the side of the Mukti Bahini was the deciding factor in the rapid victory. For a description of the war, see Jackson, *South Asian Crsis*, pp. 106–146; and Verghese, *An End to Confrontation*, pp. 41–63. For insider accounts from West Pakistan, see G. W. Choudhury, *The Last Days of United Pakistan* (Bloomington: Indiana University Press, 1974) and Hasan Zaheer, *The Separation of East Pakistan: The Rise and Realization of Bengali Muslim Nationalism* (Karachi: Oxford University Press, 1994). The movement of the American carrier The Enterprise into the Bay of Bengal during the war was viewed as a warning to India against attacking West Pakistan, a move that led to bitterness in India and Bangladesh.

[38] Riaz, *Unfolding State*, pp. 82–83.

the reliability of the central government and destroyed the idea that union with Pakistan guaranteed security from external attack. Indeed, many Bengalis came to see the cause of the Indo-Pakistan war, Kashmir, as a solely West Pakistan concern.[39] Pakistan's military forces were concentrated to protect its western sector, with the eastern flank being left wide open. The deployment of India's forces also reflected its antagonism towards the west, not east. The Indian government's studied policy to demonstrate that it did not have any quarrel with the Bengalis, especially during the 1965 war with Pakistan when it did not open a second front in the east, clearly paid dividends.[40]

Within three months of the 11-day war in December 1971, all Indian troops were withdrawn from Bangladesh, showing India's deference to Bangladeshi sensibilities. Continuing close ties to Bangladesh was also represented by the 25-year Treaty of Friendship, Cooperation and Peace signed with India shortly afterwards. Despite its own massive deficits, India's assistance to independent Bangladesh was huge.[41]

Rise and Fall of India's Political Windfall

The Bangladesh liberation movement was an ideological, political and geopolitical windfall for India. Ideologically, the Bangladesh movement vindicated India's secular platform; politically, the victorious Awami League was indebted to India; and strategically, Pakistan was cut in half. At almost every level, Indo-Bangladeshi identities were consistent in 1971. Following the military coup by General Zia in 1975, however, the orientation changed perceptibly. By 1980, Zia had introduced the notion of a South Asian Association for Regional Cooperation (SAARC) which many Indian analysts suspiciously viewed as an attempt to form a collective body to counter Indian dominance.

In relations with India, the economic sphere was an early site for political contests, from the water-sharing question which had persisted since the 1970s to controversy about Indian industrial investment. Arriving at a water-sharing deal that is ideal for both parties is impossible given the demands of Calcutta, Bangladesh's needs during the dry season and the enormous cost and technical hurdles in the way of the most ambitious schemes.[42] But water-sharing with India became so politically charged in

---

[39] Jackson, *South Asian Crisis*, p. 21; and Mohammed Ayoob and K. Subrahmanyam, *The Liberation War* (New Delhi: S. Chand & Co., 1972), p. 223.
[40] Shelley, *Emergence of a New Nation*, p. 135.   [41] Franda, *Bangladesh*, pp. 9; 78–81.
[42] See, for example, Nazrul Islam, "Indo-Bangladesh Water Treaty," in Farooq Sobhan (ed.) *Strengthening Cooperation and Security in South Asia Post-9/11* (Dhaka: The University Press, 2004): and T. Ramakrishnan, "Sharing Water Resources," *The Hindu*, October 8, 2004.

Bangladesh that it was not clear that any solution would be accepted; an unresolved water issue seemed to be convenient for political leaders and it was unclear whether they really wanted it resolved.[43] Similarly, the foreign investment proposal in 2004 by India's highly-respected Tata company and Bangladesh's lukewarm or even negative response, shows how Bangladesh's geopolitical identity needs have prevented what independent economists have uniformly hailed as a win-win situation.

In a context of declining global foreign investment in Bangladesh, Tata's $3 billion would have matched all the foreign capital that has flowed into the country since 1971. But the deal is caught up in the larger vicious cycle for Bangladesh in which it would rather not develop its gas reserves than sell it to its most logical customer, India, because gas has been elevated as a symbol of national sovereignty. Bangladesh has found it difficult to attract foreign capital and the World Economic Forum in 2004 termed Bangladesh "one of the most uncompetitive places to do business."[44] In a similar way, the plan for a regional economic cooperation group, BIMSTEC, that includes Bangladesh, Myanmar, India, Sri Lanka and Thailand has been held up in large part thanks to Bangladesh's unwillingness to let the market logic work in its relationship with India. While Bangladesh's reserves lies untapped, India is hoping to import natural gas from Myanmar in pipelines running through Bangladesh. The leadership of both the BNP and AL have made their opposition to gas exports to India clear, at least in public, going to the extent of saying "we cannot sell our wealth and become beggars."[45]

Decline of political secularism

The formulation of more hostile policies towards India and the decline of political secularism at the state level, broadly speaking, worked together to produce a geopolitical identity that made the environment more amenable to religious extremism. Relations with India became a political lightning rod, with the military and later its political creation, the BNP, introducing a new polarizing discourse into the political arena. When General Zia took power, he claimed the language of nationalism but distinguished it from Mujib's version. The purpose of the military takeover was explained as

---

[43] As one senior Bangladesh government advisor close to former Prime Minister Hasina related to this author, the question was not necessarily when the water problem would be resolved but whether political leaders wanted it resolved in the first place. Personal discussions, Washington, DC, March 2003.

[44] BBC News, October 14, 2004.

[45] Shishir K. Deb, "Political Economy of Gas Export," *Asian Affairs*, 25.3 (July–September 2003), p. 56.

safeguarding national sovereignty against foreign conspiracy (understood to be Indian dominance) and to assert the independent identity of Bangladesh. The constitutional amendments brought about by Zia sought to make subtle but important changes. Article 6 of the original constitution declared that the identity of the citizens of Bangladesh was "Bengali." Zia's amendment, which modified the identity to "Bangladeshi," was a deliberate step to de-link the identity of the country from the Bengali subregional or sub-cultural identity in India. According to one long-time observer, "Bangladeshi chauvinism implied distancing the country from Indian Bengal, it also meant restricting movement and elevating suspicions."[46]

An additional change was the replacement of the words "historic struggle for national liberation" with "historic war of national independence," denigrating the role of popular political movements (in which India was so involved) and elevating the role of the military. Together with dropping the concept of "secularism" in favor of Islamic religious terminology, a new identity was being forged. The cultivation of Bangladeshi nationalism in this fashion became bound up with an anti-Indian element for the first time. Ali Riaz puts it well, "A new ideological terrain was created by the regime to legitimize their rule. Religion, the territoriality of identity, and national security constituted the core of this new ideology."[47] Another close observer saw a similar development: "The insertion of Islamic provisions of symbolic value in the constitution only indicates the anxiety of the present government [Zia] to develop a 'multi-symbol congruence' in the Bangladesh nation differentiating it from India just as language differentiates it from Pakistan."[48]

This externalization of identity is an important explanatory factor that is not given sufficient weight by analysts of Bangladesh.[49] As the progenitor of this new thinking under Zia, the BNP and its ideology has continued to exercise a polarizing influence in the post-military political realm since 1990. Since 2001, the inclusion of Islamist parties in the BNP's ruling coalition, who harbor a lingering hostility towards India for its role in the break-up of Pakistan, has damped down relations with India. Bengali nationalism, as traditionally espoused by the Awami League, is generally understood to be more positive towards India, whereas the BNP's Bangladeshi nationalism is oriented towards the Islamic world, with an

---

[46] Lawrence Ziring, *Bangladesh*, p. 131. [47] Riaz, *Unfolding State*, p. 218, see also 216–217.
[48] Maniruzzaman, *The Bangladesh Revolution*, p. 241.
[49] Even Ali Riaz, whose work seems to be an exception, goes on to contradict his own argument by ultimately locating the contours of Islamism in purely domestic politics. See *God Willing*, p. 136.

anti-India tendency.[50] From early on, secularists were concerned that the state's attempt under Zia to find a distinct Bangladeshi identity would inexorably lead the BNP into an over-reliance on exclusivist religious ideology. Indeed Zia's campaign speeches described the Awami League and its allies in terms designed to stimulate such sentiment: "anti-national" and "irreligious."[51] In this context, Sheikh Hasina Wajed, daughter of Mujib Rahman and heir to the Awami League's leadership, suffered politically for her perceived proximity to India: the fact that she had lived in India for five years before returning to Bangladesh in May 1981 and for her father's pro-Indian position during his regime.[52]

For India, this re-orientation flew in the face of its considerable investment in Bangladesh's future. Even Zia saw the risks of a completely hostile policy and promised to honor all bilateral agreements. This political side-stepping in Bangladesh's relationship with India continues and maintains a level of instability that crops up in unpredictable ways. As in all other parts of South Asia, geography and demography have combined to influence identity politics.

India's geopolitical identity and spillovers in the northeast

India's pluralist and secular identity fits neatly with early visions for Bangladesh. Points of friction over water-sharing and economics were not colored by polarizing religious overtones. India even actively sought to bolster secular forces through its strategic policy: for example, when the secular Awami League came to power in Bangladesh in 1996, India put pressure on the United People's Party of the Chittagong Hill Tracts, which had been waging an armed revolt for two decades against Bangladeshi central rule and were finding sanctuaries in India's northeast. Backed by the Indian government's policies, the Awami League was able to bring negotiations with the tribal leaders of the insurgency to a successful conclusion.[53] Since then, the decline of the secular ethos in Bangladesh and India's rising strategic concerns on its own borderlands have come together to create new forms of tensions. This combination is illustrated well in the case of Assam.

---

[50] See Partha S. Ghosh "South Asian Muslims, 9/11 and Americanism: A Reflective Analysis," mimeo, May 2003.

[51] Franda, *Bangladesh*, p. 232.

[52] In 1981, opposition campaign posters depicted her as "Indira Wajed." Franda, *Bangladesh*, p. 323.

[53] One of the best books on this little-known conflict is by Amena Mohsin, *The Chittagong Hill Tracts, Bangladesh: On the Difficult Road to Peace* (Boulder: Lynne Rienner Publishers, 2003), pp. 13–16.

Assam and Indo-Bangladesh relations

The Indian government has seen agitation against central rule for decades in its northeast. The long border with Bangladesh is guarded by about 45,000 Indian Border Security Force troops.[54] The northeast was the least integrated area of the British India. In 1958, New Delhi passed the Armed Forces Special Powers Act specifically for the region; originally meant to last six months 50 years ago, it still remains in force. Economically underdeveloped, with peripheral political status and a patchwork of competing ethnic groups, many of the seven northeastern states have major grievances against the central government. The largest of these states, Assam, has long protested the highly uneven economic relations in which its raw materials, especially oil, are extracted with little benefit to the state.[55] In contrast, New Delhi has viewed Assam and its neighboring states through a security lens. Indian strategic anxieties have centered on China in this sensitive region and, increasingly, Bangladesh and its purported Pakistan connection. The creation of Arunachal Pradesh and Meghalaya was partly to preempt China from making claims to these border territories.[56] (China continues to be ambiguous about the status of the sensitive state of Arunachal Pradesh.) During the turbulent Sino-Indian relations of the 1960s and 1970s, China backed Mizo and Naga tribal insurgents with military, moral and economic support, ending its assistance only after bilateral relations with India improved.[57]

India's major strategic complaint against Bangladesh relates to the continuing low level insurgency in Assam, which Delhi accuses Dhaka of tacitly, if not overtly, supporting. The United Liberation Front of Assam (ULFA) has used refugee camps in Bangladesh's northeastern provinces to plan and recruit for operations, and the belief in Indian official circles is that ULFA insurgents who are captured in Bangladeshi territory are not being seriously prosecuted or dealt with.[58] (ULFA appears among the US State Department's "groups of

---

[54] Rajesh Kharat, "Developing Indo-Bangladesh Ties: The Border Issues," *South Asia*, 4 (2006), p. 6.

[55] For greater autonomy as the solution in Assam, see leading expert, Sanjib Baruah, "Autonomy for All States," *Times of India*, July 25, 2000; and *India Against Itself: Assam and the Politics of Nationality* (Philadelphia: University of Pennsylvania Press, 1999).

[56] See, for example, Maya Chadda, "Integration through Internal Reorganization: Containing Ethnic Conflict in India," *The Global Review of Ethnopolitics*, 2.1 (2002), pp. 50–51.

[57] Sumit Ganguly, *The Rise of Islamist Militancy in Bangladesh* Special Report 171, Washington, DC, US Institute of Peace, August 2006, p. 7.

[58] Interviews with senior Indian officials at the Ministry of External Affairs, October 30, 2004. See also Siddharth Varadarajan, "Border Music," regarding the capture and apparent escape of an ULFA leader in Bangladesh. *Times of India*, June 7, 2004.

concern.")[59] Some Bangladeshi analysts argue that it is the Bangladesh state's weakness that allows the ULFA to operate in Bangladesh rather than any strategic design, whereas Indian experts and officials argue otherwise. They contend that the Inter-Services Intelligence (ISI) of Pakistan is aiding the ULFA inside Bangladesh to draw India's resources away from the Kashmir conflict. They also claim that the BNP invited ISI involvement to thwart Indian dominance and that the ISI has taken advantage of Bangladesh's proximity to Assam to exacerbate the inter-ethnic conflict, fanning communal tensions.[60] It may be plausibly argued that there is a convergence of interests between Bangladesh, Pakistan and China in keeping Assam destabilized – a worst case scenario for India – and an Islamist upsurge in Bangladeshi politics may lay the groundwork for just such an outcome.

The conflict in Assam and its spillover into Indo-Bangladesh relations brings questions of sovereignty and identity closer together in rather unpredictable ways. The numerically and politically dominant Hindu Assamese are at odds with the Hindu and Muslim Bengali migrants from West Bengal and Bangladesh, and have long been disaffected with New Delhi. The Assamese are resented by plains tribes such as the Bodos but the Bodos in turn are opposed by non-Bodo tribes who fear takeover of their lands by the more populous Bodos.[61] The contentious issue of refugee and migration flows from Bangladesh into India's northeastern states has waxed and waned politically. According to India, there are approximately 16 million illegal Bangladeshis in India, a figure that Bangladesh dismisses.[62] There are demographic, economic and rising security challenges from the influx. Movement of people across the porous borders is considered one the region's biggest security threats, with migration, insurgency and terrorism being increasingly portrayed as intertwined external threats.

A major demand of the Hindu Assamese has been to identify Bangladeshis who have migrated to Assam since 1971 and to expel

---

[59] US Department of State, Office of the Coordinator for Counterterrorism, *Country Reports on Terrorism 2005* (April 2006), p. 262.

[60] Jaideep Saikia, "The ISI Reaches East: Anatomy of Conspiracy," *Studies in Conflict and Terrorism*, 25.3 (May 2002) p. 185. Imtiaz Ahmed has argued that rather than the Bangladesh state offering the ULFA sanctuary, the ULFA is taking advantage of the state's weakness to use the country as a base. See Imtiaz Ahmed, "Contemporary Terrorism and the State, Non-State and Inter-State: Newer Drinks, Newer Bottles," 2004, mimeo. There are periodic reports in the Indian media of Pakistan's involvement in the northeast via Bangladesh. See, for example, *The Hindu*, November 8, 2004 which cited a Home Ministry warning about Pakistan's alleged plan to smuggle arms to the Dhubri district of Assam bordering Bangladesh.

[61] For an excellent overview of the intricate Assam conflict, see Bajpai, *Roots of Terrorism*, pp.72–104.

[62] *India Today*, February 17, 2003, p. 19.

them. By 1977, the All Assam Students Union (AASU) and other groups launched an "anti-foreign" agitation protesting "Bangladeshi" migrants on the state's voter rolls, which became the start of a sustained insurgency against New Delhi. In response, the Indian government set up tribunals in 1978 to look into foreign migrants on electoral rolls. The intervention of Prime Minister Indira Gandhi after the general elections of 1980 and negotiations with the students bought some relief but, in 1983, the situation deteriorated dramatically when she called for state elections despite voting rolls not having been fully scrutinized.[63] Bangladesh's stand has tended to be that there are no Bangladeshi refugees in India (following the refugee return from the 1971 war) and that it is an internal Indian matter.[64]

Assam continues to serve as a flashpoint even though the original student radicals of the AASU gained political power in state elections under an accord with Prime Minister Rajiv Gandhi in 1985. The accord failed to bring about peace on different counts: the difficulty in identifying foreigners, the continuing influx of migrants and the sanctuary found in Bangladesh by the extremist ULFA, which has been agitating for a full-scale armed struggle against the Indian central government and is opposed to the AASU's adoption of the electoral path. ULFA's terrorist violence in particular has kept Assam on the boil. [65]

In Bangladesh, the unrelenting and highly polarized competition between the Awami Leage and BNP, in which "the Indian factor" also comes into play, leaves little room for either party to respond to New Delhi's concerns, even if so inclined.[66] With the inclusion of Jamaat in the ruling party in 2001, the constraints against cooperating with India increased. This stands in contrast to the joint Indo-Bhutan Armys' "Operation Flush Out" in December 2003 to dislodge ULFA camps in Bhutan.[67] (In the past decade, India, Bhutan and even the Myanmar governments have reportedly coordinated action against Assamese insurgents.) The proliferation of small arms in these adjacent areas has helped to escalate the violence, including in

---

[63] Charles Peter O'Donnell, *Bangladesh: Biography of a Muslim Nation* (Boulder: Westview Press, 1984), p. 20. The massacre of nearly 1,000 Muslim Bengalis was the most violent reaction. Bajpai, *Roots of Terrorism*, 75. Most of the migrants from Bangladesh are Hindu, with at least a third Muslims.

[64] O'Donnell, *Bangladesh*, pp. 250–251.   [65] Bajpai, *Roots of Terrorism*, pp. 76–77.

[66] For example, in late 2004, six months after ten truckloads of arms allegedly intended for insurgent groups in the northeast were seized in Bangladesh, New Delhi remained in the dark about the culprits although they reportedly belonged to ULFA. *The Asian Age*, September 13, 2004.

[67] For a detailed discussion, see Rajesh Kharat, "Countering Insurgencies in South Asia: The Case of Indo-Bhutan Co-operation," paper delivered at the 2006 Annual Meeting of the American Political Science Association, September 2006, pp. 16–23.

Bangladesh, something not entirely lost on the Bangladesh government despite its seeming unwillingness to cooperate openly with India.

There have been intermittent attempts at negotiation with the ULFA by the Indian government but none have lasted. In 2005, the group appointed an 11-member People's Consultative Group made up of prominent civil society members to represent it in talks with the central government. However, peace talks between the government and ULFA collapsed in September 2006, giving rise to a flare-up of bombings and attacks against Hindi-speaking migrant workers from other parts of India such as West Bengal and Bihar. Although the ULFA's initial agenda was to oust migrants from Bangladesh, this has become a secondary objective, dictated in large part it would seem by the need for safe havens in Bangladesh. Indeed, some Indian observers have gone as far as to suggest that Bangladeshi intelligence and the Pakistan's ISI have gained significant influence over ULFA thanks to training, funding and arms supplies and, in turn, have succeeded in pitting the group primarily against non-Assamese Indians.[68] For example, attacks against Biharis in November 2003 were surprising, given that tensions between the Assamese and thousands of Biharis who have settled in the state over the years had been almost non-existent, unlike hostility towards the Bengalis. Some have pointed out that ULFA's Bangladesh connection has "made it suspect in the eyes of the average Assamese."[69] ULFA, which could initially claim a fair amount of support among the Assamese, has steadily lost support as it has slid into terrorist violence against civilians, making the role of external backers more important than ever.

Extremism and cross-border issues

ULFA's militancy brings together India's worst fears: internal conflict in the borderlands being used as a strategic weapons by its neighbors, now coupled with concerns of Islamist extremists adding to the volatility. Suspicions surrounding the unauthorized movement of people across the Indo-Bangladesh border threaten to transform a largely demographic and

---

[68] S. K. Sinha, "Foreword," in Jaideep Saikia, *Terror Sans Frontiers: Islamic Militancy in North East India*, ADCDIS Occasional Paper, Program in Arms Control, Disarmament, and International Security, University of Chicago at Urbana-Champaign (July 2003), p. xiii. See also for Saikia's evidence from Indian intelligence and police sources for the ISI's role and ULFA's ideological shift, pp. 17–26. Saikia notes that in the absence of external geopolitics, a strong ethnic movement such as the ULFA would have likely stood in the way of militant Islam gaining strength in the area. See also B. Raman, *ULFA Terrorism in Assam: The Hindu Mercenaries of Jihadis*, South Asia Analysis Group, Paper No. 2089 (January 8, 2007), available at www.southasiaanalysis.org.

[69] See, for example, Udayan Misra, "No Military Solution for Assam," *The Hindu*, October 8, 2004.

economic issue into a strategic and religiously polarized one. Bangladesh has come under pressure from two of its neighbors on cross-border militancy – India and Myanmar. In both cases, the major concern is domestic insurgency groups that find sanctuaries in Bangladesh. The Bangladeshi government has shown sensitivity to the Myanmar military junta's conflict with the Muslim minority Rohingyas, who fled to Bangladesh.[70]

Much of New Delhi's concern is about a potential collaboration between al-Qaeda and Pakistan's ISI and the infiltration of anti-India elements into Bangladesh through its northeastern border. India has not accused the Bangladesh government of directly fomenting militancy against it but there are questions about the military–intelligence establishment having an interest in keeping anti-Indian groups alive, through inaction if nothing more. India has alleged that Bangladesh has up to 190 camps run by northeastern Indian separatist groups, allowing militants to conduct attacks in India and sneak back across the border.[71] India's underlying concern relates to the growth of Islamist influences on national policy through the inclusion of Jamaat and others at high levels of government. Given that the JeI originated in the western wing and its peculiar previous history, even some outsiders suggest that the legacy serves "as a built-in network of agents within the Jamaat and its affiliates who can be utilized to harass India along its 2500 mile border with Bangladesh."[72] Following the July 11, 2006 train bombings in Mumbai, top Indian police officials indicated that key suspects had "connections with groups in Nepal and Bangladesh, which are directly or indirectly connected to Pakistan."[73] Overlaid with this is the fear of Bangladesh becoming a safe haven from which international Islamist terrorists can attack India, with or without direct government control.

In 2004, following meetings at the home secretary level, India and Bangladesh came close to agreeing to India's suggestion for a "joint patrolling" of the border to check illegal migration, movement of Indian insurgents, trafficking and smuggling. Dhaka accuses India of exaggerating these threats and has, in turn, claimed that some anti-Bangladeshi groups are based in India. India has said that it is willing to have joint operations

---

[70] See Bertil Lintner, "Religious Extremism and Nationalism in Bangladesh," Religion and Security in South Asia – An International Workshop, Honolulu, Hawaii, Asia Pacific Center for Security Studies, 19–22 August 2002.

[71] *The Hindu*, April 19, 2005. See also Ramananda Sengupta, "Why India is Concerned about Bangladesh," (December 22, 2005), available at www.rediff.com.

[72] Selig S. Harrison, "A New Hub for Terrorism?" Op. Ed., *The Washington Post*, August 2, 2006.

[73] Harrison, "A New Hub for Terrorism?"

against and the inspection of such camps.[74] Bangladesh has been reticent to go forward with such cooperation, for reasons that may range from protection of its sovereignty to fear of what might be uncovered.

Both India and Bangladesh stand to gain from cooperation in the northeast since some of the most backward areas of the two countries are found in this region. Reciprocal concessions on transit routes are especially important. The Indian state of Tripura is landlocked and surrounded by Bangladesh on three sides; a direct bus service between Kolkata and Tripura's capital Agartala via Dhaka or cutting across Bangladesh territory would be highly beneficial to India. Conversely, India could allow Bangladesh to expand its trade with Nepal and Bhutan via Indian territory. Reciprocal transit routes would also be confidence-building measures and the two sides began exploring this option when Begum Khaleda Zia visited India in March 2006, her first official visit since assuming power in 2001.[75] For this kind of cooperation to materialize, they will have to guard against letting political rhetoric get out of hand – for Bangladesh this includes not allowing India to become a domestic foil and for India it means a coming to terms with the economic basis of most cross-border issues.

Changing discourse?

India's accusations that Bangladesh is at best turning a blind eye to Islamist extremism (including harbouring fugitive members of al-Qaeda and the Taliban, a charge that Dhaka hotly denies)[76] have made it difficult to differentiate between the historical migrant flows that have been an enduring feature of India's northeast and newer terrorist infiltration. One development at the political level is the increasing tendency to refer to cross-border migration under the all-encompassing term of *international terrorism*.[77] For Assam, the issue remains one of ethnic composition and political power in the state; for New Delhi, it is becoming one of geopolitics and strategic relations, in addition to internal conflict.

The leap from discourse on migrant flows to terrorism could be short, and in turn produce the kind of geopolitical identity compulsions that exacerbate inter-state tensions. The process of such conflation often has a political basis: for example, after the 2004 election fiasco for the Bharatiya Janata Party (BJP) in India, the party's agenda started loosely

---

[74] *The Asian Age*, September 21, 2004. See also Siddharth Varadarajan, "Border Music," interview with Morshed Khan, *The Times of India*, June 7, 2004.

[75] Kharat, "Developing Indo-Bangladesh Ties," p. 6.

[76] *India Today*, February 10, 2003, p. 40.

[77] Itty Abraham, "Illegal But Licit," *IIAS Newletter*, Leiden, International Institute for Asian Studies, p. 1.

characterizing migrants from Bangladesh as "terrorists" and part of the spread of "jihadi terrorism" on the subcontinent, a departure from the past.[78] The ruling Congress Party coalition has resisted such discourse but it is easy to see how domestic political pressure could lead to redefinitions at the state level. Apart from producing potential foreign policy distortions, it would have serious negative repercussions on innocent migrants who are caught in undefined geopolitical spaces. Further, it would reduce what have been termed "humanized spaces" carved out for undocumented migrants over long stretches of time.[79]

Between extremist and moderate outcomes

Bangladesh's 15-year experience of military rule proved critical in interjecting religion into the political system. The inheritor of this tradition, the BNP, cannot hope to calibrate its own identity politics as it suits: the extraordinary political violence of August 2004 and August 2005 are stark reminders of this fact. On August 21, 2004 the country saw unprecedented violence in a series of grenade attacks at a high-profile Awami League rally, leaving 19 people dead and 200 injured. This brazen assault against such high-value targets, for the first time in the country's history was seen as a wake-up call by insiders and outsiders, many of whom had long assumed Bangladesh's relative stability. An even more sensational string of attacks occurred on August 17, 2005, with the explosion of over 450 bombs in 63 of the country's 64 districts, all within 40 minutes of each other.

The rise of militant Islamist groups

A key question is the extent to which such violence is a symptom of the increasingly virulent hostility between the two leading political parties, the BNP and Awami League (a confrontationist political ethic), or simply a reflection of deeper changes, namely the emergence of extremist religious groups on the political scene and the greater ideological hold of militant Islam. In Bangladesh they seem to go hand in hand and, since 2001, the "global war on terrorism" and its international discourse are influencing the tide of Islamist sentiment as well.

---

[78] Neena Vyas, "Advani in a Dilemma," *The Hindu*, October 24, 2004. We may contrast this to the Janata period of 1977–1980 when the self-consciously Hindu party Jana Sangh was noticeably restrained on the Bangladesh refugee question.

[79] The manner in which cross-border interactions are governed by well-known social rules away from the purview of official state instruments is described by Abraham, "Illegal But Licit," p. 1.

The major Islamist parties in coalition with the BNP government were the JeI and the Islamic Oikyo Jote (IOJ, Islamic United Front), a small party that secured two parliamentary seats in the 2001 elections. The Jamaat obtained only 18 seats, far behind the BNP and the AL, yet it was awarded two important ministries. While both the JeI and IOJ favor an Islamic state, the latter is more radical, with the JeI favoring an incremental approach, at least publicly. The Jamaat's youth organization, the Islami Chatra Shibir (ICS), however, has allegedly been involved in a number of political and religiously motivated assassinations and bombings. During the investigation of the August 2005 bombings masterminded by a newer group, Jamaat ul-Mujahideen Bangladesh (JMB), links were reported between the accused and Shibir and even the JeI itself.[80] Until the sensational 2005 terrorist attacks in Bangladesh, the BNP government had repeatedly denied the existence of Islamist extremists in the country, attributing hostile motives to those making such charges.[81]

As the senior partner in the BNP's ruling coalition, the JeI's role in government has come under scrutiny. Jamaat's leaders do not hide their objective of establishing an Islamic state but claim that they wish to do so through the democratic process, something that is harder to accept after the large-scale violence since 2004.[82] However, the Jamaat has not been particularly successful in garnering popular support in elections, with its percentage of votes hovering around 10 percent at its height. In contrast, its five-year tenure with the BNP government restored it to a level of political respectability (denied it since 1971) and also gave it greater organizational capacity. Thus the BNP facilitated a disproportionate political role for the Jamaat and, by extension, Islamist groups. As for the Jamaat wielding excessive influence in the government, high level BNP officials are dismissive. According to one BNP cabinet minister, "We run the show; the Jamaat does not have veto power."[83] But to observers, what is troubling is the combination of Jamaat's high political profile, Shibir's strong activism in universities and private madrasas around the country and the apparent links of both organizations to underground violent groups that are hard to pin down. As elsewhere, the increasing activism of JeI and other Islamist groups politically creates a permissive and

---

[80] Liz Philipson, "Corrupted Democracy," *Himal South Asian*, August 2006, p. 4 and Ganguly, *The Rise of Islamist Militancy*, p. 5. All seven members of the Jamaat ul-Mujahideen taken in were found to have been members of either the Jamaat or the ICS.

[81] The government even banned the April 2002 issue of the well-known *Far Eastern Economic Review* for carrying an article on growing terror links in the country. The FEER and *Time Magazine* in October 2002 were among the very first to impute terrorism links to the country. See Romesh Ratnesar, "Al-Qaeda: Alive and Starting to Kick Again," *Time Magazine*, 16 October 2002.

[82] Personal interviews with high-level JeI officials, Dhaka, July 2004.

[83] Personal interview, Dhaka, July 2004.

even sympathetic environment for more radical groups to operate while at the same time circumscribing the space for political secularists. The Awami League in particular is reviled by militant groups for its secular credentials and perceived pro-India sympathies, making the League's leader, Sheikh Hasina, a prime target for assassination attempts.[84] The Awami League leader has also accused the BNP and Jamaat of sheltering the jihadist group JMB.[85]

According to various sources, more than 30 militant groups have emerged since the late 1990s.[86] In the broader context of South Asia, this is a relatively new phenomenon in Bangladesh despite radical Islamists having been steadily at work from the 1980s in Afghanistan, Pakistan and Kashmir. The geopolitical isolation of Bangladesh from these zones of conflict had insulated it to some extent. As a high-ranking Jamaat leader put it, "Afghanistan [referring to the anti-Soviet wars] and Kashmir are far away from us."[87] In contrast, the US invasion of Afghanistan and, more importantly, Iraq and its aftermath seem to have struck a deeper chord.[88] In November 2005, according to the Bangladeshi police, "suicide terrorism" struck the country for the first time, with explosions in the southeastern port city of Chittagong and outside Dhaka.

The most important of these violent jihadi groups are the Harakat ul-Jihad-i- Islami Bangladesh (HUJI-B), with a core membership of veterans from the Afghan wars, and the JMB. These two groups are on the US State Department's "groups of concern" list.[89] Both aim to establish Islamic rule in Bangladesh. HUJI-B has connections to the Pakistani militant groups Harakat ul-Jihad-i-Islami (HUJI) and Harakat ul-Mujahedin (HUM), which have similar objectives for Pakistan and Kashmir. The exact strength of the HUJI-B and JMB is unknown but some estimates suggest several thousand for the former and up to 11,000 for the latter. HUJI-B's funding is drawn from a variety of sources, including several international Islamic NGOs as well as from militant madrasa leaders in Bangladesh. The JMB emerged from the Alhe Hadith Movement in Bangladesh which has received support from a Kuwait-based NGO and probably from people of Bangladeshi origin living in Europe and the Middle East.[90]

Meanwhile, another radical group, the Jagrata Muslim Janata Bangladesh (JMJB), operates around the country's desperately poor northwestern

[84] Saikia, *Terror Sans Frontiers*, p. 34.
[85] "Bangladesh," *The Economist*, February 8, 2007.
[86] Riaz, *Unfolding State*, p. 235. For details of the key groups, see International Crisis Group, *Bangladesh Today*, Asia Report No. 121 (October 23, 2006), pp. 15–21.
[87] Author's interview in Dhaka, July 2004.
[88] This is the author's impression after a series of wide-ranging interviews in Dhaka, July 2004.
[89] US Department of State, *Country Reports on Terrorism 2005*, pp. 6–7.
[90] US Department of State, *Country Reports on Terrorism 2005*, pp. 149, 240 and 246.

region bordering India, avowedly to counter left-wing activity. Reportedly formed in the 1990s, it came into the spotlight in 2004. Led by operations chief Siddiq ul-Islam (alias Bangla Bhai or Bengali Brother), the JMJB attempted to launch an Islamist revolt in several provinces. Its spiritual leader Sheikh Abdur Rahman, who is believed to have organized both the JMB and JMJB networks, reportedly traveled to Pakistan and Saudi Arabia for studies in Arabic in the 1980s and fought in the Afghan war.[91] Rahman has declared that he wants to bring about the Talibanization of the region, beginning by trying to eliminate leftist influence. (The Purbo Banglar Communist Party is active in those areas.) This is particularly threatening in an area that is traditionally religiously diverse, and attacks in April 2004 landed Islam on the government's arrest list.[92]

The large-scale August 2005 bombings seemed designed to show the capability of the JMB in the face of the February crackdown by the BNP government. (The nature of the explosives suggested a demonstration effect rather than mass casualty terrorism.) By December 2005, the gravity of developments in the country forced the BNP government to hold a national dialogue with a number of political parties and professional groups but the effort quickly faltered. One continuing issue has been the seriousness of the BNP on this matter: some have argued that gestures are more for international public consumption. For example, the JMB and JMJB were banned in February 2005 on the day that foreign aid donors were meeting in the US to review aid to Bangladesh.

The use of suicide bombings by the JMB brought it special notoriety, earning it the label of an al-Qaeda-type organization. Although the BNP government had denied the very existence of Islam and Rahman, it finally banned the JMB and JMJB in February 2005 under intense domestic and international pressure. The government also announced a large reward for the arrest of both men. By October 2005, the HUJI-B was also banned. In March 2006, both Rahman and Islam, Bangladesh's most wanted fugitives, were captured and 21 members of the JMB were sentenced to death for carrying out the August 2005 explosions.[93]

The increasing activism of militant Islamist groups in Bangladesh caught many observers by surprise. The August 2005 bombings, in particular, shocked most Bangladeshis and may have backfired in terms of popular support. The tolerant Islamic tradition of Bangladesh had been viewed as

---

[91] *The Daily Star*, March 2, 2006; and Shamim Ahsan, "The Blasting Wakeup Call," *Star Weekend Magazine*, 4.60 (August 26, 2005).

[92] For an on-the-ground journalistic account of militancy in Bangladesh, see Eliza Griswold, "The Next Islamic Revolution?" *The New York Times Magazine*, January 23, 2005.

[93] http://english.aljazeera.net, March 2, 2006; and *Dawn*, March 1, 2006.

strong enough to withstand jihadi thrusts, although voices warning of an impending crisis were increasing as early as 2001.

An important bulwark against outright assaults on democratic institutions and culture such as the free press and religious tolerance has been the NGO sector. As the state machinery has become more openly supportive of Islamization, and new religious groups and schools are mushrooming within civil society, the earlier secular NGOs are being crowded out or intimidated. They became the direct target of attacks by conservative Islamists during the 1990s and since 2000, intimidation has reached new highs. After the BNP came to power in 2001, it has been accused of taking steps to marginalize NGOs it believes are allied with the opposition.[94]

Intimidation of minorities also became worse according to local NGOs such as the Society for Environment and Human Development. Amnesty International held the BNP coalition responsible. The JMB is accused of coordinating nationwide attacks against so-called "un-Islamic persons" and facilities, attacking a string of targets – judges, traditional folk festivals and cultural groups, government offices and NGOs.[95] The targets suggest that Islamist militants are not just poised against minorities and "westernization" but Sufi traditions as well. These targets include religious shrines, fairs and jatras (folk theater). Some JeI leaders have publicly condemned Sufi practices as "haraam (prohibited) and anti-Islam" and have urged Muslims to "resist these traditions."[96]

Effects of the BNP–Awami League competition

The sudden spike in political violence in Bangladesh is also attributable to the ruinous cycle of political competition between the AL and the BNP. Both parties have used ruthless law-and-order measures to muzzle political opponents, doing to even under the guise of anti-terrorism laws.[97] At the same time, the "blame game" between the two parties makes it that much more difficult to trace the sources of terrorist violence. The extent to which Islamist extremists are operating under the cover of party competition and political sponsorship remains an open question. What is clear is that the fighting between the AL and the BNP (the BNP ruled from 2001 to January 2007) is providing unusually fertile ground for extremists to operate, ranging from mastans (underworld figures) to

---

[94] Lewis, "On the Difficulty of Studying 'Civil Society,'" p. 310.
[95] US Department of State, *Country Reports on Terrorism 2005*, p. 149; and *The Daily Star*, February 4, 2005
[96] Quoted in Ahmed, "The Role of Education."
[97] Riaz, *Unfolding State*, pp. 235–236. An example of such measures is Operation Clean Heart, a joint army and police offensive launched in late 2002.

religious extremists and terrorists.[98] An increasing winner-take-all mentality by the two parties has led the BNP, in particular, to rely on Islamist groups for political gain. The hurried decision in August 2006 by the BNP government to equate the "Dawra degree" of the unregulated Qawmi madrasas with a masters degree in general education is likely to have far reaching repercussions, and led observers to wonder whether it was done with an eye towards elections then scheduled for January 2007.[99]

The BNP government's reaction to criticism for including Islamist elements has been to deny undue influence. As a senior cabinet minister said, "Our relationship with the JeI is an electoral alliance. What does that have to do with peace in the country? We [BNP] decide everything. They [JeI] cannot dictate anything."[100] He went on to note that although the JeI leadership is known as "anti-liberation," the government went ahead and established a Liberation Affairs Ministry. Yet, the BNP government conceded to demands of the IOJ in January 2004 and banned the publications of the Ahmadiyyas. The unprecedented suppression of this Muslim sect at the state level set the tone for what followed: the destruction of several Ahmadiyya mosques across the country in fits of rising intolerance. According to leading members of the Hindu minority, the biggest concern is such "state sponsored" insecurity.[101] They point to the lack of communal incidents during Hindu festivals such as Durga Puja when the state provides protection.

The increasing cultural activism of Islamist groups under the umbrella of the state provides a symbiotic climate between the political and cultural spheres. Besides, the JeI has a long time horizon and is putting in place grassroots organizations along the lines of the Grameen Bank and BRAC, thus competing with earlier secular NGOs it had lost ground to in the 1960s and 1970s. Its enterprises are also producing profit, allowing the JeI to continue its work and attract supporters.[102] Some analysts believe that the induction of JeI into the political arena without accountability for its "collaboration" with the Pakistan armed forces in 1971, including its participation in atrocities along with right wing groups against Bengali separatists, has left a raw nerve in the body politic, which directly feeds into questions of national identity.

---

[98] For a discussion of organized crime and politicians, see Philipson, "Corrupted Democracy."
[99] See editorial in The Daily Star, August 23, 2006.
[100] Personal interview with a senior government minister, July 27, 2004, Dhaka, Bangladesh.
[101] Interviews conducted in Washington, DC, August 2006.
[102] This is a view held by many analysts of Bangladesh. See, for example, Tariq Karim, Trip Report, US Institute of Peace, Washington, DC, August 10, 2006.

Ironically, past elections have shown a remarkable balance in the popular votes that the BNP and AL have received. If we go by electoral expressions, domestic support for Islamism is thin at best, with 90 percent of the voting population almost equally divided between supporting the Awami League and the BNP. In the lead-up to the aborted elections of January 2007, most indications gave the Awami League a better chance of victory. (This would have been entirely in keeping with the electorate consistently throwing out the incumbents since democracy was restored in 1990.) In 2001, as part of the winning combine with the BNP, the JeI found itself in a position to wield influence well beyond what the popular votes suggested. In the context of Bangladesh's first-past-the-post electoral system, however, even a slim plurality for one party allows it to walk away with a disproportionately large number of parliamentary seats.

The intertwining of political competition and religious militancy threatens to overwhelm Bangladesh's democracy. The election standoff between October 2006 and January 2007, with the BNP finally pulling back from the brink and allowing for a more neutral caretaker government prior to elections rather than continuing to stack the deck in its favor, has revealed both the erosion and resilience of democracy in Bangladesh.

The pull of post 9/11 geopolitics

The American response to the attacks of 9/11 has had two major effects on Bangladesh: it has pulled the country into a global Islamist agenda from relative isolation and severely reduced space for secular discourse. According to leading members of the intelligentsia and media in Bangladesh, the US invasion of Afghanistan and, particularly, Iraq have created a mentality that Islam is under siege, making it difficult for public criticism of domestic Islamist militancy. The introduction of suicide terrorism for the first time in Bangladesh in 2005 is a development that many connect to global trends. The term "moderate Muslim country" to describe Bangladesh (first coined by President Bill Clinton in 2000) and American calls for expanding "moderate voices" thus stand in some irony.[103] In December 2001 the cleric of Bangladesh's national mosque publicly condemned the war on terrorism, equating President Bush's actions as

---

[103] This was pointed out in numerous interviews in Dhaka with leading NGO leaders and intellectuals, July 2004. There were repeated stories of intimidation of the press and NGO leaders who spoke out against Islamist militancy, especially after September 11.

"terrorism." Bangladesh decided against contributing troops to the US-led coalition in Iraq in 2003, largely due to inflamed domestic sentiment.[104]

In the post-9/11 context, increasing Indian identification with US anti-terrorism efforts does not sit well with Bangladesh, a fact not lost on most Indian authorities. Despite its overwhelming power when measured against Bangladesh, India's central authorities have been circumspect regarding alleged terrorist sanctuaries across the border. In response to West Bengal Chief Minister Buddhadeb Bhattacharjee's demand that India enter Bangladesh to destroy terrorist camps, Indian Defense Minister Pranab Mukherjee asked, "How can we go to another country and destroy terrorist camps there? We will continue to persuade the government of Bangladesh to do it."[105] The attempt by the BJP to redefine cross border migrants as "terrorists" and the Congress resistance, also shows restraint along these lines. There is high-level Indian opinion that argues against public charges of the Bangladesh government's support for extremist groups.[106] On the other hand, there are some advocates for adopting the American discourse on terrorism, which could increase Indo-Bangladesh tension.

Unlike Pakistan, Bangladesh had never been closely linked to the Middle East Arab states and Bangladeshi nationalism had never included strong Muslim universalism.[107] Even during the years of Afghanistan's wars and the ups and downs of the Kashmir conflict, Bangladeshis did not get drawn into the region's political Islam in any notable fashion.[108] Similarly, communal riots in neighboring India did not set off reactive violence in Bangladesh (for example, in 2002, there were some disturbances after the Gujarat riots but they were quickly contained). Polls have shown that ethnic identity has dominated over religious identity, with only about 11 percent identifying Islam as their main identity. Almost 70 percent polled indicated that their preference is for Hindu Bangladeshis to remain in the country.[109] The opinion of the Hindus seems to be that while minority

---

[104] Tom Squitieri, "Nations Back Off Sending Troops to Iraq," *USA Today*, October 28, 2003, p. 8 and Mark Matthews, "Foreign Troop Relief Falls Short of US Hopes," *Baltimore Sun*, November 8, 2003.

[105] Quoted in *The Hindu*, September 9, 2006.

[106] See, for example, former Indian Prime Minister I. K. Gujral's view that Delhi made a mistake in accusing Dhaka of terrorist links, in *Daily Star*, January 22, 2003.

[107] Razia Akhtar Banu, paper presented at panel on "Religious Politics: Is Bangladesh Vulnerable to Extremism?" at a conference on *Bangladesh: Democracy, Governance and Resources*, Center for Strategic & International Studies, Washington, DC, April 29, 2004.

[108] At least rhetorically, the senior Jamaat leadership has described the Kashmir conflict as "far away" from Bangladesh. Personal interviews, Dhaka, July 2004.

[109] Banu, "Religious Politics."

insecurity has been on the rise since 2001, opposition to the BNP is also strong, reflecting a more tolerant deep popular sentiment.[110]

When ties with the Middle East began to be strengthened, it was economic not religious motivations that drove them.[111] These ties however have introduced external influences in ways that have often been detrimental to Bangladeshi traditions, similar to the experience of other South Asian states. For example, it was commonly assumed that the insertion of strongly worded Islamic clauses in Zia's Constitutional revisions, including a Constitutional commitment to pursue friendly relations with Islamic countries, was a prerequisite to Bangladesh's admission to the Islamic Conference.[112] Longstanding Sufi-based outlooks are facing twin challenges: from the stricter Deobandism of Pakistan and Wahabism from the Middle East. The rise of the latter is facilitated by the investment of oil money in Bangladesh and the unfolding global geopolitics, represented by the renewed US presence in Afghanistan and the invasion of Iraq. Together with the internal decline of secularism, this is a potent mix.

Conclusion

The competing pressures on identity seem to have been stronger in Bangladesh than in any other South Asian state. It is caught between its own past, and between India and Pakistan. Having once been a part of both India and Pakistan, its features resemble qualities of both. Politically, as in Pakistan, the civilian–military connections were strong but, like India, the civilian side ultimately dominated. Bangladesh's position between India and Pakistan, as well as its struggle between religion and secular leanings, is best captured by the notion of geopolitical identity. For instance in 1980 when Zia ur-Rahman proposed the idea of the SAARC, it was partly to have a collective mechanism that might dilute Indian power. Pakistan, however, opposed it on the grounds that India would dominate the organization.

The increasing trend of religion in political discourse has been referred to as the "Pakistanization" of Bangladesh. At a 2006 conference on developments in Bangladesh, Pakistani commentator Husain Haqqani warned the BNP and Awami League of the perils of following Pakistan's route and cautioned them to "avoid the temptation to tolerating and accepting radical Islamist ideology as a pressure tactic in settling political conflicts within

---

[110] Interview with leading Hindu Bangladeshi scholar, Washington, DC, August 24, 2006.

[111] This was the near consensus among participants at a major Conference on *Bangladesh: Democracy, Governance and Resources*, Center for Strategic & International Studies, Washington, DC, April 29, 2004.

[112] Franda, *Bangladesh*, p. 300.

the country, for example BNP painting the Awami League as Hindu agents; and shun the temptation to look upon radical Islamists as an instrument of foreign policy, such as containment of India."[113]

The icon of Bangladesh's independence, Mujib Rahman, had little hesitation in elevating the rhetoric of Indo-Bangladesh relations to romantic heights. The identity politics of Bangladesh at the time permitted such a conception because of the strong plural secularism underlying the state. The reversal of that path began at the intersection of domestic and geopolitical identities, openly for the first time under Zia. The introduction of geopolitics into Bangladesh's national identity formation occurred most pointedly under military rule, opening this space up for the civilian political parties that followed. At this stage, however, the military is caught in a bind: it cannot be seen as playing a retrogressive political role given its international role as the second largest contributor to UN peacekeeping operations, with thousands of soldiers posted around the world as an important source of foreign exchange.

The defeat of the BJP and rise of Congress in 2004 has been described by leading Bangladeshi liberals as important for "confidence building" between India and Bangladesh. Indeed, some suggest that it was more important than any action that could have been taken by India's Ministry of External Affairs.[114] However, the sentiment remains strong that as the much larger country, India has greater responsibility to be more responsive to Bangladesh's concerns rather than expecting strict reciprocity.

An immediate challenge for Bangladesh is to ensure that Islamists espousing violence are reined in before they gain long-term viability. This needs to be coupled with ensuring that intolerant Islamist agendas do not become dominant and overturn Bangladesh's longstanding preferences. For now, radical Islamists appear to be in the minority, but greater access to state power could prove to be a decisive turning point. It would allow them to not only promote their polarizing internal agenda but turn dangerously hostile and aggressive geopolitically.

[113] Husain Haqqani, *The Nation* (Pakistan), November 29, 2006.
[114] Personal interviews with a cross-section of liberal opinion leaders, Dhaka, July 2004.

8   Conclusion

The proposition that equates extremism and terrorism with ethnic and religious factors is easy to make, but harder to prove, as evidence from these cases reveal. The region's long socio-political history is revealing in its absence of strong religious identity constructions prior to the colonial period. Remarkably, this was the situation even on the eve of independence during the 1940s. But by then, conditions had already been laid for what was to become a three-way struggle in contemporary South Asia between ethno-religious, secular and geopolitical identities.

How this interaction unfolds significantly explains the key puzzles that animate the book. What accounts for the rise of extremist ethno-religious groups in societies that were historically not so predisposed? How do we account for the wide variation in ethnic and religious ideology, political strategy and the foreign-policy orientations of political groups? Most importantly, what determines the winners and losers in the overarching identity struggles that we see in South Asia and what tips the balance between more moderate and extremist outcomes?

Internal–external links

As Chapter One shows, the literature on the *politics* of ethnicity and religion is vast but inconclusive. I argue for the addition of another variable, the *geopolitics* of ethno-religious identity (or what I term geopolitical identity) that influences, and at times even determines, the trajectory of extremism in South Asia. The role of the state is critical in fashioning geopolitical identities that bring together external foreign policy considerations and internal power-seeking objectives. We find that the state has wide latitude in this role, due in part to the existence of unstable secularism across the region. In states with highly contested sovereignties and insecure elites such as Sri Lanka and Pakistan, the motivation for states to engage in polarizing and hostile identity constructions becomes especially strong.

Longstanding assimilative traditions, including even co-worship in Kashmir between Hindus and Muslims as discussed in Chapter Two, begs the question of how such structures became transformed. Despite the longevity of political secularism, along with social traditions that supported this concept, South Asia did remain susceptible to extremist ideologies thanks to the dormant instability of that secularism. Beginning with British colonial penetration, this susceptibility became much more open and institutionalized, laying the groundwork for post-colonial elites to manipulate it even more. Externally induced changes in the domestic sphere have been a recurring theme from the late nineteenth century onwards, reaching its height in post-1979 Afghanistan.

Evidence from the region

As Chapter Three indicates, current attempts at another rewriting of Afghanistan's domestic sphere is bedeviled by both previous and ongoing geopolitical challenges, and provides the strongest evidence among the cases in this book for validating Peter Gurevitch's thesis about the domestic consequences of international forces. The outcome of these challenges will determine whether or not more open and tolerant identity conceptions of the past will be reclaimed and whether groups representing the more extremist versions will be defeated or marginalized. A critical gap in the new Afghan project since 2001 is the weakness of moderate Pashtun political groups, most directly traceable to US and Pakistan geopolitical identity needs during the Afghan wars. Even at this stage, between the US's ineffective war on terrorism and the evident duplicity across the border in Pakistan, Afghanistan's fate – from how domestic institutions will evolve to the nature of the state's foreign policy – remains in the hands of outside actors.

Chaper Four demonstrates the critical importance of Pakistan to regional stability, on its western border with Afghanistan and eastern border with India. Given Pakistan's origins as a Muslim state, we would expect a strong religious tone in state identity; what is surprising is that this identity seems deeper and more polarized now than in 1947 when it might have been more relevant. The emergence of terrorist groups such as Jaish-e-Mohammed, Lashkar-e-Toiba and Sipah-i-Sahaba, as well as Islamist parties operating politically under the MMA coalition, is a recent phenomenon. The geopolitical identity needs of successive military-led governments is the single most important determinant of this development. This raises the question of whether religious groups (radical and moderate) can exist and thrive independently in Pakistan as political actors.

The tussle between President Musharraf and religious groups following his backing of the US in Afghanistan suggests otherwise. For example, when the US began bombing Afghanistan in October 2001, Maulana

Fazlur Rehman led large anti-US, anti-Musharraf and pro-Taliban rallies in Pakistan's major cities. He warned that the Pakistani chief would be overthrown if he continued supporting the Americans. The Maulana was placed under house arrest by Musharraf and charged with sedition for inciting people against the armed forces and trying to overthrow the government. The following March, Rehman was set free and all cases against him withdrawn. By the time of the national elections in October 2002 the JUI leader and the military had made up, with the religious parties getting preferential treatment during campaigning. This paid handsome electoral dividends for both, sealing Musharaff's victory. In this saga, the military not only held the critical political and institutional reins, it also showed itself to be politically agile.

We might ask why this trend towards radical Islam was not reversed during the interregnum of civilian rule in the 1990s. The experience of Benazir Bhutto is instructive: she has stated that as Prime Minister the second time around, she consciously ceded control over the two main foreign policy issues of Afghanistan and Kashmir, with the hope of focusing on domestic politics (including reining in extremist groups), only to find that it was not enough for the military. Does the ostensible turnaround since 9/11 spearheaded by Musharraf, coupled with the threat of sectarian and jihadi violence within Pakistan, presage a transformation that will finally moderate the roots of state identity? More than seven years later, opinion is deeply divided. This gives little confidence for making predictions about outcomes in Afghanistan or, on the other side, Kashmir.

Like the Afghan leadership, New Delhi's concerns about Kashmir are related to the Pakistani military's geopolitical identity needs. Chapter Five describes how both India and Pakistan's state identity requirements have worked directly at cross purposes. Pakistan's involvement in the Kashmir conflict has allowed the most polarized and violent groups space within a historically moderate and religiously tolerant setting. Kashmir's location on the geographic periphery of India has made the geopolitical aspects dominant, bringing the clashing Indo-Pakistan identities into prolonged military struggle. Ironically, one line of thinking among some Kashmiri Muslims is that while India threatens their religious identity, Pakistan threatens their ethnic identity. Against this, India could claim with justification that its strong political secularism protected the religious identity of the Kashmiris (as it did that of the large Muslim population elsewhere in India), and the lack of serious political conflict in Kashmir well into the 1980s, suggested that most Kashmiris believed this to be true. The absence of support for Kashmiri militancy among Indian Muslims, despite the episodic communal clashes from Ayodhya to Gujarat and the rise of Hindu nationalism during the 1980s and 1990s, gives this proposition even greater weight.

The Indian government's shift in strategy towards Kashmir since 2002, softening its military response with open dialogue with sections of the All Parties Hurriyat Conference, holds out the possibility of a political resolution. The defeat of the Hindu nationalist Bharatiya Janata Party in 2004 by more secular forces, and the BJP's continuing failure to seriously regroup, may prove to be an important confidence-building measure in the long run for restoring Kashmiri faith in India's political secularism. Yet when in power, even the BJP did not disturb Article 370 of the Indian constitution giving Kashmir a unique status, or push for a uniform civil code, demonstrating the unimpeachable constitutional status of Indian secularism. Besides, it was BJP stalwarts who began talks with the Kashmiri militants in 2002, laying the groundwork for a future settlement. As with Afghanistan, however, the Pakistan military's pursuit of its own competitive identity needs vis-à-vis India is likely to tip the balance one way or the other in Kashmir.

India has loomed large in the identity conceptions of not only Pakistan, but Sri Lanka and Bangladesh as well. In the case of Sri Lanka, the Sinhalese who comprise 70 percent of the population have long had a "majority-minority" complex about the over 60 million Tamils in Tamil Nadu across the narrow Palk Straits. Given the direct Indian intervention in the Sinhala–Tamil conflict in 1987, there would seem to be some justification for Sri Lanka's concern. However, all the important changes in Sri Lanka towards institutionalizing the privileges of the Sinhala Buddhist majority – from the education to the constitutional sectors – came well before India's involvement militarily or its support for Tamil militant groups inside India. Besides, India's military ended up fighting the Tamil Tigers and alienating large sections of the Tamil population. Indeed, India's on-off support for Tamil aspirations in Sri Lanka have always been carefully circumscribed to avoid a complete backing of secession, given India's own geopolitical anxieties.

Despite this reality, it is hard to entirely disentangle the rise of strident Buddhist chauvinism and its use of anti-India rhetoric from the geopolitical identity constructions of the Sri Lankan state elites. External influences on the rise of Buddhist chauvinism, and Tamil radicalism as a response, have been much more indirect than in the cases of Afghanistan and Kashmir, but should not be underestimated. Indeed, the very promising ceasefire and peace process begun with the Tamil Tigers in 2002 has been repeatedly undercut by the Buddhist nationalist parties Janata Vimukti Peramuna and Jathika Hela Urugayu, whose central platform has been the call to "protect" Sri Lanka's Buddhist character and sovereignty against outside intervention – an oblique but widely understood reference to India. By conflating Tamil demands for autonomy with India's geopolitical ambitions, these two parties make it extremely difficult for any reasonable compromise with the militants. But it was the mainstream political parties (as in Bangladesh), particularly the Sri Lankan Freedom Party, that bucked traditional Tamil–Sinhala political cooperation and elevated Buddhist religious ideology to a defining state identity. Moderate Tamil groups who had been historically dominant have found it difficult, if not impossible, to stake out any credible position within Sri Lanka's polarized polity. The result has been the rise of extremist Tamil groups, particularly the Liberation Tigers of Tamil Eelam, which a significant section of Tamils see as the only viable option.

Bangladesh offers yet another example of how long-held tolerant societal beliefs and inclusive domestic institutions have been distorted by state elites, and produced conditions that are conducive to the emergence of groups that go flagrantly against the historical grain. Although, as in Sri Lanka, a mainstream political party in Bangladesh (the Bangladesh National Party) has been complicit in perpetuating narrow and illiberal state identity, the BNP's origins are to be found squarely in the military's powerplays between 1975 and 1990. With little international attention, and surrounded by India, Dhaka's foreign policy has been almost entirely India-centric. Yet, during all of its quarter of a century in Pakistan, and for the first few years after gaining independence in 1971, Bangladesh's politically secular identity conception was practically synonymous with India's. If anything, Bangladesh stood as the antithesis of a polarized and hostile geopolitical identity vis-à-vis India, giving a glimpse of how states in South Asia are not necessarily doomed to identity competition.

Military rule, initiated by General Zia ur-Rahman, recast state identity in ways that played directly into a characteristically unstable secularism. Once again, an underlying rationale for this shift was to put distance between the strong cultural affinity with Bengalis in India, thus contributing to the cultivation of a Bangladeshi Islamic identity. Against this backdrop, even after the return of civilian government, Bangladesh's domestic political competition between the more openly secular Awami League and the military-anointed Bangladesh National Party is rife with identity struggles in which India is, at minimum, an implicit factor. Such considerations have gone so far as to make ruling Bangladesh parties reluctant to enter into economically logical deals with India to avoid the charge of "selling sovereignty" to its neighbor.

Indian exceptionalism

Among the states in South Asia, only India seems to have found a workable and stable, if not ideal, approach to the mix of religion, ethnicity and geopolitics that moderates the most pernicious identity conceptions that we find elsewhere in the region. In all the other states, what is called for is a resuscitation of their historical tolerance and a reworking of domestic structures towards greater political secularism. For this scenario, the international environment has been disastrous. US policy in the region and the war in Iraq has undermined liberal Muslim opinion and empowered radicals, shrinking the space for discourse. Secularism is denounced by ethnic and religious zealots in South Asia as a western imposition, forgetting the region's own past traditions. In the neighborhood, the concept of secularism has come to be overly identified with the Indian political project, in a strategic and short-sighted disavowal of underlying commonalities.

India has not been immune to the current wave of extremism in South Asia and the polarized international conditions. But from the December 2001 attack on the Indian parliament to the July 2006 railway bombings that rocked suburban Mumbai, the consensus among investigating authorities is that these terrorist acts were largely inspired by infiltrators. Such incidents have been successfully isolated without widespread repercussions. So far, India has been able to withstand the penetration of destructive ideologies from outside to a greater degree than its neighbors. This is explained partly by the strength of India's domestic structures and partly by its solidly independent foreign policy. The large number of distinctive caste, ethnic, social and political affiliations found in India ironically serves as a buffer against single, ideologically driven platforms. For instance, Muslims in the southwest corner of India in Kerala invariably identity themselves with other Keralites rather than with their religious compatriots in far away Kashmir. India's domestic structures are hard to influence from outside, let alone reshape.[1]

India's best bet is to maintain the integrity of its democratic pluralism. The willingness of successive Indian governments to co-opt extremists into the political arena, create layered federalist structures to meet crisscrossing ethno-religious identities and live without a uniform civil code, all contribute to Indian stability. Caste-based conflict has been contained, first under the Congress Party's umbrella of backward castes and minorities and then, by the 1990s, the emergence of strong independent caste and regional parties vying for state power via the ballot box. In the current context, the Indian state will have to avoid overreacting to terrorist challenges despite persistent provocations. As India's (military) hard power grows, many within the country and outside recognize the attraction of India's (politico-economic and cultural) soft power as well. At a 2006 Leadership Summit in New Delhi, United Nations Undersecretary General Shashi Tharoor

---

[1] This is not to say that there has not been increasing cultural isolationism of sections of Muslims as a reaction to Hindutva forces and the global "war on terrorism."

and former Japanese Foreign Minister Yoriko Kawaguchi both saw the management of diversity as India's singular civilizational achievement.[2]

The traditional Indian obsession with achieving strategic autonomy (found across the political spectrum) has also paid dividends domestically, although at times it has been frustrating internationally. In contrast to many political elites in the developing world who have been condemned by their people for an excessive dependency on the US or other great powers, the Indian leadership can claim special legitimacy. At present, this would mean continuing the traditional ideological distance from US foreign-policy distortions and blunders in the Persian Gulf and Middle East, while at the same time forging ahead with the evolving Indo-US partnership, epitomized by the pathbreaking deal on civilian nuclear technology and trade. In this regard, Washington's present stand-off with Iran and India's attempt to keep a balanced approach to this critical energy supplier and key friend in the Islamic world, is clearly testing Indian diplomacy. From a regional viewpoint the US resistance to a potential Iran–Pakistan–India natural gas pipeline is a huge stumbling block to one of the biggest confidence-building measures imaginable in the troubled neighbourhood.

It is no secret that India likes diversified partnerships – its renewed relationship with a resurgent Russia is a case in point. There is little evidence that India will compromise its autonomy. Its decision against sending troops to support the US in Iraq despite intense pressure from Washington is likely to be the rule, not the exception. As India acquires new geo-strategic importance, such a stance will only be strengthened. The US National Intelligence Council's "Mapping the Global Future" projects that the rise of India and China will transform the international strategic landscape with an impact comparable to unified Germany in the nineteenth century and the US in the twentieth century.[3]

Looking ahead

There is no escaping the conclusion that without understanding that the fates of countries in the region are linked, we can make little progress to counter the destructive identity conflicts that are being waged across South Asia. This has to occur at the level of the state but, as we have found time

---

[2] According to Tharoor, "Our democracy, our thriving free media, our NGOs, our energetic human rights groups and the repeated spectacle of our remarkable general elections have all made India a rare example of successful management of diversity in the developing world." *The Hindustan Times*, November 18, 2006.

[3] National Intelligence Council, *Mapping the Global Future: Report of the National Intelligence Council's 2020 Project* (Washington, DC: US Government Printing Office, December 2004), p.47.

and time again, state actors are fashioning exclusivist, ahistorical identities because of their perceived utility in shoring up the state or mobilizing political power. With South Asia's insecure states and unstable secularism, we end up seeing the kind of geopolitical identities in Sri Lanka, Afghanistan, Pakistan and Bangladesh that create more permissive conditions for extremist groups than ever before. Inter-state rivalries all too often go well beyond strategic factors to the identity and domestic sociopolitical realms, making them that much more difficult to resolve.

For too long, regional interests and narrow national interests have been at loggerheads, but there are glimmers of countervailing developments: the increasingly robust Indo-Sri Lankan economic relations since 1998 are worth noting. That situation demonstrates how states may circumvent or create a *modus vivendi* even after the experience of explosive geopolitcs and chauvinistic nationalism. The positive "security externalities" from their expanded trade ties have been cited by close analysts.[4] From a policy perspective, we cannot minimize the importance of economic relations, despite the weakness of the South Asian Association for Regional Cooperation so far. India's rapid economic ascent could hold the key as an engine of growth for the region. Indeed, the managing director of the International Monetary Fund has gone further, expecting "China, and increasingly India to grow in importance as engines of global growth."[5] The growing weight of economic diplomacy in Indian foreign policy suggests that New Delhi is finally ready to seize the opportunity. Since none of India's neighbors share a boundary, regional trade ultimately comes down to the other states developing commerce with different regions of India.[6] The underlying view in Islamabad that economic cooperation with India should wait until Kashmir is resolved is becoming more self-defeating by the day.

Surprisingly, there is still scant popular support regionally for extremist politics if electoral performance or public opinion polls are anything to go by – in Afghanistan, Pakistan, Bangladesh, Sri Lanka and Kashmir, we rarely find public support for religious parties (let alone radical religious parties) crossing single digit figures in percentage terms. This makes it easy for another policy prescription: the democratic

---

[4] See Devesh Kapur and Kavita Iyengar, "The Limits of Integration in Improving South Asian Security," in Ashley Tellis and Michael Wills (eds.) *Trade, Interdependence and Security Strategic Asia 2006–07* (Seattle: National Bureau of Asian Research, 2006), p. 257.

[5] This statement was made by Rodrigo Rato, *International Business Times*, August 3, 2007.

[6] Rakesh Sood was an Indian government official who recognized the importance of India in regional economics early on; among strategic analysts, C. Raja Mohan has been an articulate proponent of the value of regional economic cooperation led by India. See for example, "Stability and Challenge," IISS Global Strategic Review, (September 13–15, 2002) and *The Hindu*, September 23, 2004 respectively.

process has to be promoted. When we find state elites manipulating the political system or militant groups shunning open elections, we have to ask the question: why are they afraid of the democratic process? Given the unmistakable footprint of Pakistan's military in the rise of extremism in the region, America's sponsorship of the military over democratic institutions comes at a huge price.[7] There is no respite in sight even though some violent Islamist groups are now on a direct collision course with the Pakistani military leadership as graphically demonstrated by the Lal Masjid (Red Mosque) clashes in the heart of the capital city. The problem is that the military would like to have it both ways – retain its influence with selected extremist groups for foreign policy purposes and simultaneously appear to be responsive to US pressures on fighting terrorism.[8] As a regime under international scrutiny, this kind of dual track policy becomes harder to conceal. The threat by Musharraf to impose emergency rule as late as August 2007, however, shows that the military prefers to take the predictable road in a crisis rather than overhaul Pakistan's political structures. Even the transition to civilian leadership in 2008 after Benazir Bhutto's shocking assassination is no guarantee that the military has relinquished its hold on foreign policy. If at all, it is more likely to be a temporary and strategic retreat.

From an immediate US policy perspective, there is another compelling lesson that this book offers. Despite the extensive analysis of contemporary extremism and terrorism by American government agencies and think tanks since 9/11, Washington's understanding appears wholly inadequate. This lack of understanding stems in large part from a fundamental confusion about whether terrorist violence now is characterized by decentralized groups and individuals who meet and plot locally or on the Internet; by a profusion of dispersed groups controlled by al Qaeda's central command structure; or by organized but shadowy groups with ties to motivated state actors and other powerful institutions. Increasingly, the debate seems confined to the first two alternatives, but as evidence from South Asia shows, we ignore or miss the role of the state at our peril.[9]

---

[7] Many activists in Pakistan criticize what they believe is a dominant feeling in Washington that democracy cannot work in Pakistan.

[8] Ahmed Rashid provides a devastating account of how Pakistan has been arming and aiding extremist groups, in particular the Taliban, while remaining America's most important ally in the war on terrorism. See his *Descent into Chaos: The United States and the Failure of Nature Building in Pakistan, Afghanistan and Central Asia* (New York: Viking Penguin, 2008).

[9] For a lively journalisitic debate on some of these issues, see Elaine Sciolino and Eric Schmitt, "A Not Very Private Feud Over Terrorism," *The New York Times*, June 8, 2008.

In order to advance our understanding of the rise of ethnic and religious extremism at this historical juncture, this book has argued that we need to look beyond ethnicity and religion, and beyond the domestic realm to the impact of geopolitics that we all too often assign solely to the external arena. The intermingling of identity and security perceptions, mediated by the state, is a significant predictor of the level of extremism. Weak secularism, combined with competitive external politics, makes for worst case outcomes. From what we know of state behavior elsewhere, these findings on the critical role of the state and identity formation should have important relevance beyond the South Asian context.

Bibliography

Aall, Pamela and Ollapally, Deepa (eds.), *Perspectives on the Role of Education and Media in Conflict Management in South Asia* (Washington, DC: US Institute of Peace Press, forthcoming 2008)

Abdullah, F. H., "Affirmative Action Policy in Malaysia: To Restructure Society, to Eradicate Poverty," *Ethnic Studies Report*, 15.2 (1997)

Afzal, M. Rafique, *Pakistan: History and Politics 1947–1971* (Karachi: Oxford University Press, 2001)

Ahmad, Imtiaz and Reifeld, Helmut (eds.), *Lived Islam in South Asia: Adaptation, Accommodation and Conflict* (New Delhi: Social Science Press, 2004)

Ahmed, Imtiaz, "Governance and the International Development Community: Making Sense of the Bangladesh Experience," *Contemporary South Asia*, 8.3 (1999)

"The Role of Education in Conflict: Bangladesh," in Aall and Ollapally (eds.), *Perspectives*

Akbar, M. J., *Kashmir: Behind the Vale* (New Delhi: Lotus Collection of Roli Books, 2002)

Alexander, Yonah (ed.), *International Terrorism: National, Regional and Global Perspectives* (New York: Praeger, 1976)

Allen, Charles, "The Hidden Roots of Wahhabism in British India," *World Policy Journal*, 22.2 (2005)

Antonio, Robert J. "After Postmodernism: Reactionary Tribalism," *American Journal of Sociology*, 106.2 (2000)

Asia Foundation, The, *Voter Education Planning Survey: Afghanistan 2004 National Elections, A Report Based on a Public Opinion Poll* (The Asia Foundation: New York, 2004)

Ayoob, Mohammed, "Political Islam: Image and Reality," *World Policy Journal*, 21.3 (2004)

Ayoob, Mohammed and Subrahmanyam, K., *The Liberation War* (New Delhi: S. Chand & Co., 1972)

Azad, Abdul Kalam, *India Wins Freedom: An Autobiographical Narrative* (Bombay: Orient Longman, 1959)

Bajpai, Kanti P., *Roots of Terrorism* (New Delhi: Penguin Books, 2002)

Balachandran, G., "Religion and Nationalism in Modern India," in Basu and Subrahmanyam (eds.), *Unravelling the Nation*

Banerjee, Mukulika, *The Pathan Unarmed: Opposition and Memory in the North West Frontier* (Karachi: Oxford University Press, 2000)

Banu, Razia Akhtar, *Islam in Bangladesh* (Leiden: E. J. Brill, 1992)
  "Jamaat-i-Islami in Bangladesh: Challenges and Prospects," in Jussain Mutalib and Tajul Islam Hashmi (eds.) *Islam, Muslims and the Modern State* (London: Macmillan Press, 1994)
  Paper presented at a panel on "Religious Politics: Is Bangladesh Vulnerable to Extremism?" at *Bangladesh: Democracy, Governance and Resources,* Center for Strategic and International Studies, Washington, DC, April 29, 2004
Baruah, Sanjib, *India Against Itself: Assam and the Politics of Nationality* (Philadelphia: University of Pennsylvania Press, 1999)
Basu, Amrita and Kohli, Atul, "Community Conflicts and the State in India," *The Journal of Asian Studies,* 56.2 (1997)
Basu, Kaushik and Subrahmanyam, Sanjay (eds.), *Unravelling the Nation: Sectarian Conflict and India's Secular Identity* (New Delhi: Penguin Books, 1996)
Behera, Navnita Chadha, "Kashmir: Redefining the US Role," The Brookings Institution Policy Brief No. 110 (Washington, DC: The Brookings Institution, 2002)
Benjamin, Daniel and Simon, Steven, *The Age of Sacred Terror* (New York: Random House, 2002)
Bhargava, Rajeev (ed.), *Secularism and Its Critics* (New Delhi: Oxford University Press, 1999)
  "What is Secularism For?" in Bhargava (ed.), *Secularism and Its Critics*
Bhuiyan, Md. Abdul Wadud, *Emergence of Bangladesh and Role of Awami League* (New Delhi: Vikas Publishing House, 1982)
Bilgrami, Akeel, "The Clash Within Civilizations," *Daedalus,* 123.3 (2003)
Blackburn, Robin (ed.), *Explosion in a Subcontinent* (New York: Penguin Books, 1975)
Blank, Jonah, "Kashmir: Fundamentalism Takes Root," *Foreign Affairs,* 78.6 (1999)
Bose, Sumantra, *The Challenge in Kashmir* (New Delhi: Sage Publications, 1997)
  Kashmir: Roots of Conflict, Paths to Peace (Cambridge, MA: Harvard University Press, 2003)
Bradsher, Henry S., *Afghanistan and the Soviet Union* (Durham, NC: Duke University Press, 1983)
Brass, Paul, *Ethnicity and Nationalism* (New Delhi: Sage Publications, 1991)
  (ed.), *Riots and Pogroms* (New York University Press, 1996)
Bullion, Alan J., *India, Sri Lanka and the Tamil Crisis 1976–1994: An International Perspective* (London: Pinter, 1995)
Burr, William (ed.), *The September 11th Sourcebooks, Volume IV: The Once and Future King? From the Secret Files on King Zahir's Reign in Afghanistan, 1970–1973,* National Security Archive Electronic Briefing Book No. 59, October 26, 2001
Byman, Dan, *Deadly Connections: States That Sponsor Terrorism* (New York: Cambridge University Press, 2005)
Callinicos, Alex, *Against Postmodernism* (New York: St. Martin's Press, 1990)
Center for Economic and Social Rights, *Human Rights and Reconstruction in Afghanistan* (New York: CESR, May 2002)

Center on International Cooperation, *Regional Approaches to the Reconstruction of Afghanistan*, Summary of a conference to discuss regional peacebuilding held in Istanbul, June 3–5, 2002 (New York: CIC, 2002)

Chadda, Maya, "Integration through Internal Reorganization: Containing Ethnic Conflict in India," *The Global Review of Ethnopolitics*, 2.1 (2002)

Chandhoke, Neera, *Beyond Secularism: The Rights of Religious Minorities* (New Delhi: Oxford University Press, 1999)

Chandran, Suba, "Recent Developments in Kashmir I: Hizbul Ceasefire – Why?," Article No. 401 (New Delhi: Institute for Peace and Conflict Studies, 2000)

Choudhury, G. W., *The Last Days of United Pakistan* (Bloomington: Indiana University Press, 1974)

Coelho, Vincent, *Across the Palk Straits: India–Sri Lanka Relations* (New Delhi: Palit & Palit, 1976)

Cohen, Stephen, *The Idea of Pakistan* (Washington, DC: Brookings Institution Press, 2004)

Coll, Steve, *Ghost Wars: The Secret History of the CIA, Afghanistan and bin Laden, from the Soviet Invasion to September 10, 2001* (New York: Penguin Books, 2004)

Committee for Rational Development, "Selected Documents of the Committee for Rational Development July 1983–March 1984," in Committee for Rational Development (ed.) *Sri Lanka*

(ed.), *Sri Lanka: The Ethnic Conflict* (New Delhi: Navrang Publishers, 1984)

Cooley, John, *Unholy Wars: Afghanistan, America and International Terrorism* (London: Pluto Press, 2002)

Coomaraswamy, Radhika, "'Through the Looking Glass Darkly:' The Politics of Ethnicity," in Committee for Rational Development (ed.), *Sri Lanka*

Cooper, Barry, *New Political Religions, or an Analysis of Modern Terrorism* (Columbia: University of Missouri Press, 2004)

Cossman, Brenda, and Kapur, Ratna, *Secularism's Last Sigh? Hindutva and the (Mis)Rule of Law* (New Delhi: Oxford University Press, 1999)

Crenshaw, Martha, "The Psychology of Terrorism: An Agenda for the 21st Century," *Political Psychology* 21.2 (2002)

Cronin, Audrey Kurth, *The Diplomacy of Counterterrorism: Lessons Learned, Ignored and Disputed*, Special Report No. 80 (Washington, DC: US Institute of Peace, January 14, 2002)

Crossette, Barbara, "Sri Lanka: In the Shadow of the Indian Elephant," *World Policy Journal*, 19.1 (2002)

Davis, Craig, "'A'" is for Allah, 'J' is for Jihad," *World Policy Journal*, 19.1 (2002)

Desai, A. R., *Social Background of Indian Nationalism* (Bombay: Popular Prakashan, 1991)

De Silva, C. R., "Sinhala–Tamil Relations and Education in Sri Lanka: The University Admissions Issue – the First Phase, 1971–1977," in Robert B. Goldman and A. J. Wilson (eds.), *From Independence to Statehood* (London: Pinter Publishers, 1984)

De Silva, K. M, *A History of Sri Lanka* (London: C. Hurst & Co., 1981)

Deb, Shishir K., "Political Economy of Gas Export," *Asian Affairs*, 25.3 (2003)

DeVotta, Neil, "Ethnolinguistic Nationalism and Ethnic Conflict in Sri Lanka," in Michael E. Brown and Sumit Ganguly (eds.), *Fighting Words: Language Policy and Ethnic Relations in Asia* (Cambridge, MA: MIT Press, 2003)

Dharmadasa, K. N. O., *Language, Religion, and Ethnic Assertiveness: The Growth of Sinhalese Nationalism in Sri Lanka* (Ann Arbor: University of Michigan Press, 1992)

Dupree, Louis, *Afghanistan* (Princeton University Press, 1973)

Edwards, David B., *Before Taliban: Genealogies of the Afghan Jihad* (Berkeley, CA: University of California Press, 2002)

Emadi, Hafizullah, *Culture and Customs of Afghanistan* (Westport, CT: Greenwood Press, 2005)

Embree, Ainslie, *Utopias in Conflict: Religion and Nationalism in Modern India* (Berkeley, CA: University of California Press, 1990)

Engineer, Asghar Ali, "Hindu–Muslim Relations Before and After 1947," in Sarvepalli Gopal (ed.), *Anatomy of a Confrontation* (Delhi: Penguin Books, 1991)

Fair, C. Christine, "Militant Recruitment in Pakistan: Implications for Al-Qaeda and Other Organizations," *Studies in Conflict & Terrorism*, 27 (2004)

Faruki, Kemal A., "Pakistan: Islamic Government and Society," in John L. Esposito (ed.), *Islam in Asia: Religion, Politics and Society* (New York: Oxford University Press, 1987)

Feldman, Shelley, "NGOs and Civil Society: (Un)stated contradictions," *Annals of American Academy of Political and Social Science*, 554 (1997)

Fradkin, Hillel, Haqqani, Husain, and Brown, Eric, *Current Trends in Islamist Ideology*, Vol. I (Washington, DC: Hudson Institute, 2005)

Franda, Marcus, *Bangladesh: The First Decade* (New Delhi: South Asian Publishers, 1982)

Friedman, Thomas, *The World is Flat: A Brief History of the Twenty-First Century* (New York: Farrar, Straus and Giroux, 2005)

Gandhi, Rajmohan, *Revenge and Reconciliation* (New Delhi: Penguin Books, 1999)

Ganguly, Sumit, *The Crisis in Kashmir: Portents of War, Hopes of Peace* (New York: Cambridge University Press, 1997)

The Rise of Islamist Militancy in Bangladesh, Special Report 171 (Washington, DC: US Institute of Peace, 2006)

Ghani, Ashraf, "Afghanistan: Islam and Counterrevolutionary Movements," in John L. Esposito, (ed.) *Islam in Asia: Religion, Politics and Society* (New York: Oxford University Press, 1987)

Ghosh, Partha S., *BJP and the Evolution of Hindu Nationalism: From Periphery to Center* (New Delhi: Manohar Publishers, 1999)

Gilley, Bruce, "Against the Concept of Ethnic Conflict," *Third World Quarterly*, 25.6 (2004)

Gopal, S., "Nehru, Religion and Secularism," in R. Champakalakshmi and S. Gopal (eds.), *Tradition, Dissent and Ideology* (Delhi: Oxford University Press, 1986)

Gopinath, Meenakshi, "Restoring the Canvas of Coexistence: A Role for Education in India," in Aall and Ollapally (eds.), *Perspectives*.

Gourevitch, Peter, "The Second Image Reversed: The International Sources of Domestic Politics," *International Organization*, 32.4 (1978)

Griffin, Michael, *Reaping the Whirlwind: Afghanistan, Al Qa'ida and the Holy War* (London: Pluto Press, 2003)

Guha, Ramachandra, "Opening a Window in Kashmir," *World Policy Journal*, 21.3 (2004)

Gurr, Ted R., *Why Men Rebel* (Princeton University Press, 1970)
  Minorities at Risk (Washington, DC: US Institute of Peace Press, 1993)

Gurr, Ted R., and Harff, Barbara, *Ethnic Conflict in World Politics* (Boulder CO: Westview Press, 1994)

Habibullah, Wajahat, *The Political Economy of the Kashmir Conflict*, US Institute of Peace Special Report 121 (Washington, DC: US Institute of Peace Press, 2004).
  "Siege: Hazratbal, Kashmir 1993," *India Review*, 1.3 (2002)

Hafez, Mohammed, *Why Muslims Rebel: Repression and Resistance in the Islamic World* (Boulder, CO: Lynne Rienner Publishers, 2003)

Haqqani, Husain, *Pakistan: Between Mosque and Military* (Washington, DC: Carnegie Endowment for International Peace, 2005)

Harvey, David, *The Condition of Postmodernity: An Enquiry into the Origins of Cultural Change* (Oxford: Basil Blackwell, 1989)

Hasan, Mushirul, "Competing Symbols and Shared Codes: Inter-Community Relations in Modern India," in Sarvepalli Gopal (ed.), *Anatomy of a Confrontation: The Babri Masjid–Ramjanmabhumi Issue* (New Delhi: Penguin Books, 1991)

Hasan, Mushirul and Roy, Asim (eds.), *Living Together Separately: Cultural India in History and Politics* (New Delhi: Oxford University Press, 2005)

Hewison, Kevin and Rodan, Garry, "Closing the Circle: Globalization, Conflict and Political Regimes," presented at the Conference on Asia Pacific Economies: Multilateral vs. Bilateral Relationships, City University of Hong Kong, May 19–21, 2004.

Hewitt, Vernon, *The New International Relations of South Asia* (Manchester: Manchester University Press and Palgrave Press, 1999)

Hiro, Dilip, *Holy Wars* (New York: Routledge, 1989)
  War Without End: The Rise of Islamist Terrorism and Global Response (London: Routledge, 2002)

Hoffmann, Bruce, *Inside Terrorism* (New York: Columbia University Press, 1998)

Horowitz, Donald, *Ethnic Groups in Conflict* (Berkeley, CA: University of California Press, 2000)
  Deadly Ethnic Riots (Berkeley, CA: University of California Press, 2001)

Huntington, Samuel P., *The Clash of Civilizations and the Remaking of World Order* (New York: Touchstone, 1997)

Hussain, Hamid, "Afghanistan – Not So Great Games," *Defence Journal (Pakistan)* (April 2002), available at www.defencejournal.com

Ikenberry, G. John, Lake, David A. and Mastanduno, Michael, "Introduction: Approaches to Explaining American Foreign Economic Policy," *International Organization* 42.1 (1988)

International Crisis Group, *Pakistan: Madrasas, Extremism and the Military*, ICG Asia Report No. 36, July 29, 2002
  The Afghanistan Transitional Administration: Prospects and Perils, Afghanistan Briefing, July 30, 2002
  Kashmir: The View from Srinagar, ICG Asia Report No. 41, November 21, 2002

Afghanistan: Judicial Reform and Transitional Justice, ICG Asia Report No. 45, January 28, 2003

Afghanistan's Flawed Constitutional Process, ICG Asia Report No. 56, June 12, 2003

Afghanistan: The Problem of Pashtun Alienation, ICG Asia Report No. 62, August 5, 2003

Authoritarianism and Political Party Reform in Pakistan, ICG Asia Report No. 102, September 28, 2005

Bangladesh Today, ICG Asia Report No. 121, October 23, 2006

Islam, Nazrul. "Indo-Bangladesh Water Treaty," in Farooq Sobhan (ed.) *Strengthening Cooperation and Security in South Asia Post 9/11* (Dhaka: The University Press, 2004)

Jackson, Robert, *South Asian Crisis* (London: Chatto & Windus, 1975)

Jahan, Rounaq, *Pakistan: Failure in National Integration* (Dhaka: The University Press, 1972)

Jalal, Ayesha, *The Sole Spokesman: Jinnah, the Muslim League and the Demand for Pakistan* (New York: Cambridge University Press, 1994)

Democracy and Authoritarianism in South Asia: A Comparative and Historical Perspective (New York: Cambridge University Press, 1995)

Jalali, Ali A. "The Future of Afghanistan," *Parameters*, 36.1 (2006)

Jayatilleka, Dayan, "The Ethnic Conflict and the Crisis in the South," in Committee for Rational Development (ed.), *Sri Lanka*

Jha, Prem Shankar, *In the Eye of the Cyclone: The Crisis in Indian Democracy* (New Delhi: Viking Books, 1993)

Kakar, M. H., "The Fall of the Afghan Monarchy in 1973," *International Journal of Middle East Studies*, 9.2 (1978)

Kaplan, Robert, "The Taliban," *The Atlantic Monthly*, September 2000, available at www.theatlantic.com

Kapur, Devesh, and Iyengar, Kavita, "The Limits of Integration in Improving South Asian Security," in Ashley Tellis and Michael Wills (eds.), *Trade, Interdependence and Security Strategic Asia 2006–07* (Seattle: National Bureau of Asian Research, 2006)

Katznelson, Ira and Shefte, Martin (eds.), *Shaped by War and Trade: International Influences on American Political Development* (Princeton University Press, 2002)

Keck, Margaret, and Sikkink, Katherine, *Activists Beyond Borders: Advocacy Networks in International Politics* (Ithaca, NY: Cornell University Press, 1998)

Khan, Adeel, *Politics of Identity: Ethnic Nationalism and the State in Pakistan* (New Delhi: Sage Publications, 2005)

Khan, Riaz M., *Untying the Knot: Negotiating Soviet Withdrawal* (Durham, NC: Duke University Press, 1991)

Kharat, Rajesh, "Countering Insurgencies in South Asia: The Case of Indo-Bhutan Co-operation," delivered at the 2006 Annual Meeting of the American Political Science Association, Philadelphia, PA, September 2006

Khilnani, Sunil, *The Idea of India* (London: Hamish Hamilton, 1997)

Kodikara, Shelton, *Foreign Policy of Sri Lanka: A Third World Perspective* (Delhi: Chanakya Publications, 1982)

"The Continuing Crisis in Sri Lanka: the JVP, the Indian Troops and Tamil Politics," *Asia Survey*, 29.7 (1989)

Koon, H. P., "The New Economic Policy and the Community in Peninsular Malaysia," *The Developing Economies*, 35.3 (1997)

Kottegoda, Shantha, "Sri Lanka's Conflict in the North and East and Challenges to the Army," *International Relations in a Globalizing World*, 1.2 (2005)

Koul, Sudha, *The Tiger Ladies* (New York: Beacon Press, 2002)

Kronstadt, K. Alan, "Pakistan's Domestic Political Developments: Issues for Congress," Congressional Research Service Report for Congress, January 5, 2004

Kronstadt, K. Alan, and Vaughn, Bruce, "Terrorism in South Asia," Congressional Research Service, Library of Congress, August 9, 2004

Laqueur, Walter, *The Age of Terrorism* (New York: Little, Brown and Co., 1987)

Lau, Martin, "The Fifteenth Constitutional Amendment in Pakistan and its Implications," presented at The South Asia Forum Seminar, Department of Law, School of Oriental and African Studies, London, October 26, 1998

Lewis, David, "NGOs, Donors, and the State in Bangladesh," *Annals of American Academy of Political and Social Science*, 554 (1997)

"On the Difficulty of Studying 'Civil Society': Reflections on NGOs, State and Democracy in Bangladesh," *Contributions to Indian Sociology*, 38.3 (2004)

Liphart, Arend, *Democracies: Patterns of Majoritarian and Consensus Government in Twenty One Countries* (New Haven, CT: Yale University Press, 1984)

Loganathan, Ketheshwaran, *Sri Lanka: Lost Opportunities* (Colombo: Centre for Policy Research and Analysis, University of Colombo, 1996)

Lyotard, Jean-Francois, *The Postmodern Condition* (Minneapolis: University of Minnesota Press, 1984)

Madan, T. N. "Secularism in its Place," *Journal of Asian Studies*, 46.4 (1987)

Maley, William, *The Afghanistan Wars* (New York: Palgrave Macmillan, 2002)

Mamdani, Mahmood, *Good Muslim, Bad Muslim: America, the Cold War and the Roots of Terror* (New York: Doubleday, 2005)

Maney, Gregory M., "International Sources of Domestic Protest," *Mobilization* 6 (2001)

Maniruzzaman, Talukder, *The Bangladesh Revolution and Its Aftermath* (Dhaka: Bangladesh Books International Ltd, 1980)

Mann, Michael, "The Autonomous Power of the State," in John A. Hall (ed.), *States in History* (Cambridge: Basil Blackwell, 1986)

Manogaran, Chelvadurai, *Ethnic Conflict and Reconciliation in Sri Lanka* (Honolulu: University of Hawaii Press, 1987)

Manor, James, *The Expedient Utopian: Bandaranaika and Ceylon* (Cambridge University Press, 1989)

McGregor, Andrew, "Jihad and the Rifle Alone: Abdullah Azzam and the Islamist Revolution," *The Journal of Conflict Studies*, 23.2 (2003)

Misra, Ashutosh, "Rise of Religious Parties in Pakistan: Causes and Prospects," *Strategic Analysis*, 27.2 (2003)

Mohsin, Amena, *The Chittagong Hill Tracts, Bangladesh: On the Difficult Road to Peace* (Boulder, CO: Lynne Rienner Publishers, 2003)

Mukharya, P. S., "Contributions of Sant Prannath to the Composite Culture of India," in Settar and Kaimal (eds.), *We Lived Together*

Muni, S. D., "India and the Post Cold War World: Opportunities and Challenges," *Asian Survey*, 31.9 (1991)

Muni, S. D. *Pangs of Proximity* (New Delhi: Sage Publications, 1993)

Nandy, Ashis, "The Politics of Secularism and the Recovery of Religious Tolerance," *Alternatives* 13 (1998)

Romance of the State and the Fate of Dissent in the Tropics (New Delhi: Oxford University Press, 2003)

Bonfire of Creeds: The Essential Nandy (New Delhi: Oxford University Press, 2004)

National Commission on Terrorist Attacks Upon the United States, *The 9/11 Commission Report, Final Report of the National Commission on Terrorist Attacks Upon the United States*, Official Government Edition (Washington, DC: US Government Printing Office, 2004)

Nayyar, A. H., "The Making of the Pakistani Mind," in Aall and Ollapally (eds.), *Perspectives*

Nayyar, A. H., and Salim, Ahmed, "Glorification of War and the Military," in Nayyar and Salim (eds.), *The Subtle Subversion*

The Subtle Subversion: The State of Curricula and Textbooks in Pakistan (Islamabad: Sustainable Development Policy Institute, 2003)

Nehru, Jawaharlal, *The Unity of India: Collected Writings 1937–1940* (London: Lindsay Drummond, 1948)

Nizami, K. A., "Contributions of Mystics to Amity and Harmony in Indian Society," in Settar and Kaimal (eds.), *We Lived Together*

Nojumi, Neamat, *The Rise of the Taliban in Afghanistan: Mass Mobilization, Civil War, and the Future of the Region* (New York: Palgrave, 2002)

Obeysekera, Gananath, "Political Violence and the Future of Democracy in Sri Lanka," Committee for Rational Development (ed.), *Sri Lanka.*

O'Donnell, Charles Peter, *Bangladesh: Biography of a Muslim Nation* (Boulder, CO: Westview Press, 1984)

Olesen, Asta, *Islam and Politics in Afghanistan* (Surrey: Curzon Press, 1995)

Ollapally, Deepa, *Confronting Conflict: Domestic Factors and US Policymaking in the Third World* (Westport, CT: Greenwood Press, 1993)

"India's Strategic Doctrine and Practice: The Impact of Nuclear Testing," in Raju G. C. Thomas and Amit Gupta (eds.), *India's Nuclear Security* (Boulder, CO: Lynne Rienner Publishers, 2000)

"Combating Warlordism and Regionalism in Afghanistan," paper presented at the US Institute of Peace, Washington, DC, November 1, 2002

US–India Relations: Ties That Bind? The Sigur Center Asia Papers No. 22 (Washington, DC: George Washington University, 2005)

Ostby, Gudrun, "Horizontal Inequalities and Civil Conflict," paper prepared for the 46th Annual Convention of the International Studies Association, Honolulu, HI, March 1–5, 2005

Parekh, Bhikhu, "The Cultural Particularity of Liberal Democracy," *Political Studies*, 40 (1992)

Pasha, Mustapha Kamal, "Islamic Extremists: How Do They Mobilize Support?" Current Issues Briefing (Washington, DC: US Institute of Peace, 2002)

Peiris, G. H., "Economic Inequalities and Ethnic Conflict in Sri Lanka," *International Relations in a Globalizing World*, 1.2 (2005)

Perera, Jehan, "Exploring the Solution to the Communal Problem," in Committee for Rational Development (ed.), *Sri Lanka.*

Perito, Robert, *The US Experience with Provincial Reconstruction Teams in Afghanistan: Lessons Identified*, US Institute of Peace Special Report No. 152 (Washington, DC: US Institute of Peace, 2005)

Philipson, Liz, "Corrupted Democracy," *Himal South Asian*, August 2006, available at www.himalmag.com

Poullada, L. B., *Reform and Rebellion in Afghanistan, 1919–1929* (Ithaca, NY: Cornell University Press, 1973)

Prabha, Kshitij, "Defining Terrorism," *Strategic Analysis*, 24.1 (2000)

Pratap, Anita, *Island of Blood: Frontline Reports from Sri Lanka, Afghanistan and Other South Asian Flashpoints* (New York: Penguin Books, 2001)

Punjabi, Riaz, "Kashmir: The Bruised Identity," in Thomas (ed.), *Perspectives on Kashmir*

Puri, Balraj, "India, Kashmir and the War Against Terrorism," *EPW Commentary*, October 27, 2001

Rahmani, Waliullah, "Helmand Province and the Afghan Insurgency," *Terrorism Monitor*, 4.6 (2006)

Rais, Rasul Bakhsh, *War Without Winners: Afghanistan's Uncertain Transition After the Cold War* (Karachi: Oxford University Press, 1994)

Rajeshwari, B., *Communal Riots in India: A Chronology (1947–2003)*, IPCS Research Papers (New Delhi: Institute of Peace and Conflict Studies, 2004)

Rashid, Ahmed, *Taliban: Militant Islam, Oil and Fundamentalism in Central Asia* (New Haven, CT: Yale University Press, 2001)

   Descent into Chaos: The United States and the Failure of Nation Building in Pakistan, Afghanistan and Central Asia (New York: Viking Penguin, 2008)

Raychoudhary, S. C., *History of Modern India: A Detailed Study of Political, Economic, Social and Cultural Aspects* (Delhi: Surjeet Publications, 1992)

Regani, Sarojini, "We Lived Together – Deccani Culture and the Qutb Shahs of Golkonda," in Settar and Kaimal (eds.), *We Lived Together*

Riaz, Ali, *God Willing: The Politics of Islamism in Bangladesh* (Lanham, MD: Rowman & Littlefield, 2004)

   Unfolding State: The Transformation of Bangladesh (Ontario: de Sitter Publications, 2005)

Richardson, John, *Paradise Poisoned: Learning About Conflict, Terrorism and Development from Sri Lanka's Civil Wars* (Kandy: International Centre for Ethnic Studies, 2005)

Rose, Leo, "The Politics of Azad Kashmir," in Thomas, *Perspectives on Kashmir*

Rosenau, Pauline Marie, *Postmodernism and the Social Sciences* (Princeton University Press, 1992)

Roy, Asim, *Islamic Syncretistic Tradition in Bengal* (Princeton University Press, 1983)

Rubin, Barnett, *The Fragmentation of Afghanistan* (New Haven, CT: Yale University Press, 1995)

   "Crafting a Constitution for Afghanistan," *Journal of Democracy*, 15.3 (2004)

Rubin, Barnett R., Hamidzada, Humayun and Stoddard, Abby, *Through the Fog of Peace Building: Evaluating the Reconstruction of Afghanistan* (New York: Center on International Cooperation, New York University, 2003)

Rubin, Michael, "Who is Responsible for the Taliban?" *Middle East Review of International Affairs*, 6.1 (2002)

Ryan, Stephen, *Ethnic Conflict and International Relations* (Aldershot: Dartmouth Publishing Co., 1995)

Sabaratnam, Lakshmanan, *Ethnic Attachments in Sri Lanka: Social Change and Cultural Continuity* (New York: Palgrave, 2001)

Sageman, Marc, *Leaderless Jihad: Terror Networks in the Twenty-first Century* (Philadelphia: University of Pennsylvania Press, 2008)

Said, Edward W., *Orientalism* (New York: Vintage Books, 1978)

Saikia, Jaideep, "The ISI Reaches East: Anatomy of Conspiracy," *Studies in Conflict and Terrorism*, 25.3 (2002)

Salim, Ahmed, "Historical Falsehoods and Inaccuracies," in Nayyar and Salim (eds.), *The Subtle Subversion*

Sambanis, Nicholas, "Poverty and the Organization of Political Violence," *Brookings Trade Forum* (2004)

Santhanam, K., Sreedhar, Saxena, Sudhir and Manish, *Jihadis in Jammu and Kashmir: A Portrait Gallery* (New Delhi: Sage Publications, 2003)

Sayeed, K. B., *Pakistan: The Formative Phase* (Karachi: Pakistan Publishing House, 1960)

Schurmann, Franz, *The Logic of World Power: An Inquiry into the Origins, Currents and Contradictions of World Politics* (New York: Pantheon, 1974)

Schwedler, Jillian, *Faith in Moderation: Islamist Parties in Jordan and Yemen* (New York: Cambridge University Press, 2006)

Scruton, Roger, *The Dictionary of Political Thought* (New York: Hill & Wang, 1982)

Sen, Amartya, "Secularism and Its Discontents," in Kaushik Basu and Sanjay Subrahmanyam (eds.), *Unravelling the Nation*

Settar, S. and Kaimal P. K. V. (eds.), *We Lived Together* (Delhi: Pragati Publications, Indian Council of Historical Research, 1999)

Shastri, Amita and Wilson, A. J. (eds.), *The Post-Colonial States of South Asia* (London: Curzon and Palgrave Press, 2001)

Shelley, Mizanur Rahman, *Emergence of a New Nation in a Multi-Polar World: Bangladesh* (Dhaka: Academic Press and Publishers Ltd., 2000)

Sieghart, Paul, *Sri Lanka: A Mounting Tragedy of Errors*, (London: International Commission of Jurists and JUSTICE, 1984)

Sikand, Yoginder, *Sacred Spaces: Exploring Traditions of Shared Faith in India* (New Delhi: Penguin Books, 2003)

Simon, Steven and Benjamin, Daniel, "America and the New Terrorism," *Survival*, 42.1 (2000)

Singh, K. S., "Diversity, Heterogeneity and Integration: An Ideological Perspective," in Settar and Kaimal (eds.), *We Lived Together*

Singh, Tavleen, *Kashmir: A Tragedy of Errors* (New Delhi: Viking, 1995)

Sinha, S. K., "Foreword," in Jaideep Saikia, *Terror Sans Frontiers: Islamic Militancy in North East India*, ADCDIS Occasional Paper, Program in Arms Control, Disarmament and International Security (University of Chicago at Urbana-Champaign, 2003)

Sisson, Richard, and Rose, Leo E., *War and Secessions: Pakistan, India and the Creation of Bangladesh* (Berkeley, CA: University of California Press, 1992)

Skocpol, Theda, "Bringing the State Back In: Strategies of Analysis in Current Research," in Peter B. Evans, Dietrich Rueschemeyer and Theda Skocpol (eds.), *Bringing the State Back In* (Cambridge University Press, 1985)

Stern, Jessica, "Pakistan's Jihad Culture," *Foreign Affairs*, 79.6 (2000)
  Terror in the Name of God: Why Religious Militants Kill (New York: Ecco/ HarperCollins Publishers, 2003)
Takeyh, Ray, "Two Cheers from the Islamic World," *Foreign Policy*, 128 (2002)
Tambiah, S. J., *Ethnic Fratricide and the Dismantling of Democracy* (University of Chicago Press, 1991)
Thapar, Romila, *Interpreting Early India* (Delhi: Oxford University Press, 1993)
Thomas, Raju G. C., *Perspectives on Kashmir: The Roots of Conflict in South Asia* (Boulder, CO: Westview Press, 1992)
  "Competing Nationalisms," *Harvard International Review*, 28.3 (1996)
  "The 'Nationalities' Question in South Asia," in Shastri and Wilson (eds.), *The Post-Colonial States of South Asia*
Tilly, Charles, (ed.), *The Formation of National States in Western Europe* (Princeton University Press, 1972)
Titus, Paul, "Routes to Ethnicity," in Paul Titus (ed.), *Marginality and Modernity: Ethnicity and Change in Post-Colonial Baluchistan* (Karachi: Oxford University Press, 1997)
Tripathi, Dwijendra, "The Crisis of Indian Polity: A Historical Perspective," in Settar and Kaimal (eds.), *We Lived Together*
US Department of State, *Annual Report on International Religious Freedom for 1999: India*, Bureau for Democracy, Human Rights and Labor, Washington DC, September 9, 1999.
  International Religious Freedom Report 2005, Bureau of Democracy, Human Rights and Labor, Washington, DC, November 8, 2005.
  Country Reports on Terrorism 2005, Office of the Coordinator for Counter-terrorism (2006).
Van der Veer, Peter, "Riots and Rituals: The Construction of Violence and Public Space in Hindu Nationalism," in Brass (ed.), *Riots and Pogroms*
Vanina, Eugenia, "Communal Relations in Pre-Modern India," in Settar and Kaimal (eds.), *We Lived Together*
Varshney, Ashutosh, *Ethnic Conflict and Civic Life: Hindus and Muslims in India* (New Haven, CT: Yale University Press, 2002)
Verghese, B. G, *An End to Confrontation: Restructuring the Sub-Continent* (New Delhi: S. Chand & Co., 1972)
Waltz, Kenneth, *Theory of International Politics* (Reading, MA: Addison-Wesley, 1979)
Waslekar, Sundeep, and Futehally, Ilmas, *Reshaping the Agenda in Kashmir* (Mumbai: International Centre for Peace Initiatives, 2002)
Widmalm, Sten, "The Rise and Fall of Democracy in Jammu and Kashmir," *Asian Survey*, 37.11 (1997)
  "The Kashmir Conflict," *SIPRI Yearbook 1999* (Oxford University Press, 1999)
Wilber, Donald, *Afghanistan* (New Haven, CT: HRAF Press, 1962)
Williams, Brian Glyn, "Jihad and Ethnicity in Post-Communist Eurasia: On the Trail of Transnational Islamic Holy Warriors in Kashmir, Afghanistan, Central Asia, Chechnya and Kosovo," *The Global Review of Ethnopolitics*, 2.3–4 (2003)
Wilson, Jeyaratnam A., *The Break-Up of Sri Lanka: The Sinhalese–Tamil Conflict* (Honolulu, HI: University of Hawaii Press, 1988)

Wilson, Jeyaratnam, "Politics and Political Development since 1948," in de Silva, K. M. (ed.), *Sri Lanka: A Survey* (London: C. Hurst Co., 1977)

Wriggins, W. Howard, *Ceylon: Dilemmas of a New Nation*, (Princeton University Press, 1960)

Yousaf, Mohammad, and Adkin, Major Mark, *The Bear Trap: Afghanistan's Untold Story* (London: Leo Cooper, 1992)

Zaheer, Hasan, *The Separation of East Pakistan: The Rise and Realization of Bengali Muslim Nationalism* (Karachi: Oxford University Press, 1994)

Ziring, Lawrence, *Bangladesh: From Mujib to Ershad, An Interpretive Study* (Karachi: Oxford University Press, 1992)

Index